Body-Poetics of the Virgin Mary

Body-Poetics of the Virgin Mary

Mary's Maternal Body as Poem of the Father

Jane Petkovic

FOREWORD BY
Ben Quash

PICKWICK *Publications* · Eugene, Oregon

BODY-POETICS OF THE VIRGIN MARY
Mary's Maternal Body as Poem of the Father

Pickwick Publications
An Imprint of Wipf and Stock Publishers
199 W. 8th Ave., Suite 3
Eugene, OR 97401

www.wipfandstock.com

PAPERBACK ISBN: 978-1-5326-9922-1
HARDCOVER ISBN: 978-1-5326-9923-8
EBOOK ISBN: 978-1-5326-9924-5

Cataloguing-in-Publication data:

Names: Petkovic, Jane. | Quash, Ben, foreword.
Title: Body-poetics of the virgin Mary : Mary's maternal body as poem of the father / Jane Petkovic.
Description: Eugene, OR : Pickwick Publications, 2021 | Includes bibliographical references and index(es).
Identifiers: ISBN 978-1-5326-9922-1 (paperback) | ISBN 978-1-5326-9923-8 (hardcover) | ISBN 978-1-5326-9924-5 (ebook)
Subjects: LCSH: Mary, Blessed Virgin, Saint—Theology. | Human body—Religious aspects—Catholic Church.
Classification: BT613 .P475 2021 (print) | BT613 .P475 (ebook)

Table of Contents

List of Poems in Order of Appearance

Foreword

Ben Quash

IN A SERIES OF lectures in the early 1950s, Jacques Maritain asserted that "rational language" is "burdened with social and utilitarian connotations, ready-made associations, and worn-out meanings."[1] Poetry, by contrast, can admit us to different domains. Poetic images and forms cannot be left behind in favor of their "interpretation." They remain resilient and fecund—continually generating new resonances, associations, and trajectories of thought and feeling.

This opens onto a larger issue, that goes beyond the particular case of poetry as an artform to other strands of the arts as well. Whether literary, visual, musical, architectural, cinematic (the list could go on)—each artistic form harbors particular resources for breaking open our set assumptions about the way the world is, and our functionalist reductivism about how we are to live in it.

So in any really open engagement with the arts there must be a readiness to learn from the *way the artform works* and not just from *what it says*. The latter would inevitably risk a betrayal of the artform's particularity in the interests of a "translation," or even a "generalization," of some supposed core message. The form cannot be dispensed with. Thus poets' concerns incarnate themselves in the forms of their poems. They are bodied forth in them. And in theological terms this bodying forth should command respect. It is an entailment of any high view of incarnation that bodies must be treated with reverence.

1. Jacques Maritain, *Creative Intuition in Art and Poetry* (New York: Pantheon, 1953), 74.

xi

Jane Petkovic, in this book, models just such respect. She has written an original and far-reaching work whose value to its readers as a scholarly stimulus will be matched by its value as a spiritual resource. Her book is also a valuable reminder that these two things do not have to be in tension with each other.

Petkovic succeeds in focussing us on the connections between two kinds of reflection: reflection on bodies, and reflection on poems. She offers detailed and nuanced reflections on the material and meaningful continuities of poetry with bodies, through focussed readings of specific Marian poems.

In much Christian tradition, Mary's maternal body is held up as a paradigm of our highest human possibility, which is to be perfectly responsive to the divine life's movements towards and within us. In this way, Mariology is at the same time theological anthropology. It is by being reciprocal, self-donating, and receptive beings that all humans are best able to image God, and Mary is paradigmatically such a human being.

Petkovic is beautifully attuned to this tradition—and refreshingly so, because she has roots in Anglican evangelicalism, and it is all too rare to find Mary treated so generatively outside Roman Catholic and Orthodox theological circles. She argues that Mary is consummately "in the image" of God (*imago Dei*) because of the supreme way she is available for relationship.

Her next, and ambitious, step is to make the connection between this "open-textured" way of realizing the human vocation, embodied in Mary, and the character of poetry itself. Mary is transformed through her energetically participative openness in a way that is comparable to how human language is transformed, extended, tried, and elevated in great poetry, such that she can aptly be described as herself a "poem," and human destiny as "poetic." Mary is, in Petkovic's phrase, "the poem of God the Father." Petkovic asks us to view ourselves as likewise called to be "poetic" in our being. It is on this basis that this book can offer an inspirational theology of the *imago Dei* as something that can be articulated in the language and the categories of poetry.

Yet it also stays unflinchingly attentive to the realities of human bodies. Theological wonder is here untainted by sentimentality or idealization. For Petkovic, the obstetric and the epiphanic are interwoven, and the epiphanies she shares in the pages that follow are all the more profound for the fierce honesty with which corporeal processes are explored and honored.

It is not just that poems are like bodies; it is that bodies are like poems. That includes our bodies. And one of the ways in which we can learn to live our embodied lives well—with the right kind of speed and the right kind of slowness; the right kind of vagueness and the right kind of precision; the right kind of boundaries and the right kind of porousness—is by attending to poetry.

We can do this in discipleship of the one who was Word-become-flesh—a Gospel who walked the earth before he was turned into text, and who, even when we meet him *through* text, presses to be made incarnate again in and through us. When this happens, our embodied existence becomes a sign of what will abide when all else falls away. To adapt R. S. Thomas's words, our bodies can become the locus of a "brightness" that is "the eternity that awaits you."[2]

That brightness is intimated throughout this book, whose tracings of poetic language are as intensively pursued—and as subtle—as its tracings of the body's rhythms, sacrifices and joys.

2. R. S. Thomas, "The Bright Field," in *Collected Poems 1945–1990* (London: Phoenix, 2000), 302.

Acknowledgments

GRATEFUL ACKNOWLEDGMENT AND THANKS are offered to the following people who have contributed to the realization and completion of this work: Professor Jeremy Begbie, Dr. Susannah Ticciati, Professor Emeritus Oliver Davies, Dr. Sarah Jane Boss, the late Professor Peter Alexander, Professor Emerita Christine Alexander, and to Professor Ben Quash, without whom, naught. Several friends have shown tenacious encouragement, support and interest—thank you for all you have generously given. To family, both here and departed, thank you for all you are, and all you have been.

Abbreviations

CCC   *Catechism of the Catholic Church.* Latin ed. approved and promulgated by John Paul II, August 15, 1997. English translation ©1997. 2nd ed., revised with Glossary and Index Analyticus ©2000. Reprint, Vatican: Libreria Editrice Vaticana, 2007.

CE   Herbermann, George, et al., eds. *The Catholic Encyclopedia.* New York: Robert Appleton, 1908.

FR   John Paul II. "*Fides et Ratio:* On the Relationship between Faith and Reason." Encyclical Letter given September 14, 1998.

MD   John Paul II. "*Mulieris Dignitatem:* On the Dignity and Vocation of Women." Apostolic Letter given August 15, 1988.

SM   Kristeva, Julia. "Stabat Mater." Translated by Leon S. Roudiez. In *The Kristeva Reader*, edited by Toril Moi, 160–86. 1986. Reprint, Oxford: Blackwell, 1996.

     Citations are to this edition.

TOB   John Paul II. *Man and Woman, He Created Them: A Theology of the Body.* Translated by Michael Waldstein. Boston, MA: Pauline, 2006.

     Citations are to this edition. The abbreviation is followed by catechesis number and paragraph number.

Documents of the Second Vatican Ecumenical Council

DV   *"Dei Verbum*: Dogmatic Constitution on Divine Revelation." Solemnly promulgated by Pope Paul VI on November 18, 1965.

GS   *"Gaudium et Spes*: Pastoral Constitution on the Church in the Modern World." Promulgated by Pope Paul VI on December 7, 1965.

LG   *"Lumen Gentium*: Dogmatic Constitution on the Church." Solemnly promulgated by Pope Paul VI on November 21, 1964.

NA   *"Nostra Aetate*: Declaration on the Relation of the Church to Non-Christian Religions." Proclaimed by Pope Paul VI on October 28, 1965.

SC   *"Sacrosanctum Concilium*: Constitution on the Sacred Liturgy." Solemnly promulgated by His Holiness Pope Paul VI on December 4, 1963.

1

Of Bodies and Words

Meaning and Mattering

High on the end wall hangs / the Gospel, from before He was books
—LES MURRAY, "CHURCH"

AT HIS WEDNESDAY GENERAL audiences, held between 1979 and 1984, Pope John Paul II delivered a sequential catechetical series on the human person in relation to God; a theological anthropology. The weekly instalments were adapted from an unpublished book manuscript he had written prior to his papal election in 1978. Originally given the title, *Man and Woman He Created Them*, a direct citation of Genesis 1:27, it has become generally known, and referred to, by a phrase that recurs more than one hundred times in the text: a "theology of the body."[1] As the subject of Wednesday audiences, John Paul's catechetical series was unusual for its duration, content, and register. Attendant pilgrims and visitors at Wednesday audiences, often at that time numbering in the thousands, would customarily expect to receive a papal greeting, short address, prayer, and blessing. Weighty catechetical instruction was not what they expected but was what they received. Substantial in content and academic references, John Paul's talks fused pastoral occasion and

1. The most reliable, academically-annotated edition of the work, translated, introduced, and indexed by Michael Walstein, combines both phrases in its title. The title used throughout this book is *Theology of the Body*.

1

catechetical intent—implicitly, a call to conversion—with grounding in biblical texts, philosophy, and theology.

It may be surprising that a series of talks on the meaning of the human body gives no simple definition of its key term. Michael Waldstein's edition lists four index headings for *body*; each entry having multiple subheadings. The first entry deals with "fundamental concepts." These are: that the person is an embodied entity who does not *have* a body but *is* a body among other bodies; that the body "determines man's ontological subjectivity and participates in the dignity of the person"; and that the body expresses the person. These concepts were identified by John Paul II in scriptural exegesis. The pope saw his task in writing a theology of the body to, in Waldstein's words, "unfold and explain" the scriptural revelation of the body, "helped by reflecting upon human experience." John Paul II therefore had two broad foci: the meaning of the body, and the human experience of the body. The experience of being embodied is how we experience the body's meaning; an experience John Paul refers to as "(re)-reading the meaning of the body."

A foundational premise of John Paul's *Theology of the Body* is that the body in its natural state functions as a sign. This natural body has objective meanings, against which any cultural construal can be measured. John Paul recognizes that prevailing cultural norms may proclaim a different meaning for the body or claim the body's meaning is alterable by cultural fiat. If, though, the body has objectively true meanings, then deviation from these is a falsification. If, as John Paul argues, the body's meanings *are* objectively, so invariantly true, then it is not possible to subscribe to a theory of the body's being a social construct, unstable and variable in meaning. John Paul recognizes how social paradigms, within which bodies are situated, shape societal attitudes toward the body. These attitudes, in turn, shape ethical codes pertaining to how persons are treated socially and legally. The overarching motivation for John Paul's theological anthropology was to repudiate social attitudes which he saw as damaging to persons through their misrepresentation of the body's meaning.

The pope's immediate intention in writing was to defend Paul VI's 1969 Encyclical, *Humanae Vitae*. That encyclical's reception had been neither smooth nor uniform. Its continuing, and for some, unexpected and unwelcome, proscription against artificial contraception had alienated large numbers, not only outside the church, but within it. The controversy it aroused contributed to a growing disconnect between the sexual praxis of increasing numbers of Roman Catholics, and church teaching, as became clear to John Paul in the exercise of his priestly pastoral duties. He therefore sought not only to defend church teaching from the infiltration of opposing ideas from without, but to reaffirm the coherence and strength of catholic teachings, more particularly those concerned with sexual ethics, to those within the church who did not see their value, or continued relevance. To achieve this aim, he followed Jesus's gospel lead by going back to "the beginning"; to the first book of holy scripture, the first story of which deals with the starting point of creation. John Paul likewise began his talks with extensive meditations upon the mythological creation narratives of Genesis, using them to contextualize church doctrine. By comparing the biblical vision of "the beginning" with the contemporary alternative vision, the pope invited thinking into how the one differs from the other, what difference this makes, and why such difference matters. This method also served John Paul's wider purpose of providing the intellectual and faith resources to defend Roman Catholic sexual ethics. He presented a robust theological anthropology, underpinned by the Western philosophic tradition, along with scholarship more recent to his time of writing.

Theological anthropology—the study of man in relation to God—has tended to rely upon intellectual disciplines as its chief way of knowing. *Anthropology*, a social science, seeks knowledge through a study of all aspects of human existence; material and organizational, as well as intellectual. John Paul draws upon both approaches, constantly referring to trends in philosophical and theological discussion, contemporary to his time of writing, as well as describing experiences common in daily living. This balancing of different ways of knowing has been strongly present within the Roman Catholic Church, which tests intellectual knowledge against the church's collective memory. The Catechism of the Catholic Church recognizes several sources which accessibly store this collective memory: holy scripture, tradition, the magisterium, sacramental liturgy, prayer, the ministries and charisms of the church, the signs of apostolic and missionary life, and the witness of the saints (*CCC* 688).

John Paul draws upon this collective repository in his scriptural exegesis. He freshens scriptural revelation by putting it in dialogue with the experience of living. In this way, he hopes to assist his audience and readership towards a truer and deeper understanding of what it means to be human. His method draws upon the internal intellectual resources of memory and imagination as a way to make sense of, and process, external sense data gleaned from living. This is the phenomenological method: studying how phenomena disclose themselves through being concretely experienced. As John Paul's immediate aim was to defend *Humanae Vitae*, his major task is to set out how, in the experience of love, man realizes his meaning. The expression of love he focuses on is sacramental marriage, including its sexual dimension. This is not because he considers marriage to be determinative of human existence, but because it is what he calls the "primal sacrament" (*TOB* 96:6, *inter alia*). Present since the beginning of the world, it confirms the nature of man's origin in perfect love.

Hermeneutics—the analysis and interpretation of texts—is central to John Paul's endeavor. His extensive interpretation of the two creation myths of Genesis is interspersed with many other wide-ranging scriptural references. His commitment to the phenomenological method extends the range of his interpretative field, so that ordinary life experiences, such as speaking and other acts, provide a potentially huge volume of material for analysis. Through this method, John Paul tries to kindle an imaginative spark of understanding about how the body is meaningful, and what truths it manifests. Although John Paul's *Theology of the Body* is a multifaceted exercise in hermeneutics, that discipline is not his primary interest; hermeneutics and phenomenology are put to the service of theology.

The fact of embodiment determines how man knows anything of the world, including knowing what kind of creature he is; what he means. This knowledge is radically available for all persons, as everyone is embodied. Church teaching would add that scriptural revelation leads persons to arrive at right understanding of themselves. Additionally, although the body is the means of man's knowing, the body itself also *knows*. It has an innate awareness of itself. A primary life task of the person is to correctly interpret his or her own meaning, in the light of divine revelation. The key phrase John Paul repeatedly uses to express this hermeneutical task is: "rereading the body in truth."[2] In this phrase, John Paul expressly connects the body with language, treating the body metaphorically as text. Two different types of things: literary text, and the human body, are related to each other by the cognitive practice of interpretation; each treated of as text to be decoded. In thinking of the body in this way, John Paul's hermeneutic enters the domain of body-poetics. The

2. The phrase "rereading the body in truth" is used on forty-nine separate occasions in John Paul's theology of the body; "reading the language of the body" is used three times in *TOB* 118:4, and once in 118:6 (Waldstein, "Index," s.v. "Body 3").

body, that is, communicates on a metaphorical level as a sign, pointing to its own nature, and to its origin beyond itself. Metaphor and poetics are not an alien imposition upon John Paul's theological anthropology but are intimately entwined in it.

The key findings of John Paul's theological anthropology, his hermeneutic strategy of "reading the body in truth," and his reliance upon phenomenology to clarify and confirm his findings, form the basis of the claims made in this book. These claims are that John Paul's two-pronged method of reading scripture as revelatory of the body, and treating the body as a revelatory text to be read, support the idea that reality can be accessed through poetics. Poetic articulations may be literary, as in the case of scripture, for example, or physical, as in the case of the body. Related to this claim is one that proceeds from it: that fruitful theological reflection can take place in the experience of reading literature and/or in the experience of embodiment. If, as upheld by this author, poetics may disclose some aspects of reality that literalist, or scientific approaches alone cannot, then a hermeneutic of body-poetics is a legitimate resource to expand theological knowledge. On the basis of the three preceding claims, it is further claimed that the maternal body of the Virgin Mary is given *for* Christ's body and that her body is well-expressed as "poem of the Father."

These four claims are addressed by first of all, contextualizing John Paul's theological anthropology with the philosophic ideas which shaped it, and within the ecclesial assumptions that inform his work. His scriptural engagement and his core concept of *reading* the body invite some analysis of the place of metaphor in John Paul's hermeneutical exercise. His premise, as articulated in this book, that poetic expressions can disclose the Real and the True, is put to the test with a series of poetry readings. John Paul's further premise, that the body reveals the Real and the True, is tested by a detailed reading of the poetics of the obstetric body, as seen through the lens of the Virgin Mary. Several issues arise in these tests of claims.

John Paul's implicit interest in, and commitment to, the truth-bearing potential of literary poetics as a resource for theological anthropology, has prompted this writer to look at poetics through a reading of selected literary poems, all of which deal in some way with the Virgin Mary as their subject. Two issues arise. The first is why poems were chosen, rather than any other literary genre; is there some quiddity that makes poems an especially suitable means of disclosing reality? The second is why these particular poems were chosen; does their subject, the Virgin Mary, prejudice the outcome?

A further issue pertains to the focus this book gives to the obstetric body of the Holy Mother; that is, to those body organs and that body system that distinguish the Virgin Mary as a woman. Traditionally, the focus of the catholic faithful has been Mary's perpetual virginity and her spiritual, rather than somatic, motherhood. The twentieth century saw a prolific output in Roman Catholic publications on the subject of Mariology, and the formation of a large number of Marian societies to promote her veneration. These did not, though, attend to Marian maternity in terms of its full womanly embodiment. Her obstetric body, though, distinguishes her especial contribution to salvation history. It therefore warrants theological scrutiny as it was *this* body in which, uniquely, the God-man dwelt bodily. It is therefore consistent with catholic orthodoxy to redress this omission.

The first chapter of part 1 of John Paul's *Theology of the Body* gives a close and extended theological and philosophical exegesis of the two creation narratives of Genesis. From his reading, John Paul extracts the essential qualities that, according to those texts, distinguish man, marking him off as different in kind from other living things: that man receives himself from the excess outpouring of divine love; that man, likewise, inclines towards others to whom he wants to give himself; that the body is a sacramental sign. These qualities can be summed up as the body's having a spousal meaning. It is one of the aims of this book to show how the obstetric body expresses these qualities, and how specifically a female body manifests them in a particular way.

It becomes clear, says John Paul, that the person, at a fundamental level, is correctly known by what he calls the "hermeneutic of gift." *Givenness* is the nature of the cosmos, and the foundational metaphor that shapes how the person is to be treated. Each person is a gift. John Paul's theological anthropology probes this metaphor, analyzing what it means by "reading" the *text* of the body. Metaphor lies at the heart of John Paul's investigations, prompting consideration of how its ubiquity gives a window into the nature of the embodied person. Metaphor is seen not as dispensable motif but as indispensable hermeneutical strategy. This book seeks to extend the application of John Paul's central metaphoric strategy of "reading," and of the implicit metaphor on which it relies: that the body is a text, by making a strong claim that the text as which the body is best understood is a *poem*, and that the Virgin Mary is the human poem par excellence.

The years since the delivery and publication of the *Theology of the Body* have seen a renewed interest by theologians in the body as a subject of theological investigation. John Paul is now one among a range of newer, contemporary voices, which also promote a renewed interest in the sexed body. These newer voices tend to differ in their approach to the body. Historic theological engagements with the body have tended towards moral polemic, aimed at encouraging the avoidance of concupiscence. (John Paul's theological anthropology is consistent with that inheritance: one chapter is devoted to the change effected by the primeval lapse into sin.[3] His overall approach, though, is oriented far more positively on how the good of sexual relations within marriage contributes to the good of spouses and the good of society.) While some of these contemporary theologians may share John Paul's broad motivation of affirming the importance of the body, and of lived experience, several pointedly diverge from him in their aim of changing ecclesial norms so as to expand the range of sexual practices endorsed by the church. Such theologians therefore differ profoundly from John Paul II in how they read the body. I share the interest of these contemporary theologians in issues of embodiment and am sympathetic to some of their concerns (reaffirming the centrality of the body as a legitimate focus of theological enquiry; attending to the sexed body; redressing imbalances in masculine biases). However, I arrive at significantly different conclusions: that the body is not well thought of as being a social construction; that the "spousal" meaning of the body does not prejudice women; that the obstetric body is a rich resource for poetics; that the obstetric body as seen in the light of the Virgin Mary is a resource to further and better understand her, and that it sheds light on the meanings of motherhood, womanhood, and being human.

In looking at the body-poetics of the Virgin Mary, it is the finding here that Mary serves Christ's body; body-physical, and body-mystical. Her life's orientation and purpose are *for* Christ. This is detectable in her actualized desire, as expressed in her body-acts; in the sum realization of

---

3. Adam and Eve were originally free from concupiscence (that is, yearning for temporal things to gratify one's sensuous appetites, rather than satisfying the good of reason). Freedom from concupiscence has not been restored to humanity, which is, though, given abundant grace to succeed in struggling against it. See Ming, "Concupiscence."

her earthly life; and in the glorified life that the Catholic and Orthodox churches believe her now to live. Marian orientation toward God recapitulates primal man's original orientation. Restoring a correct orientation is the perpetual task of salvation history in each generation, and in each individual. Mary's unwavering orientation makes her the prototype of loyal discipleship and foremost of the saints. Such has been taught and upheld in church tradition. While ecclesial tradition and the veneration of the faithful have properly focused on her personal holiness, her sacred body has been much reduced in the catholic imaginary. Personal holiness, though, does not bypass the body; it suffuses it. The body manifests the person, and a person sufficiently conformed to Christ, infused with the Holy Spirit, is materially holy, not just spiritually so. It is therefore both desirable, and consistent with tradition, that Mary's maternal body be incorporated, centered, within theological anthropology.

Although the Virgin Mary has historically been much venerated by laity and consecrated religious, Joseph Cardinal Ratzinger (Pope Benedict XVI) remarked regretfully in 1977 the decline in her veneration over the course of the preceding years.[4] Her ecclesial diminution coincided with a period of social upheaval in the West, which notably included a societal reconfiguration of sexual boundaries and practices. These changes were embraced by substantial numbers within the church. John Paul II had long been sustained by a personal devotion to the Virgin Mary. On his elevation to the papacy, he had dedicated his pontificate to the Immaculate Heart of Mary, adopting as his papal motto, *Totus tuus*. He encouraged the faithful to likewise venerate and imitate Mary, perceiving a need to restore Mariology to its proper place within the church.[5] To omit, or minimize, Mary's presence within theological anthropology is to forfeit particular insights she can best offer, whether as a specific person (*Mary*), as a representative figure (*woman; mother*), or as typological figure (*church*). Woman's unique capacity to bring forth human life touches upon the mystery of life itself. The experiences of, and facts of, gestation and birth give essential perspectives on being human, and on human being in relation to God. To overlook these foundational and universal life events is to neglect what is "purely and simply feminine."[6]

4. Ratzinger, *Daughter Zion*, 7.
5. Bulzacchelli, "Mary and the Acting Person."
6. Ratzinger, *Daughter Zion*, 25.

While Mariology was not overlooked at the Second Ecumenical Council of the Vatican (hence, Vatican II), neither was it afforded a discrete Vatican II document. Instead, it was incorporated within *"Lumen Gentium:* Dogmatic Constitution on the Church." This placement resituated her *horizontally* within the church, as fellow disciple. Mariology horizontally contextualized within theological anthropology could be seen to have a positive effect upon all women who may indirectly benefit when Mary is affirmed and honored. Venerating Mary may also contribute to redressing the over-articulation of the male both within the church, and more broadly, as figuring humanity.

Mary is seldom contemplated as woman, or as mother, in a corporeal sense. Doing so within the context of theological anthropology broadens the scope of that enquiry and helps to flesh out its portrait of *anthropos.* Within the terms of the Roman Catholic Church's self-understanding, this type of expansion, provided it is not a deviation, is legitimate. Although God's public revelation was declared complete upon the formation and closure of the catholic scriptural canon, that revelation can be clarified, or some aspect of doctrine made more explicit, as the church continues to collectively grow in understanding. As *motherhood* is a key metaphor for the church's self-understanding, by including the Virgin Mary's maternal body within theological anthropology, the valences of maternal symbolics are expanded, contributing to a renewed, and fuller, somatically grounded anthropology.

Chapter 2 outlines the contextual background of John Paul II's theology of the body that is relevant for the scope of this work: his philosophic foundations; his hermeneutical presuppositions; his ontological presuppositions; the distinctive inclination, and ability, of humans to make intransitive signs. *Myth* is also analyzed as a genre, especially in terms of how it may disclose truth.

Chapter 3 analyzes John Paul's exegesis of scripture generally, and *myth* in particular, as they appear in part 1, chapter 1, of the *Theology of the Body.* The chief human characteristics that John Paul reads from the Genesis creation myths: original solitude, original unity, original somatic harmony, and the spousal meaning of the body are outlined. Two aspects of John Paul's theology as it relates to construal of the *imago Dei* and human sex distinction, are considered from others' critical perspectives. The chapter ends by analyzing what John Paul means by "language of the body," a key phrase that he introduces in part 2, chapter 2, of the *Theology of the Body*. The philosophic underpinning of the concept, and its connection with symbolic thought, are considered.

Chapter 4 opens with a brief introductory recapitulation of the claims of this book, as have been outlined here, concerning the admissibility of reading poems in the hope, or expectation, that they may disclose or manifest, some aspect of reality. The poetry readings which then follow are done in the belief that literary poems can be looked at as embodied ways of knowing. This speaks to the prime theological interest of articulating and presenting truth. The poems chosen for the readings are treated as forms of linguistic embodiments that speak theologically, by virtue of their being poems, not only in relation to their subject matter.

Chapter 5 sees John Paul II's heuristic principle: that the body speaks, applied to the gestational and birthing body (referred to as the *obstetric* body). This body is looked at through a Marian lens. The obstetric body makes concrete, and expands the horizon of, John Paul's term for the structure that spousal sexual union brings about: "uni-duality." The obstetric body, looked at as a revelatory and communicative entity, opens the way for an enriched appraisal of Mary as a woman; of her divine motherhood of the incarnated God; and of her spiritual motherhood of the church.

The final chapter draws together the claims, and tests of claim, of this book by putting the poetic valences of the poems in conversation with the poetic valences of the Virgin Mary's maternal body, seeing how each speaks to each. Mary's body is argued to be well expressed by the metaphor, "poem of the Father."

2

Contextual Background to John Paul II's *Theology of the Body*

Philosophical Foundations: Debt to Phenomenology

PRIOR TO HIS ELEVATION to the papacy, John Paul had published two books known in English as *Love and Responsibility* (1960; English edition 1981) and *The Acting Person* (1969; English edition 1979) that provide the philosophical foundations for, and are precursors of, his theological anthropology. John Paul offered both a critique of, and an alternative to, the dominant twentieth-century attitude toward materiality, derived from Bacon and Descartes, that it is value-free and exterior to the person. The Cartesian mechanistic view of nature posited matter as an object over which the human could, and should, exercise power; the world being on this account, inhospitable. According to such a worldview, there is no network of relations in which man and the rest of the natural order participate, so there is no conception of a unified natural order. The beauty of nature that man perceives is held to have no meaning; worse, to be a deceit. Man's only hope of finding meaning, on this account, is to find it within himself, in his own rational thought and will. As every person, though, is embodied, constituted as matter, this scheme splits the subject into a dualism of physical exterior, and spiritual interior.

Contra Gnostic and Cartesian tendencies, somatic unity points instead to the physical affecting the spiritual, and vice versa. It rejects any simple dualism that associates the physical with negativity, the spiritual

11

with positivity, or that limits physicality to mere externality. John Paul II, following Thomas Aquinas, upholds the unity of the person. In his "Letter to Families," *Gratissimam Sane* (1994), John Paul wrote that "man is a person in the unity of his body and his spirit. The body can never be reduced to mere matter."[1]

John Paul sought to explicate the Judeo-Christian alternative to pervading notions of the person derived from the philosophies of Immanuel Kant (1724–1804) and Max Scheler (1874–1928). Kant's anti-trinitarian notion of personhood prioritized the autonomous, rather than the relational, self. The Kantian conception of autonomy meant the exercise of one's will without reference to data gleaned from the senses or emotions. In order to be autonomous, an act had to proceed from pure will, with no concern for that act's goodness or badness, as such a consideration would constitute a curb against the subject's will, so, according to Kant, limiting the person's freedom to act. Such limitation was deemed an infringement of personal dignity.[2] Experience, in the Kantian view, is properly subjected to, and over-ruled by, rationality. This extended to all sexual acts, even those within marriage. As sexual union entails the giving of each participating self to the other, Kant saw in sexual relations an inevitable diminishment of personhood by virtue of each experiencing diminished autonomy. Sexual partners, Kant deemed, became "property" for each other's use.

While John Paul II also repudiated any notion of a person's being used as a means for sexual gratification, he departed sharply from Kant's conception of marital sex. Instead, decades before writing his *Theology of the Body*, John Paul held that, while each spouse does renounce his or her autonomy, such renunciation does not diminish the persons. As the renunciation, or self-limiting, proceeds from love for the other, the persons are paradoxically enlarged. Spouses do not *use* each other but give themselves to each other and, in this freely given, sacrificial, and total self-gift, find themselves.[3]

The philosophy of Max Scheler had been closely studied by John Paul II and was the subject of his habilitation thesis. Scheler's thinking provided a foundation for the development of John Paul's thinking about phenomenology, as later presented in *The Acting Person*. Scheler, contra

---

1. GS 19.
2. See Waldstein, "Introduction," 49–51.
3. See Wojtyła, *Love and Responsibility*.

Kant, claimed that love was at the heart of philosophy, and that the philosopher was positively motivated to understand and contemplate given phenomena. Whereas for Kant, emotions had been an embarrassment, dismissed to the realm of the irrational, for Scheler, they were more fundamental to the person than willing or knowing.[4] These intentional feelings manifest a *value* of a thing or person. A personal subject is conscious of experiencing these values, this experience being that which constitutes the subject as a person.[5]

It was Scheler's reduction of the person to consciousness, and the consequence of this: a lack of moral responsibility for his or her acts, against which Wojtyła constructed his conception of the "acting person." Wojtyła had seen the value in the phenomenological method of Scheler, particularly the central position he accorded love. Scheler envisaged love as a feeling at the person's inner core. The phenomenological method he used was applauded by John Paul II late in his life as showing "a relationship of the mind with reality . . . [which is] an attitude of intellectual charity to the human being and the world, and for the believer, to God."[6] Even so, the younger Wojtyła had concluded that phenomenology must be subordinate to theology, as it is the latter which deals with the real, who is God. Scheler's philosophy had raised consciousness to the supreme status, substituting it for the real person in the process.[7]

John Paul II's Hermeneutical Presuppositions

John Paul II's chief hermeneutical presupposition is that it is possible for any person to come to knowledge of truth owing to the nature of personhood and of the world. To discern meaning in life presupposes a world invested with meaning, and so organized and structured so as to make itself intelligible. The Christian belief in a meaningful world is based upon the two-fold scriptural revelation: that the world, and all within it, was intentionally created by God; and that God then lived within, and as, his own created material.

4. Waldstein, "Introduction," 66.

5. Waldstein, "Introduction," 68.

6. Waldstein, "Introduction," 65. Waldstein cites a 2003 address of John Paul II to the World Institute of Phenomenology.

7. Waldstein, "Introduction," 75–76.

That we inhabit a meaningful and accessible universe is inferred from the way humans speak; human speech indicates what sort of universe we inhabit. Augustine's analysis of the relationship between language and reality has been the subject of ongoing reflections by Rowan Williams, who says that how we live and speak suggests that "matter and meaning do not necessarily belong in different universes."[8] Words are signs that we are given; language is an inheritance, passed on to us.

Calling the universe *created* is an acknowledgement that it, too, has been received. By virtue of its givenness, each part of it points to the giver. Therefore all created things are, in a primary way, signs, pointing beyond themselves to their ultimate referent, God. Completing an exegetical circle, human words follow this pattern. They function by indicating a referent, pointing beyond themselves. It is therefore possible to say that the "essential quality" of the world is *sign*.[9] Thinking along these lines seems to have informed the creation story in Genesis 1, where the world is seen as the speech-act of God. Beyond this, but in continuity with it, Christians believe that God made matter his own in the fullest and most extraordinary way by entering into it. The Incarnation is God speaking himself into the language of his own creation.

John Paul's *Theology of the Body* is premised upon the nexus of *gift, language, matter,* and *sign*; an inter-relationship between those who receive the gift; take part in the conversation; are material; interpret the signs; and participate in making further signs. Such a premise allows for no such thing as "mere biology" as the cosmos, including the human body, is alive with meaning. A world that is a matrix of signs, inviting and awaiting understanding, (and *understanding* not in a shallow sense, such that "when you know the code, you read off the content"[10]) is a world that warrants and rewards close observation. Metaphor is one of the chief outgrowths and enablers of attentive observance. John Paul gives such close watchfulness to the Scriptures and to the body. Included within *body* are its potentialities, signed in the type of body it is, and the realizations of those potentialities in relations with others.

The *Theology of the Body* is heavy with scriptural references and quotation. The first chapter of part 1 comprises some ninety pages of theological commentary and exegesis of the Genesis creation narratives.

8. Williams, *Edge of Words*, x.

9. Williams, "Language, Reality and Desire," 141.

10. Williams, "Language, Reality and Desire," 146.

Normatively, Christians relate to scripture as that which anticipates and responds to, the coming into the world of God's definitive sign, Jesus. Again, Rowan Williams is helpful in his gloss of Augustine's view of scripture, that it is "a paradigm of self-conscious symbolic awareness: it is a pattern of signs organized around—and by—the incarnate Word."[11] Scripture, in an especial way, invites participation in its play of signs in order that the reader or hearer may be led towards an ever-deepening love of the world and of God.

For Christian communities, biblical scriptures are believed to have been divinely revealed, communicating knowledge of God that would otherwise be unattainable. These writings are therefore regarded as being foundational for man's knowledge of God. Believed to have been divinely inspired, the Holy Spirit is also believed to be present within the words, and to act as an indispensable aid in forming a correct interpretation. They are therefore believed to be texts unlike any other, and as such, are accorded exceptional status. They also, though, share properties of non-canonical texts, in being conditioned by the times and cultures in which they were written. They may therefore be subjected to fields of academic textual enquiry, ranging from the historical, to the literary, to communication theories. In these senses, they may be regarded as texts like any other.

John Paul's reading of scripture in his *Theology of the Body* accords with the parameters outlined in the Vatican II document, *Dei Verbum*: that scripture should be read in the "sacred spirit" in which it was written (*DV* 12); that its content forms a unified whole; and that its content harmonizes with other aspects of the faith. *Dei Verbum* acknowledges the trends of twentieth-century biblical scholarship, endorsing the application of the historical-investigative method, and form criticism. Attention, it says, should also be paid to the human aspects of the language used, as well as to authorial intent. Scriptural texts, even though separated by many generations in their composition, may be read intertextually, as scripture is one unified whole. Paragraphs 7–10 of *Dei Verbum* deal with textual transmission: the church is to serve scripture by guarding it, listening to it, teaching it, and explaining it. In keeping with these responsibilities, the teaching office of the church has exclusive authority to approve scriptural interpretations. Sacred tradition, scripture, and magisterium are seen as interdependent, and mutually supportive.

---

11. Williams, "Language, Reality and Desire," 147.

What *Dei Verbum* makes clear is that scripture belongs to the ecclesial body corporate. It is communal property prior to, and above, its being individual; an instantiation of what Janet Martin Soskice has felicitously called the "profoundly social religious epistemology" of Christianity.[12] The Bible is therefore not only an historical or a literary text. Its communal dimension sets the bounds of exegetical endeavor, which is always subject to the judgement of the church. Its oversight is defensive, ordered to preventing the transmission of error. Its hermeneutical task, of seeking better understanding and explanation of scripture, is directed to furthering the ultimate aim of biblical hermeneutics, which is maturation of the faith.

So much for the authority of scripture. What, though, of the powers of poetry and prayer? *Dei Verbum* accorded a subordinate place to exegetes. The bounds of exegesis approved by the church may imply overly circumscribed possibilities for the imagination, and so, curtailed opportunities for expressing new insights. However, John Paul's readings of Genesis in his *Theology of the Body*, militates against this concern. By imaginatively rereading the Genesis texts, John Paul is able to enrich the idea of the *imago Dei* and to apply it in a new way to the married couple. He also offers a more detailed and nuanced reading of the narrative specifics of the texts, using this to advance the discipline of theological anthropology. He is not primarily interested in historical questions about the texts, but in their poetic disclosive power.

John Paul is thereby making an implicit, in-principle claim for the licitness of using the imaginative faculty as a means to advance the church's understanding of God. His reading of the Genesis stories is imaginative, analytical, and informed by orthodox personal faith. His faith-commitment does not render his reading suspect or unreliable, but rather the reverse: a fuller knowledge of God is liable to grow precisely in as far as it proceeds from a mind regenerated by faith.[13] While scripture is open to rational inspection, and a rational reading could lead a reader to an intellectual assent to God's existence, knowledge of God that is limited to intellectual assent is not the *telos* of scriptural revelation, which is saving knowledge of God, expressed as obedient faith.[14] Scriptural exegesis

12. Soskice, "Monica's Tears," 450.

13. Truth's formulations are "produced by human reason wounded and weakened by sin" (*FR* 51). Consequently, "reason needs to be reinforced by faith, in order to discover horizons it cannot reach on its own" (*FR* 67).

14. There is always the possibility that human reason alone, apart from revelation

is therefore best conducted not only as an intellectual exercise, but as a practice of faith and a participation in grace. Proper receptive reading calls for a proper disposition. Prayer for faithful interpretation is therefore urged by John Paul.

The nature of John Paul II's approach expresses the relationship between phenomenology and hermeneutics. A phenomenon of the world, scripture is received and responded to by a human subject who embarks upon a hermeneutical task. John Paul's hermeneutical exercise is carried out in the expectation of first, discerning meaning, then receiving truth from the sacred text. The hope and purpose of this process is to more fully know truth, and that this expanded knowledge would deepen the church's public teaching.

The truth-bearing capacity of scripture holds, regardless of the compositional genre of its various texts. For the contemporary mind, this presents a problem when it comes to the genre of myth, such as the Genesis creation texts. According to George Steiner, the distinctive characteristic of this genre is "openness to unknowing."[15] Such openness is the ground of a quest for meaning that lies beyond the scope of the visible world to provide. Myth presses beyond the frontiers of the known, and of the knowable. It deals with the weighty questions of man's existence and demise, how one is to live and why one must die. Mythic construction is a hermeneutical strategy to open a community's apprehension of truths that cannot be empirically demonstrated. Myths makes available that which cannot be accessed by other means, mediating erstwhile inaccessible truths as poetic narrative.

Mythology as a form of reflection about the world is not superseded with the progress of science. Scientific methodology gives revisable, partial access to truths about the world. The *telos* of the natural sciences is to arrive at knowledge via demonstrable theories or verifiable explanations. This is clearly not a methodology suitable for all areas of knowledge (as, for example, the affective or the philosophic). There has been recent theological interest in identifying epistemes common to the sciences and the arts, such as the "critical realism," proposed by Anthony Monti.[16] Likewise, Rowan Williams in *The Edge of Words* has argued that the universe is "inherently symbolic," in a move that recasts "symbolism"

---

and grace, could lead a person to knowledge of God. See Pius XII, "*Humani Generis*" 2, 25, 29.

15. Steiner, *Real Presences*, 222.

16. Monti, *Natural Theology of the Arts*.

as an episteme not only for the arts, but for the sciences. A symbolic world is inherently allusive and representative, and, like the genome of which Williams writes, is "structured as a complex of patterns inviting recognition and constantly generating new combinations of intelligible structures."[17] This suggestive quality implies a world ordered for some recipient, "it *becomes* a pattern only when there is a receiving and decoding 'partner.'"[18] This concept of symbolic materiality is as far removed as possible from what Williams admonishes is the "decadent" Cartesian concept of materiality as alien exteriorization.

The notion of inherent symbolism in the world was the currency of medieval Christianity. Its trace is present in the notion of the world as gift, where the world represents and expresses the love of the divine giver.[19] On this view, the order of nature is more than a context in which mankind dwells. As it is a gift, participation in the world is a participation in the set of relations that proceed from the created order's common source. This divine source is held, to a greater or lesser degree, to pervade the created order. Grace is still present, even after the world is wounded by sin. Owing to this presence of graced goodness, the natural order is a constantly available resource pointing beyond itself and toward God. On this account, the natural order is not something to distrust or despise, but something to gratefully receive and learn from, as the Creator intended the meaning of the cosmos to be intelligible to, and progressively penetrable by, human understanding.

The concept of creation's giftedness is secured by the Judeo-Christian concept of creation *ex nihilo*. To say creation proceeded from nothing is to say that it was not a necessity; it was created without any help; and it is not an extension of God's own being. It is ontologically distinct from its maker. David L. Schindler sees this real giftedness of the creature from nothing as securing the possibility of creaturely participation in his own self-realizing: "his own self-constitution [occurs] only from 'inside' the act of creation."[20] The act of being is both given to, and exercised by, the creature. This paradox of creation Schindler dubs

17. Williams, *Edge of Words*, 103.

18. Williams, *Edge of Words*, 102.

19. The giftedness of creation is strongly expressed in the theology of Spanish Carmelite mystic, St John of the Cross (1542–1591), on whose theology of faith Karol Wojtyła wrote his first doctoral thesis.

20. Schindler, "Being, Gift, Self-Gift," 238.

"receptive self-constitution."[21] That is, the creature is both profoundly other than God—a receptive subject "in and by means of which God's act is received"[22]—and simultaneously dependent through and through on God's communication of being. The giftedness, and therefore implicit reception, of creation is an expression of generous Love. The constitutive meaning of the creature is therefore, in Schindler's words, "*to be loved by* and *to love* (the Creator)."[23]

John Paul II's Ontological Presuppositions: Grace and Participation

Two related ontological principles of creation are that the created order, which proceeded from God, is infused with God's sustaining grace, and that the human creature participates in this in a distinctive way.[24] Owing to its being divinely infused, the world is inherently meaningful; a site of meaningful truths. That is to say that the created order has epistemic potential; that being structured according to the hermeneutic of gift, it is something to be received and understood, although, as the Catechism of the Catholic Church cautions, not without effort.[25] The human body is not exempted from bearing this epistemic potential. Not only is the body-person the site where such understanding takes place, the body itself is an object towards which understanding can be directed. It is a manifestation of intelligible materiality; in Rowan Williams's phrase, it is "a *meaning* portion of matter."[26]

The Christian dogma of the incarnation—the belief that the Second Person of the Holy Trinity was incarnated as the man, Jesus of Nazareth—both underwrites, and confirms, the meaningfulness of the body. God's definitive self-revelation (see John 1:18) is flesh before being translated into literary text. Christ's enfleshment occasioned theological debate in the early centuries of the church about the implications of this for

21. Schindler, "Being, Gift, Self-Gift," 244.

22. Schindler, "Being, Gift, Self-Gift," 238.

23. Schindler, "Being, Gift, Self-Gift," 250.

24. The Catechism states, "Creation comes forth from God's goodness, and it shares in that goodness" (*CCC* 299).

25. The Catechism says that humans "can understand what God tells us by means of his creation, though not without great effort and only in a spirit of humility and respect before the Creator and his work" (*CCC* 299).

26. Williams, "On Being a Human Body," 406.

the common valuing of corporeality. Those tensions and disagreements finally favored an affirmation of the goodness of the body, even while acknowledging its limitations. The incarnated Christ is held to be the definitive expression of human personhood, as well as mediating divine personhood, precisely through his body. The necessity for a hermeneutic of the body is therefore confirmed and fortified by the Incarnation as it is Jesus's body that was, and so Christians believe, continues to be, the instantiation of God's redemptive self-gift. Owing to the Incarnation, the study of God and the study of the body are not only properly linked, but inseparably so: "Through the very fact that the Word of God became flesh, the body entered theology . . . through the main door" (*TOB* 23:4).

What also entered through the main door is hermeneutics; specifically, the relationship between phenomenology and hermeneutics. As persons are phenomena in the world, God in the Incarnation made himself subject to common interpretation. In Augustinian terms, as Rowan Williams explains, Jesus in his divinity is "supremely 'res'; the context of all else that exists." Simultaneously, Jesus as God's incarnated Word is also "a unique *signum* which is the speech of God."[27] Jesus is a sign that stretches hermeneutical capacity, so implicitly leading us towards an activation of the imagination. God manifest as Jesus confounds understanding, incapacitating linguistic expressivity (cf. Luke 2:34). His *call* is that of the definitive master-work of art that confronts our stumbling efforts at interpretation (cf. Mark 8:27; Matt 16:13). To answer the call is to make a hermeneutic commitment.

John Paul's hermeneutical commitment affirms the worthiness of the body. The pope's attitude is distinguished from some negative views of the early church, influenced by Gnosticism or Platonism, such as, for example, that expressed in the *Epistle to Diognetus* in the late second-century, that "the flesh hates the soul, and wars against it," and "the soul is imprisoned in the body."[28] Christopher Gousmett's doctoral research parsed differing attitudes to the body in patristic texts. Some patristic theologians, such as Irenaeus (c. AD 120–200), Theodore of Mopsuestia, (c. AD 350–428), and Ephrem of Syria (c. AD 306–373), expressed an integrative, unitary view of the body (body as a composite of body and spirit). However, not all patristic writers who held a unitary view of the body affirmed the body's value. Some, such as Melito of Sardis (died c.

---

27. Williams, "Language, Reality and Desire," 140–41.

28. Mathetes, "Epistle to Diognetus" 6.

AD 180) and Tertullian (c. AD 155–240), considered the body to be unworthy, and so ineligible for inclusion within the concept of the *imago Dei*. John Paul II's anthropology takes an integrative, unitary view of the body. His patrimony is by way of Irenaeus, Tertullian, and Cyprian (c. AD 200–258), each of whom held a unitary view and also included the body within the *imago Dei*.[29]

Some of the early church's priest-theologians did attest to the epistemic nature of creation; its truths discoverable, or discernible, in a unique way by humans who have the fullest creaturely capacity to receive and respond to them. One such was Justin Martyr (c. AD 100–165) who, in his *First Apology*, wrote that the created order showed forth the Resurrection in the daily transition from night to day, and the seasonal transitions from planting to harvest. This attestation of the world's openness to interpretation implies the necessity of a hermeneutic of *text*; (*world* understood as that which is read). This involves a commitment to a certain way of understanding texts, and of the relationship between author, text, and reader. Such a textual hermeneutic implies, *a priori,* a hermeneutic of language. If the world is meaningful, its meanings discoverable and communicable, then *language* is implicated from the world's beginning.

Meaningfulness is often mediated linguistically via symbol and metaphor. Once thought of as dispensable surface adornments, so arbitrary communication tactics, metaphor is now seen to be strongly rooted in thought structures.[30] The broad definitional frame of Paul Ricoeur in *The Rule of Metaphor* is that metaphoric predication draws into relationship two terms that are not alike, and in this difference, pronounces a perceived similarity. The enigmatic union between the literal meanings of each term, and their metaphoric meaning, forges a tensile relationship. Ricoeur borrows the term, "semantic impertinence," to describe the semantic challenge of the relationship between metaphoric terms which, he says, establish "proximity" in spite of "distance." Ricoeur, that is, proposes that at the heart of metaphor is paradox, or logical inconsistency. His suggestion is supported by a cognitive science model which has found the initial reading of a metaphor to be "typically inconsistent."[31]

Ricoeur seems to be suggesting that the surprise element ("impertinence") dominates, but the force of such surprise is ordered towards

29. Gousmett, "Shall the Body Strive," 22–27.

30. According to Gentner and Bowdle, metaphor is "a way of deriving new abstractions" ("Metaphor as Structure-Mapping," 110).

31. Gentner and Bowdle, "Metaphor as Structure-Mapping," 111.

persuasiveness. His account of metaphoric structure relies upon contrast ("distance") at two levels: between, using I. A. Richards's terms, the tenor and vehicle, and between their literal and metaphoric meanings. That the terms of a metaphor productively interact within the mind of a reader is nuanced differently by different theorists but is uncontentious. What has proven to be contentious is the idea Ricoeur advances of two levels of meaning, the literal and the metaphoric; the interaction between the two is what gives metaphor its force.[32] Recent cognitive science has indicated that the whole of a metaphoric statement is imaginatively grasped at once, both the literal meaning and the metaphorical. This involves cognitive processing that can process literality within a metaphor, even while leaping beyond it.[33] Metaphor appears to be processed in the same way as literal comparisons. A reader can simultaneously grasp both a literal and a metaphoric interpretation. The reader registers that the statement is literally false while also registering that that is not the point.

Michael Polanyi's (1891–1976) theory of metaphor seems closer to the recent findings of cognitive science. Polanyi theorized that the performance of linguistic tasks, such as processing a metaphor, involved the same cognitive skills and processes as the performance of physical tasks. Polanyi suggested that a masterly performance of a physical task involved two levels of awareness, the "focal" and the "subsidiary." These are interactive, mutually-supportive, and simultaneously present. It is the latter subsidiary, or background, awareness that gives the performer a tacit understanding of the task that is occupying him. Anthony Monti expresses this as the activation of "intuitive perception rather than correct deduction."[34]

Polanyi opened a door to a new way of understanding the complexity of how the body *knows* in the performance of tasks, and how such knowing has similarities with how the mind knows. Polanyi's schema of two mutually supportive types of attention is helpful in understanding the dual levels of attention which the mind gives to the literal and metaphoric meanings of metaphor. The indicators from cognitive science suggest confirmation of Polanyi's theory, and lend credence to the intuition of Hans-Georg Gadamer (1900–2002) that metaphor is the primary way we engage with the world. Viewed from the reverse perspective, if the world

32. Monti, *Natural Theology of the Arts*, 63.

33. Gentner and Bowdle, "Metaphor as Structure-Mapping," 112.

34. Monti, *Natural Theology of the Arts*, 57.

we inhabit is intrinsically metaphoric, then that dimension seems to be readily accommodated in human acts of knowing.

Metaphor is the primary strategy for communicating an insight or extending understanding. It expands thought in the same structural way that human-world relations take place: whatever is new (*unknown*) we seek to understand via something familiar (*known*). What is newly known redounds to what was previously known, modifying our perception of it. Metaphor is a linguistic construct but prior to this, it is a thought structure. We speak metaphorically because we think metaphorically. Persons experience the world as multiple acts of interpretation. Metaphor is the primary hermeneutic which conditions and shapes how we make sense of the world.

Poeisis: Divine and Human

The two Genesis creation texts speak of the world as being an intentional production proceeding from the creative force of God; analogically, the cosmos is the art-work of God. There is ancient precedent in the tradition for this. As noted by Margaret Miles, Ambrose (c. AD 340–397) spoke of the human body as being superlative divine art.[35] The biblical texts present the cosmos as an ordered unity proceeding from God. Human art productions (*art* understood broadly as any medium of visual or literary art, including poetry) echo in their finite way this structure of taking material, ordering it, or fitting it together, "to form a new unity that the human agent intends to serve some purpose."[36] This is not to imply that art is ideologically driven (the hall-mark of propaganda) but that it hopes to present something in such a way that a truthful new vision of some reality takes place. It invites and facilitates; it does not impose. Art, that is to say, is a gift.

The reciprocal acts of giving and receiving are anchored in the *a priori* given-ness of creation. The structure of relationality is therefore intrinsic to the world as it proceeds from somewhere to elsewhere, from Source to terminus. The two principles of creation: that it is the created-from-nothing work of God, and that it is given from, by, and through God, imply a moral obligation on the part of the created order to respond to this act of love. George Steiner sees just such a moral obligation

---

35. Miles, *Augustine on the Body*, 87.

36. Gurtler, "Plotinus on the Limitation of Act of Potency," 38.

attaching to works of art. Recalling Ricoeur, beholding an art-work is an act of encounter. A type of relation is formed, and with it, says Steiner, attendant moral accountability. This, Steiner calls art's "answerability."[37]

Steiner's claim rests upon an assumption that art is not neutral material; it is distinguished from other objects. Its distinction lies in its having been configured as an object of meaningful matter that "speaks," which presupposes someone who will hear, and maybe listen. This is one dimension of the moral force art exerts: being a meaningful, speaking presence. There is no moral compulsion to reply, as art does not coerce. One may discern, though, an attractive force, an allure, to respond in such a way as to honor the labor of the work's creation.[38] The late, prolific Australian poet, Les Murray, suggests that contemplation may be the most suitable response.[39] It is the type of response the Lucan gospel attributes to the Virgin Mary (Luke 2:19).

The moral force of art is also related to its gratuity. The *factum est* of an artwork is the rationale for its existence: *being* is the reason for being. While God is the only instance of absolute predication ("I Am Who I Am") the human, God's supreme creation, is imbued with his own irreducibility: the fact of his being secures his right to be. This is one way in which art analogically images the human, the divine image. Art is that production which befits humanity's stature. Neither a human being, nor art, serve a utilitarian purpose. Art's philosophic stance of repudiating the utilitarian, accounts for its being politically engaged in its substratum. It does not exist to generate profit (for this reason, poetry-writing is a purer artform than the visual arts which are more readily absorbed into, and corruptible by, art markets). To the extent that it does not compromise its nature as a gratuitous object, gratuitously made, art resists becoming an object of power. That very failure of power-structures to contain it, imbues it with its own authority, making it dangerous for those who aspire to totalitarianism.

An embedded paradox of an artwork is that although it is a thing set apart from other things, it is also a thing with a conversational structure. Art, by its nature, is public. Its very presence within someone's sensory field is already a way of person and object initiating a relationship.[40] This

37. Steiner, *Real Presences*, 8.

38. Murray, "On Being Subject Matter," 40.

39. Murray, "Embodiment and Incarnation," 322.

40. Cognitive linguists and philosophers George Lakoff and Mark Johnson have argued that metaphor is fundamental to human self-perception and to the way the

implies surrendering something of the self to that relationship: time, effort, mental space. The nature of such an artistic relationship is transient; a receiver may directly encounter it only intermittently, and may need repeated rests from it, as has been the experience of Les Murray.[41] The attractive force of the relationship, though, may last a lifetime. Appreciation of the art need not imply any concomitant moral commitment as to its content. Even art fashioned so as to express particular values or truths may not necessarily realize its maker's intention.[42]

In his 1955 essay enquiring into the nature of art, artist and poet, David Jones (1895–1974) attributed art's moral value both to its gratuitous presence, and to the intransitive nature of its signing. It is an insight echoed by Graham Pechey: art (as is an intransitive verb) is "the subject and object of its own activity."[43] Animals and birds also make things, but their creations are only functional ("transitive")[44] so do not qualify as sign-making. The uniqueness of man's sign-making leads Jones to say that "*poeta*" is the title best befitting the human. Acts of *poeisis* necessitate a body; disincarnate entities cannot make. Owing to sign-making's reliance on the human body, art signifies and affirms the body's goodness. In Jones's uplifting words, "the body is not an infirmity but a unique benefit and splendor."[45] If, in making signs, man realizes a distinctive creaturely capacity, and if this capacity is possible only by virtue of embodiment, then the body is not something unworthy of man's stature, nor obstructive to the realization of holiness. Jones's philosophical endorsement of the body's goodness, and his celebratory affirmation of it, accords with John Paul's reading of the Genesis creation accounts.

If artworks do call for a response, then human embodiment is doubly implicated as persons are both receptors, and generators, of art. Persons have a unique creaturely capacity to cognize intransitive signs

---

mind works. They claim that persons think of their "visual field" as a container within which they perceive themselves to be. Persons are conscious both of being a seeing subject and of being an object within that field of vision; that sight is inherently relational, reaching beyond the body's boundary. See Lakoff and Johnson, *Metaphors We Live By*.

41. Murray, "Poems and Poesies," 374.

42. Paul Ricoeur makes a distinction within the category of "signification" between what an author intended to signify and what a text does actually signify. Ricoeur, "Problem of Hermeneutics," 12.

43. Pechey, "Frost at Midnight," 232.

44. Jones, "Art and Sacrament," 149.

45. Jones, "Art and Sacrament," 165.

(whereas functional signs of, for example, smoke signaling fire, are cognized by animals, as well as persons), and to echo divine sign-making in the finite order. Converging the metaphors of Augustine and Steiner, we can say that humans are doubly answerable to the divine artwork of creation, both by virtue of living within it, and of being creation's highest-order artwork.

To make a response implies a prior cognitive act of recognition. This recognition constitutes, at the least, a putative form of knowledge. Understanding can develop when such knowledge becomes the subject of contemplation.[46] A response is an act of interpretation, and interpretation is, according to Paul Ricoeur, the central problem of hermeneutics. Turning his attention to the hermeneutics of biblical revelation, Ricoeur's 1977 essay, "Metaphor and the Central Problem of Hermeneutics," reflected upon the theological import of biblical genres in which the revelatory function of the texts is modulated differently. Ricoeur argues that genre is not just "a rhetorical façade" but functions within the text theologically. When the form of revelation (genre) is taken seriously, the concept of revelation is revealed to be "polysemic and polyphonic."[47]

A major advantage of this approach for Ricoeur is that his hermeneutical method does not disconnect regular human experiences from acts of biblical interpretation. Persons order and make sense of their own lives in multiple daily acts of interpretation. Ricoeur is therefore able to claim that he approaches revelation in an "a-religious sense."[48] Ricoeur calls attention to the nature of the Christian biblical texts as "originary"; that is, having been written closer in time to the events they record, and so closer to the primary effects of those events. These texts are not written as neutral records of events but as the first interpretations of the definitive events that shaped the Christian community's belief, and grounded its self-understanding. Using Gadamer's term, they are "engaged" texts (text and interpreter engaged in a dialogue to arrive at truth). In their engagement, they mimic the way in which persons experience ordinary life. Anyone can experience a sense of having been "seized" by some event and have a sense that the seizure will prove life-shaping. In the case of the biblical texts, Ricoeur claims it is only their subsequent systematization

46. Ricoeur sees interpretation as "the alternating of the phases of understanding and those of explanation along a unique 'hermeneutical arc'" ("Problem of Hermeneutics," 9).

47. Ricoeur, "Metaphor and the Central Problem," 129.

48. Ricoeur, "Metaphor and Hermeneutics," 133.

into propositional faith claims that "neutralizes" them by dissociating them from their expressive genres. John Paul II was alive to the different expressive force of different literary genres so would not have shared any implicit censure of formal faith statements (a different genre, serving a different purpose). He did, though, share a concern for reinvigorating faith claims, some of which no longer seemed to "seize" many of the faithful.

Ricoeur's thinking about how different genres differently reveal reclaims ground for the medium of the message, seen not in reductive terms as a means to the end of delivering certain content, but as a contributor to, and shaper of, that content. Ricoeur is theorizing a symbiotic relationship between message-content and message-form. His approach, as noted, engaged a single paradigm by which all acts of interpretation, secular or sacred, are made. In arguing that genre and content form a single, symbiotic, expressive unity, Ricoeur's theory contributes to restoring of a sense of the sacramental. David Jones had argued that improper fragmentation of that which should properly be united, wounds a sacramental sense (a sacrament being a sign which confers the grace it signifies).[49] Ricoeur's theory also recasts the propositions of faith so they more nearly resemble what they originally were: something forcefully experienced within a living community. His hermeneutical method re-sites faith claims within the whole body, not only within the mind.

The act of reading a text provides an analogy of the person's ability to objectify his or her own body. Each person's body is the fundamental text of encounter. The manner of this encounter differs in kind from any other, as, in Rowan Williams's words, "the body is never simply an object in my field of perception."[50] Williams reflects that this difference means that our perception of occupying space is the unconscious backdrop of our engagement with the world, while also shaping that world in which we live and move. Being oriented in space, having to face a direction, means that we are constantly navigating obstacles. This *facing-toward* is already a form of relationship with what we see or move towards (or away from). Our bodies, he claims, are therefore constantly bound up with "attitudes, projects, and relationships."[51] The body is inherently intelligent as a site from which negotiations with the world are conducted. The implication

49. Jones, "Art and Sacrament," 176.
50. Williams, "On Being a Human Body," 404.
51. Williams, "On Being a Human Body," 405.

of this, for Williams, is that the natural body is never a neutral organism; it is always already engaged with culture. Persons organize and symbolize their engagements with the world, not excluding their bodily needs and desires, as, for example, in eating's symbolization as social bonding.

While the body from birth is entangled with culture, caution should be exercised so as not to over-state culture's role. The extreme expression of their entanglement would be to claim culture as determinative of the body. Bodies function physiologically, though, in predictable ways for demonstrable reasons, regardless of the culture in which they are present. The same logic applies (although perhaps, less straightforwardly) to the psychological functioning of persons. Culture schools the body (such as in which functions may be exercised publicly, which privately; which body parts may be visible to whom and where) but even so, the *body*—an acting person—can resist, or choose to selectively disengage from some, if not all, of its cultural entanglements. A discriminatory cultural appropriation could be seen as a moral imperative for each life and as informing the primary task conferred on the church: the evangelical commission to reach (therefore, change) all cultures. The form of cultural resistance that Christianity advocates is to turn to, and embrace, the *a priori* culture of faith that constituted "the beginning." The need for cultural *metanoia* is the starting point from which John Paul II begins his theological-anthropological task; that contemporary culture has a distorted and erroneous conception of the body, which is manifest most clearly in its misrepresentation of sexual relations.

One way in which the thinking of Rowan Williams, and John Paul II does lightly converge is their shared perception that the body and its functions is, in Williams's words, "part of language,"[52] and therefore entwined with culture. John Paul, though, understands something different by *culture*. In the biblical origin myths, which so absorbed John Paul, God's *language* is the originary event; the works of creation are the *what-God-spoke*. On this account, language *is* entwined with the body but the culture within which the body negotiates the world is that of prevenient grace which precedes and grounds human culture.

The task John Paul set himself (and his readers) is to "read the 'language of the body' in the truth" (*TOB* 118:6).[53] This language of the body speaks its filial-spousal meaning, which was inscribed in it by God who

---

52. Williams, "On Being a Human Body," 407.

53. "Rereading" the language of the body has sixty entries in *TOB*.

is the ultimate source of all persons (the "filial" meaning). This same God is also the *telos*, or end-point, in whom and with whom, all persons may experience complete unity in love (the "spousal" meaning). This dual relational metaphor is a way of expressing the intimate participatory nature of personhood in God's self-giving love. Drawing upon Williams's spatial terms, we can say: creatureliness is an orientation towards others by virtue of humans being kin to divine otherness.

3

John Paul II's *Theology of the Body*

PART 1 OF JOHN Paul's *Theology of the Body* opens with his exegesis of the two creation stories in the book of Genesis. As those myths form part of the scriptural canon, they are held to be revelatory. All holy scripture is understood to be a *living* text in an especial and elevated sense, as the Holy Spirit is believed by the church to be present and active within it. For this reason, the scriptural texts are held to be reliably truth-bearing in a way that secular or non-canonical texts are not. Placed at the beginning of the canon, the creation texts provide the meta-context and theological under-pinning for Judeo-Christian self-understanding. John Paul II acknowledges that the creation stories are ancient myths (cf. *TOB* 3:1n4). Affording them serious attention is not intended to affront, nor contend with, a rational, scientific and historical world-view. It *is* to imply the limits of operating exclusively within those boundaries, and to affirm the importance of the imagination in communicating meaning; it is to attest to the truth-bearing potential of mythology.

John Paul is following the gospel injunction of Jesus who, when interrogated by the Pharisees about contemporary marriage practices and their implications (Matt 19:3–12; Mark 10:1–12), directed them to the Genesis accounts of man's beginning. Jesus reversed the direction of interrogation, recasting the religious experts as students, while implicitly contrasting their present practice and attitudes with original practice and divine intention. It was a tactic designed to reorient and correct his questioners by reminding the enforcers of the law that they, too, fall short of the original standard of love. In referring them to their myths of origin,

Christ is indicating that present practice should be interpreted by the scriptural texts.

The transcendent atemporality of myth reminds man he is circumscribed by time and space, and points to his fleeting earthly existence. Myth also attests to the macro-continuity of that existence; that every human life, as Edwin Muir has observed, "begins at the beginning . . . the same problem of good and evil . . . the same need to learn how to live"[1] and follows the same developmental arch or "ancestral pattern."[2] Jesus's directive to his questioners implies they need to reacquaint themselves with who they are, which, as they will read, is no less than the image of God; that the only way in which they (or anyone) can know themselves is in relation to God. The intended outcome is the restoration of proper order; that contemporary cultural practices and ideas will be assessed according to whether, or not; how extensively, or not, they cohere with the truths expressed in the narrative. Jesus clearly regards the texts as being authoritative and having "normative meaning" (*TOB* 1:4) and in citing both accounts, treats them as organically connected. This internal biblical warrant may not seem persuasive for those who do not subscribe to the authority of Judeo-Christian scripture, though. The warrant may appear more persuasive, and less misaligned with the late-twentieth-century context within which the pope wrote, if the genre of myth is analyzed.

Myth and Meaning

In his essay, "Genesis as Myth," Edmund Leach defines myth as that which seeks to communicate knowledge of some reality which is not observable in terms which are observable.[3] Two features of myth are that they occur in a variety of versions ("redundancy") and are expressed according to a series of binaries or opposing categories. When the messages they express are believed to be God's Word, multiple versions are reassuring in so far as the different versions reinforce the essential meaning. Leach himself proceeds to read the Genesis texts as inter-related, forming a complex of repetitions, inversions and variations where, within a common structure, patterns recur.

---

1. Muir, "Poetry and the Poet," 87.
2. Muir, "Poetry and the Poet," 88.
3. Leach, *Genesis as Myth and Other Essays.*

While not explicitly dealing with myth, Edwin Muir's essay, "The Natural Estate," explores the connection between traditional folk ballads and the communities which generated them.[4] This forms part of his wider project to investigate the distance between the poet and the public. Muir's own Orkney childhood, steeped in folkloric tales and ballads, had uniquely equipped him to comment upon this. The communal and familial life he experienced there, tied closely to the land and sea, and governed by the seasons, contrasted sharply and favorably with the Glasgow slum life he witnessed and lived alongside as a teenager. There, he was able to understand the distancing effects of the huge number of manufactured objects which serve to isolate people from the natural world, and consequently adversely affect the imagination. The most potent myths survive in various versions, largely attributable to the oral tradition of ballad transmission; each generation actively contributes to the final modified version. Muir notes an economy of expression and structure in the best ballads: "extreme simplification of form and content," or again: "an ancestral vision simplified to the last degree."[5] Muir concludes that the traditional ballad demonstrates that "great poetry can, or once could, be a general possession,"[6] which invites a reconsideration of the radical availability of the ancient mythic poetic texts of the Bible.

In his early essay, "Myths, Signs and Significations," Gerard Loughlin contrasts a literal reading of a text, where the text is read as a sign (so, a signifier expressing the signified; form expressing meaning), with Roland Barthes's alternative explanation of the differing way a text is read when it is a myth. For Barthes, says Loughlin, mythical texts are read as significations (so, a signifier and a signified; form and meaning), so as to express a so-called "second signified." In the case of mythology, the text as sign is turned by the reader-interpreter into a signifier. Together, *form* and *meaning* comprise a single entity that expresses a "second" mythological meaning. Loughlin summarizes Barthes's analysis as: "Myth properly can only be read as one complete thing, in the conjunction of signifier, signified and signification."[7] According to this thesis, *myth* as a genre functions as do poems, each element bound as a whole—a spliced unity of form and meaning. The idea of a second meaning being simultaneously

---

4. Muir, "Natural Estate."

5. Muir, "Natural Estate," 14.

6. Muir, "Natural Estate," 22.

7. Loughlin, "Myths, Signs and Significations," 273.

grasped also harmonizes with more recent neuroscientific research, as touched upon in chapter 2. Applying this understanding to the human person, as presented in the Genesis myths, each person is a physical sign (signifier) which refers to the Ultimate Referent (signified), which means that the person's signification is the image of God.

The different literary genres that make up the Judeo-Christian Scriptures are attempts to interpret events and persons; to give them a meaning (or to communicate a revealed meaning). The Genesis creation myths are exercises in self-understanding; etiological stories seeking to interpret who *man* is. The preservation of two creation myths offers different metaphorical frameworks, each one taking a different perspective on man in relation to God. John Paul II is mindful of the differences between them (*TOB* 2:2), noting the greater maturity of the Elohist, or Priestly, account of Genesis 1:1–2:4. Although this is first in the canonical ordering, it is the more recent of the two texts. He relates to the texts as revelatory communication, disclosive of truth, which, perforce, have contemporary relevance.[8] His scriptural exegesis follows the approach of literary analysis, rather than biblical studies. He freely probes the texts, composed many years apart, inspecting closely the arrangements of the words, and the meanings they generate, expecting the texts to be truth-bearing. In the case of the Elohist text, rendered according to the formulae of Hebrew poetry, it seems an especially apt method; active investigation operative alongside active receptivity. His methodology assumes the openness of the text, pauses for reflection, and invites further meditation, making it especially suited to the manner of its initial delivery by weekly instalments.

As well as assuming the privileged status of canonical scripture as text, this literary-analytical methodology assumes the text to still be capable of speaking to contemporary readers; to still *live*. This introduces the possibility that a later reading may diverge from an earlier consensus of a text's meaning. This divergence need not simply equate with contradiction. If God's Spirit is held to be distinctively present within scripture,

---

8. In *TOB* 3:1, John Paul explicitly links "deeper reflection" on the earlier Yahwist text" with modern concerns: "We find there 'in nucleo' almost all the elements of the analysis of man to which modern, and above all contemporary, philosophical anthropology is sensitive." In similar fashion, John Paul also saw a parallel between his own attempt to "penetrate" Genesis with the deliberations, then in progress, of a synod of bishops gathered to discuss family relations. See *TOB* 2:5.

then grace is operative.[9] Through the operation of grace, a reader may suddenly apprehend a text differently, or more completely, finding something hitherto unnoticed. This leads to the second assumption behind the pope's methodology: a certain philosophical understanding of language. To arrive at meaning, attention is paid not only to the words written, but to use J. L. Austin's terms, to "*the force*" of the words, and to their intended "*effects*." A reader who is a well-intentioned interpreter enters into dialogue with the text, aiming to faithfully understand it.[10]

Graeme Marshall finds in late Wittgenstein a great help in articulating how it is that texts can disclose more of themselves the more they are read; an idea which is applicable not only to scriptural texts. The challenge comes from the text itself having remained constant—the same words on the page—while the perspective from which it is viewed or read *has* changed and this change has allowed things previously unseen to become visible. Wittgenstein used the spatial analogy of "aspect perception" to illuminate how concepts are fixed. Marshall expresses Wittgenstein's insight:

> Any particular thing has a manifold of aspects each of which presents the whole thing anew. The emphasis shifts from the properties a thing has . . . to what it increasingly is in all its aspects. Its properties are either obvious or to be discovered by proper investigation; its aspects are revelatory of the thing itself.[11]

Different aspects become apparent when a viewer changes vantage point. This spatial analogy can be applied less obviously by imagining not a moving viewer, but a moving text. Once a reader apprehends a text presenting differently, it seems to alter, as, for example, in the perceptual puzzle known as "Rubin's vase," where viewer perception slips between seeing the vase as a positive shape, or seeing it as negative space between two facial profiles, depending on how the relation between the spaces is read. It is an apt metaphor for how different readings of a text may not be

9. Kevin Vanhoozer identified grace as being the missing element in Hans-Georg Gadamer's account of textual interpretation (Vanhoozer, "Discourse on Matter," 31).

10. The consensus of speech-act theorists is that language is more than referential or representational; *action* is the operative concept. Beyond the propositional content of any text is an energy or force. This accounts for words in usage being more than signs or encoded thoughts. For a systematic account of the force of words, see Austin, *How to Do Things*.

11. Marshall, "Look at It This Way," 9.

immediately apparent, but when they are, they cannot be unseen. Apprehending the different aspects, or presentations, expands understanding, bringing, in Marshall's words: "new aspects, awareness of new relations, enrichment of meaning."[12]

Furthermore, authentic dialogue with a text is a two-way flow of interpretation. A contemporary reader of an historic text does not exercise hegemony over it, as though its sole interpreter; contemporary readings stand alongside, and within, historic readings. Any given text, then, resembles a palimpsest. The text co-exists with its accretion of readings.[13] This constitutes one axis of critical enquiry. The other pertains to the text itself which interprets the reader and offers a critique of the historic present.[14] This may be difficult to recognize, requiring developed textual sensibilities, as any *now* tends to appear normal to those living within it. We enter into a text, but that text also enters into us; recognizing what it is saying to us is the textual challenge. This is paradigmatically so when that text is scriptural. The Christian understanding is that scriptural words are perpetually animated by God, their ultimate author (and definitive divine *text*) whose self-determined aspiration is to be admitted inside us.

Texts vary in their capacity to support reader dialogue, depending on their degree of openness. Some types of language, especially those associated with specialisms, are opaque to the non-specialist, or can be manipulated to close down third-party understanding and to obscure meaning—one part of Wendell Berry's thesis in his essay, "Standing By Words."[15] Commitment to textual openness is the operative hermeneutic argued for by Susannah Ticciati in her reading of the Book of Job.[16] Ticciati offers a reversal of the usual assumption—that the book is seeking to deliver answers to the problem of evil—by arguing instead that it seeks to alter the way we ask questions about it (which is the purpose of poetry, according to Australian poet, Bruce Dawe). She argues, therefore, that the text is designed to be read and re-read in a dynamic interaction between text and interpretation, where the text is not shut down upon

12. Marshall, "Look at It This Way," 10.

13. "Any text is an intertext; other texts are present in it, at varying levels, in more or less recognisable forms: the texts of the previous and surrounding culture. Any text is a new tissue of past citations" (Barthes, "Theory of the Text," 39).

14. James Hanvey speaks of the "convergence of horizons" in the kairos, where past, present, and future are present to each other ("Tradition as Subversion," 62).

15. Berry, "Standing by Words."

16. Ticciati, *Job and the Disruption of Identity*.

having provided supposed answers, but is always open to re-reading and the possibility of revised or divergent interpretations—a methodology she implements, in her own reading of Job.

The drawbacks of such openness to new possibilities is that real efforts to engage with a text may only lead to a disheartening exegetical circle where knowledge is frustratingly elusive; textual interpretation can become diffuse and individualistic, prone to the idiosyncrasies and proclivities of any given reader, or group of readers, at any given time. Textual meaning becomes an elusive *telos*. The ultimate implication of perpetual textual uncertainty is a crisis of language; *word* decoupled from *meaning*. *Meaning* subsumed into interpretation becomes a construct of the reader. Such an approach struggles to validate and uphold any one interpretation as normative, or better, and, *verso*, to identify and discard a misreading. The relativism of such interpretations would make it difficult to identify and uphold any textual truth; my truth may not be your truth.[17]

The accretion of interpretations can distract from a text, especially when the history of interpretation is long and varied. In cases of such distraction and/or confusion, a return to the primary text is called for. Perhaps that need is implicitly recognized by Jesus in his instruction to return to "the beginning." While it may not be possible to engage with a text in a state of interpretive amnesia, denuding the text of its history of reception, it is possible to temporarily suspend those memories so as to return to a text in a state of openness, prepared to be surprised. A certain tension may remain, though, as biblical Scriptures are foundational texts, relied upon to provide continuity and connection within the believing community across time and place. Yet one of the chief benefits of textual openness is the possibility of new insights being generated as those texts come into contact with minds shaped by new disciplines, new social attitudes, and new contexts of living. Textual openness is therefore both a grace—even texts composed in a social context long-gone can offer more than dry, historic interest—and risk, so that any new interpretations do not mislead with their novelty. The interpretative task navigates a path between integrating fresh insights, which enrich extant readings, without erasing those other readings. Joseph Cardinal Ratzinger encouraged mindfulness in biblical interpretation; that biblical exegetical models

---

17. Roland Barthes resists the notion of a single, or paramount, truth: "Textual analysis impugns the idea of a final signified." He posits the relation between text and critic as "entering into the play of the signifiers . . . but not hierarchising them. Textual analysis is pluralistic" (Barthes, "Theory of the Text," 43).

from any given period follow the dominant thought-patterns of their time. Church discernment must be exercised, he has said, in identifying and removing any "contemporary ideology" from interpretations, and to assess their compatibility with what he calls "the base memory of the Church."[18]

Imago Dei

One of the most striking instances of John Paul's re-reading disclosing a new insight, or a different way of taking the text, concerns his interpretation of the *imago Dei*. The term has eluded precise definition, or theological consensus, as to its meaning. It not only situates mankind in a special, privileged position *vis-à-vis* the rest of creation, but distinctively defines him through his relation to God, from whom and through whom he was created, in order that God may share the super-abundant divine life. The specifics of the content of *image* are not elaborated in scripture although its meaning can be extrapolated from what the Bible says of God. The reliability of this method rests upon an understanding that the Bible is God's self-revelation, and therefore not a text just like any other. In his 1988 Apostolic Letter, "*Mulieris Dignitatem*: On the Dignity and Vocation of Women," John Paul discusses the link between human resemblance to God and the anthropomorphic language and concepts used of God in the Bible. If man resembles God in some way (as an image must resemble its original) then God can in some way be humanly known, and *verso*, the original in some sense resembles the likeness. The biblical language and concepts used of God do not obstruct understanding but facilitate it. The check on this knowledge is present in the concept, *likeness*, which implies its own limitation. The analogy reaches its own boundary, allowing for the ways in which God is incomprehensibly Other, or *unlike* man.[19] This is particularly pertinent, says John Paul, concerning "*comparisons that attribute to God 'masculine' or 'feminine' qualities*" (*MD* 8).

Historically, the divine image has been seen variously as: inhering in a substantive quality that manifests the image, such as spirit; as a functional quality, such as authoritative leadership; or as creaturely

18. Ratzinger, *Called to Communion*, 19–20.

19. *CCC* 370 states "in no way is God in man's image. . . . But the respective 'perfections' of man and woman reflect something of the infinite perfection of God: those of a mother and those of a father and husband."

relationality (where the focus is not upon having the capacity for relationships, but being within them from the moment of conception). The first of these, man's spiritual dimension, or immateriality, is indicated in the distinctive and unique powers of the human intellect.[20] Human intellectual knowledge is capable of grasping abstract concepts such as *truth*. This type of knowledge—ideas—differs from the sense knowledge that other animals acquire through living in the world. While some other creatures have developed rudimentary forms of communication, none of them can generate abstract concepts, and none of them use abstract sign-systems. Human language therefore strongly indicates human singularity.[21] This singularity is confirmed in Genesis 1: that man, though a creature in the world, also occupies a heightened position "above" the world (see *TOB* 2:3) and can never be merely reduced to the world (*TOB* 2:4).

The second marker of the divine image referred to above, authoritative leadership, can be, and too often has been, corrupted into utilitarian unconcern for other species and biospheres. Perhaps with this in mind, John Paul shifts the emphasis away from seeing human domination of the world (Gen 1:28) as the marker of the divine image, and towards seeing the key marker as inalienable human dignity, and a concomitant moral imperative to safeguard it. Likewise, John Paul resists any distorted interpretation of the *imago Dei* which would reserve it as primarily man's over woman's. John Paul, rather, carefully restates the equality of man and woman before God, seeing man in his personhood imaging God precisely "inasmuch as he is male and female" (*TOB* 9:3). The nature of the image is one of unity in diversity where the *esse* of each of the persons is differentiated, a given, and of the nature of the person, not a role or an adjunct to the person. As far as persons, male and female together, image God, they do so by virtue of living together in a community of symbiotic harmony.

John Paul deduces from the two Genesis texts "that *man became the image of God not only through his own humanity, but also through the*

---

20. For a clear exposition of distinctive human faculties, see George, "What Does 'Made in the Image of God' Mean?"

21. Academic psychologist David Premack has observed that, of the microscopic studies of neural structures conducted since the latter decade of the twentieth century, "virtually all the newly discovered human singularities are located in areas [of the brain] associated with either complex social cognition or language" ("Human and Animal Cognition," 13861).

communion of persons, which man and woman form from the very begin-ning" (*TOB* 9:3). This focuses upon dynamism, rather than the *stasis* im-plied with substantive accounts of the divine image. While the rationale for seeing dynamic relationality as imaging God appears to draw upon Trinitarian theology, the words of Genesis contain under-articulated hints of a differentiated unity in God.[22] These hints open the way for the very much later articulation of the Trinity (*TOB* 9:3). In John Paul's read-ing, inter-personal communion is not just one faculty among others, but is the bedrock, "the very bone marrow" (*TOB* 9:4) of the divine image. To be human is to seek out *"reciprocal enrichment"* (*TOB* 9:5).[23]

A term which summarizes man's distinctive, and superlative crea-turehood, is *person.* Personhood is constituted by the subject's unity of the spiritual, physical, social, and historical dimensions.[24] The person is an agent endowed with free will, moral responsibility, and the capacity to give and receive love. Reciprocal self-giving *for* another finds fullest corporeal expression within marriage, the paradigmatic sign and instan-tiation of which is spousal sexual union. Although this is a relation, and a metaphor, of particular depth, John Paul does not claim it to be the ex-haustive, or exclusive, metaphor by which to understand the *imago Dei.* It is, though, a unique, so uniquely revealing, metaphor. Single persons also image God; each person is endowed with a capacity and a desire for love, and is set within a matrix of relations. John Paul devotes a number of catecheses to explaining how the universal longing to love can lead some, such as he, to forego marriage and all sexual relations in chaste virginity and/or chaste celibacy (*TOB* 73–85). While the totality of self-giving is strikingly manifest in spousal sexual relations, self-giving is not simply equatable with them; in Genesis 1, *"adam* is the divine image of God in his responsibility to obey God, to imitate him, and to worship him."[25] The spousal relationship provides a coherent context for responding to the blessing-command to multiply the divine image. Response to the

22. In Genesis 1, evening and morning form one day, and in Genesis 2:24, man and woman become one flesh. Each of the singularities contains two components. See Atkinson, "Experience of the Body and the Divine," 320.

23. John Paul II's emphasis on reciprocity within the complementarity of male-female relations has been found to contrast favorably with the hierarchical under-standings of Karl Barth and Balthasar. See Sutton, "Complementarity and Symbolism of the Two Sexes."

24. International Theological Commission, "Communion and Stewardship" 9.

25. Martin, "Male and Female," 249.

command is both an imitation of, and participation in, God's free, loving, creative act. John Paul's distinctive contribution to theological anthropology is to see in marital sexual union a strongly revelatory manifestation of the *imago Dei*. John Paul recognizes that he is, in effect, proposing "a theology of sex" (*TOB* 9:5).[26]

One critic of John Paul's theological anthropology, more especially of his treatment of the *imago Dei*, is Gerard Loughlin. Loughlin's 2012 essay, "Nuptial Mysteries," charges the pope with altering the concept of the divine image—a move, he alleges, that excludes some categories of persons. Much in Loughlin's argument relies upon his reading of the Genesis creation stories, and his handling of metaphor. His critical engagement with John Paul II's theology illuminates their different handling of scriptural text.

Loughlin argues that the *Theology of the Body* amounts to an "anthropology of nuptiality."[27] While neither the term, *nuptial mystery*, nor the word, *nuptial*, appear in Waldstein's translation, the concept is central to John Paul's seeing spousal union as a metaphoric sign for the unity and totality of divine revelation.[28] Loughlin expresses concern that the principle of nuptiality as applied to the *imago Dei* is a novelty that breaks with tradition.

John Paul's comfort with, and appreciation of, the fullness of human bodiliness, including its sexual dimension, does contrast with some of the early church fathers, several of whom Loughlin cites in a footnote. One of those not mentioned is Gregory of Nyssa who found the intimacy and ecstasy of sexual expression analogical not only of intra-Trinitarian relations, but of creaturely longing for communion with God, a resource Sarah Coakley has drawn upon.[29] Later mystics, St Bernard of Clairvaux and St John of the Cross, found the biblical nuptial figure of Israel-Church as the bride of Christ a rich resource for theological reflection. Nuptiality

---

26. John Paul most often uses the expression, "conjugal act." Waldstein explains that the term is not a euphemism but is intended to indicate "sex in its full moral nature and goodness as a personal act in the determinate circumstances of conjugal life" (Waldstein, "Index," 687; cf. "Index," s.v. "Conjugal Act").

27. Loughlin, "Nuptial Mysteries," 174.

28. Angelo Scola notes, "The expression 'nuptiality' refers in the first instance to the relationship between the man and the woman." Later development in theological thinking transfers the concept, applying it metaphorically to "the 'sacred marriage' between heaven and earth to the Judeo-Christian theme of the nuptial relationship between Yahweh and his people" (Scola, "Nuptial Mystery," 631).

29. See Coakley, "Creaturehood Before God," 344.

is a metaphor that has been used to theological purpose in scripture and tradition. The figure is more fully elaborated by John Paul II who traces its suitability back to the Genesis texts. He is explicit in seeing the bonding of man and woman together as a potent image of the loving God. Allowing for the inclusion of spousal sexual relations within what is meant by *imago Dei* is not, then, a deviation from normative Christian belief, but more an instance of showing how all human relations, including the most intimate, are understood properly only in relation to God.

A further objection, for Loughlin, in the application of nuptiality to the *imago Dei* is that the sexual relations are exclusively heterosexual. Loughlin sees this as implying that anyone who does not engage in heterosexual acts is excluded from the divine image, so is not fully human. As noted above, John Paul does not mandate spousal sexual relations in order to more fully image God. He does argue insistently, though, for the equal and inalienable dignity of all humans, irrespective of their state or condition of life. John Paul sees in the Genesis stories a principle of the "priority of the *soma*," meaning that human dignity is *a priori* of sexual differentiation: "*The fact that man is a 'body' belongs more deeply to the structure of the personal subject than the fact that in his somatic constitution he is also male or female*" (*TOB* 8:1). This principle importantly secures the moral status of all persons, irrespective of sexual functionality or inclination, including persons of indeterminate sex.

Loughlin also finds it a labored reading to interpret the Genesis text as giving an account of "the inauguration of matrimony."[30] When he speaks of *marriage*, John Paul is referring to the unique relationship between the man and the woman inaugurated "in the beginning." This relationship, a *communio personarum*,[31] predates the foundation of any social order. The married couple most fully expresses this communion of persons in their unique relational unity. *Marriage* is the paradigmatic metaphor by which man gains epistemic access to certain qualities of God, such as cohesion, endurance, and fruitfulness. The relational nature of the intra-Trinitarian life grounds the spousal analogy: "Man becomes an image of God not so much in the moment of solitude as in the moment of communion" (*TOB* 9:3)

Loughlin is further troubled by how the nuptial metaphor is invoked within magisterial teachings, looking at the *Letter to Bishops of the*

30. Loughlin, "Nuptial Mysteries," 175.

31. John Paul II adopted the term from the Vatican II document *Gaudium et Spes* (*GS* 12).

Catholic Church on the Collaboration of Men and Women in the Church and the World (2004) as an exemplum. The letter was issued by the Congregation for the Doctrine of the Faith while under the prefecture of Joseph Cardinal Ratzinger, during the papacy of John Paul II.[32] The final paragraph of number 9 refers to the bridal and covenant metaphors as being, "more than simple metaphors"; the bridal symbolism is "indispensable for understanding the way in which God loves his people." The metaphor of the marriage covenant is, as written earlier in number 9, one "among the many ways in which God reveals himself to his people." The letter expresses the church's belief that the relation established between the terms (*Christ* and *Church*; *God* and *people of God*) is in some sense interior to the nature of the relationship; that what the metaphor expresses is unavailable using any other analogy.

In *Mulieris Dignitatem*, John Paul II notes that biblical bridal imagery is analogical, and that "analogy implies a likeness, while at the same time leaving ample room for non-likeness" (*MD* 25). The *bride*, whether the people of Israel (Isa 54:5) or the church (Eph 5:27), is a collective noun that foregrounds the community (possibly as extensive as the whole of humanity), as God's intended spouse. Loughlin acknowledges as much in a footnote.[33] When the many form a coherent group, by virtue of sharing one or more characteristics, they can be referred to as a single entity. This is the logic of collective nouns. The many referred to as a singular (*bride* of Christ) are bound together by the Holy Spirit, the principle and ground of their unity. They share more than a characteristic; they share in the covenant. The principle of a collective noun is unity, not multiplicity, hence its governing a singular, not a plural, verb.

Loughlin's reading side-steps this singularity, focusing instead on the many who comprise the bride, leading to his grave mischaracterization of the Christic-ecclesial relationship as "polygamous and bisexual."[34] For the purposes of the bridal analogy, *sex* is relevant in that marriage effects the unity of a differentiated two, such that their union changes their ontological status ("the two will become one"). In a marriage between a man and a woman, each spouse takes on that which he or she is not, yet without losing that which he or she is. This is what makes marriage an apt analogy for the relationship that is possible between the divine

32. Ratzinger, "Collaboration of Men and Women."

33. Loughlin, "Nuptial Mysteries," 183n46.

34. Loughlin, "Nuptial Mysteries," 183.

persons and human persons. The materialization of this principle and this metaphor was, for the Christian church, the Incarnation when the Word became human (the what-is-not) without losing divinity (the what-is).[35] When *bride* is used as a collective noun to refer to the church, the salient quality is not sex distinction, it is faithful obedience (although the image does also give a coherent relational account through its sexual referents: God in Christ pours himself out into the believing community, which is a corporate figuration of receptive femininity). Meaning in metaphor is relational, derived positively from the connection between terms, but also negatively, from operative constraints. Loughlin's reading cannot be upheld as it seriously distorts the integrity of the bridal analogy. Polygamy is, in John Paul's words, contrary to the "equal personal dignity of men and women" and radically contradicts the nature of the spousal relation which is unique and exclusive.[36] Instead of the unity of the collective noun, Loughlin's reading signs the inverse: multiplicity ("polygamy"). Figuring the community of believers as one bride signs the radical cohesion of that singularity.

Loughlin's reading of the Genesis stories contrasts unfavorably with that of John Paul II. Ambivalent about the spousal analogy, Loughlin selectively retrieves from it features of social endorsement, intimacy, sexual expression, and generation while rejecting the principle of unity-within-diversity and the necessity of that for generation. That same-sex couples have no organic possibility of generating issue is glossed over by Loughlin: "same-sex couples can have children by many of the same means as employed by other-sex couples." The noun-choice ("means") reveals the hidden ethical problem. Any intervention or procedure that uses a person as a "means" to a desired outcome has damaged that person's dignity. Artificial reproductive methods use persons of either sex as a means to someone else's end. Loughlin himself has to allow that all persons "are the children of mothers." Using one (or more) woman's procreative potential, whether through gamete-sourcing, or using her as a gestational surrogate, instrumentalizes and depersonalizes her. Instead of women being treated as equals, Loughlin's proposal renders them both "needed and not needed," the very criticism he had levied against the 2004 *Letter to Bishops*.

---

35. Norris, "Mariology a Key to the Faith," 195.
36. John Paul II, "*Familiaris Consortio*" 19.

Original Solitude

John Paul identified three original states in the Genesis texts which determined man's condition: solitude, unity, and nakedness without shame.
Original solitude appears early in his catechesis (*TOB* 5:1), and is given a
total of thirty-two entries. John Paul reads man's solitude before God as
having two meanings: "*one deriving from man's very nature,* that is, from
his humanity . . . and *the other deriving from the relationship between male
and female*" (*TOB* 5:2). In the earlier Yahwist story of Genesis 2, man
experiences himself as in some sense alone within abundant creation.
Man's consciousness of his difference is marked and confirmed by his being the only creature capable of cultivating the land (Gen 2:5).[37] This idea
reappears in Genesis 1:28 where man was mandated by God to "fill the
earth and subdue it; and have dominion over" all living creatures. As intentional transformation of the land is a specifically human activity, and
as God enjoined man to work the land, this capacity for work is part of
the meaning of his own bodiliness (*TOB* 6:4). Man comes to knowledge
of his own solitude when carrying out his first divine task: naming the
other creatures (Gen 2:19). John Paul sees this task as one amounting
to a "test" by God (*TOB* 5:4) as it takes place after the conditions of the
covenant have been set: that the man will till and keep the garden, and
refrain from eating of the tree of the knowledge of good and evil (Gen
2:15–17). Man passes this test, coming to realize that he differs from
animals in a profound way. The task of naming the animals guides man
towards self-knowledge through attentive observation of each animal's
"*specific differentia*" (*TOB* 5:6). God accepts the names the man confers,
confirming that he was learning correctly. It is in gaining knowledge of
the world of creatures that man learns that there is no creature like himself. This consciousness of his difference was detected through what he
saw.[38] Although the biblical text does not explicitly speak of man's body,

37. *Man* here refers to the human rather than the male. The first man is only defined as male after the woman has been created (Gen 2:21–22). See *TOB* 5:2.

38. Seeing brings knowledge. The assumption that this is so has been challenged
by some late-twentieth-century feminists, beginning with Donna Haraway (1988). Vision, they have pointed out, takes place from one perspective, so it gives only partial
knowledge. Even the potential to arrive at this knowledge is dependent upon the viewer's readiness to see and possibly be challenged by what is seen. Vision as a politically-
situated action is not relevant in the Genesis text, which deals with primordial man,
the first and only of his species. As there are no others whose vision may differ from
his own, what he sees is to be read straight-forwardly. His vision leads him to authentic
knowledge about himself and the world he inhabits.

it is "precisely as a body among bodies" (*TOB* 6:3) that man arrives at his own self-definition; that he is "*a person with the subjectivity character-izing the person*" (*TOB* 6:1).

God's provision of the tree of the knowledge of good and evil grants man the status of subject. Up until then, man had been only the object of God's creative act; now, he can freely exercise his subjectivity within the limits of the covenant, able to "consciously discern and choose between good and evil, between life and death" (*TOB* 6:2). The hierarchy within creation: man above other creatures, but dependent on God and subject to God, is ordered towards balance. Man is a subject constituted, by virtue of the covenant, "according to the measure of 'partner of the Absolute'" (*TOB* 6:2) but balanced against this stature, he also faces the possibility of a "dimension of solitude that was unknown to him up to this point" (*TOB* 7:3). Even within his constitutive framework of communion with God, man had experienced solitude. There is now the possibility of all communion with God ceasing in the absolute solitude of death if the fruit of the forbidden tree is eaten. Man has already learnt that he can, by virtue of the structure of his body, "*be the author of genuinely human activity*" (*TOB* 7:2). Embodied man is a person, not only self-conscious but self-determinative, who may determine against God.

Man's original solitude is reprised in the exceptional solitude of the Virgin Mary. *Solitude* as a Marian characteristic has received criticism from some feminist theologians. As the title of her 1976 book, *Alone of All Her Sex,* indicates, Marina Warner sees Mary as an isolated figure whose very isolation keeps her from being a serviceable role model for contemporary women. Warner sets out her objections in her preface: that because Mary's predicates are superlatives, then "in the very celebration of the perfect human woman, both humanity and women were subtly denigrated."[39] Similarly, Elizabeth Johnson is motivated by a feminist hermeneutic in her 2006 book, *Truly Our Sister.* Johnson shares Warner's unease when Mary is, in Warner's assessment, venerated as "feminine perfection personified."[40] Johnson and Warner see Marian elevation as unhelpful for women, and wish to see a rebalancing of Marian figura-tion, with the emphasis less upon her uniqueness and creaturely perfec-tion. Johnson therefore focuses upon Mary's discipleship. As "sister," embarking on her own pilgrimage of faith, she is seen as relating in a

---

39. Warner, *Alone of All Her Sex,* xxi.
40. Warner, *Alone of All Her Sex,* 159.

non-hierarchical scheme within a structure of equality with other women. Marian modes of relation in this scheme are associative, partnering and befriending. Warner and Johnson are intent on reclaiming the horizontal axis of the Mary figure as an essential balance to the vertical axis which had dominated her veneration in the Roman Catholic and Orthodox Churches.

Johnson could be seen as extending the work begun at Vatican II concerning Mary's place within the church. While the final chapter of Vatican II's *Lumen Gentium*, which deals with Mary, retains exalted language, such as "the splendor of an entirely unique holiness" (*LG* 56), there is an explicit effort to balance the tropes used of her, so the mother is also the "daughter" (*LG* 53), and fellow-sojourner who "advanced in her pilgrimage of faith" (*LG* 58). Whilst being "pre-eminent" and "wholly unique" (*LG* 53), she is also "closest to us" (*LG* 54). Johnson endorses such a redressing of the balance but remains critical of what she sees as "gender-inflected notions of masculine and feminine"[41] which she deems characteristic of conciliar texts, such as *Lumen Gentium*.

The solitude of Mary, object of veneration, exalted in splendid isolation, troubles Warner and Johnson. When considered through the prism of John Paul's analysis of man's original solitude, much in the two beginnings is seen to align: in the Annunciation, Mary's experience reflects the Adamic experience of his constitutive solitude which provoked a reflective self-awareness. Mary is similarly self-aware, asking the angel how, as she is a virgin, the angelic prophecy could be fulfilled in her. While Mary's task was unique and exalted, she was asked to exhibit faith in the impossible-being-made-possible by God. Her singular experience anticipated a time not far in the future when all persons would be faced with making a similar assent in faith to the impossible-made-possible resurrection of her son.[42] The grammar of the figural work the Annunciation does within the meta-narrative of the salvation story parallels the primordial beginning. Mary is aware of her difference (a betrothed virgin); is given a particular task to do (conceive and bear a son); has a distinguishing quality which especially suits her for this task (being "Full of grace"), and exercises her free choice in assent ("May it be done to me according to Your word"). The primeval man of Genesis becomes aware of his difference (being man, not beast); is given a particular task (to act as God's

41. Johnson, *Truly Our Sister*, 66.

42. The theme of the impossible-made-possible as a theme of the Annunciation was explored by Jean-Luc Marion. It has been developed in Dunn, "Let It Be."

deputy, filling the earth and subduing it, Gen 1: 28); has a distinguishing quality that fits him for the task (being the *imago Dei*; that is, being full of grace), and was free to assent or decline (through the boundary presence of the forbidden tree). The Annunciation can therefore be read as a recapitulation of man's creation in Genesis 2:7. The newly-created human is realized anew at the Annunciation where the modality is not the male but the female. Mary at the Annunciation is figured not only as the new Eve, but as the new Adam.

Likewise, while the superlative dogmatic titles by which Mary is known in the church: "Mother of God" and "Immaculate Conception," and her honorific devotional titles such as "Queen of Heaven," do focus upon her elevated solitude, they have their roots in the primordial condition of man before the breaking of the covenant. Humans were the only creatures able to worship God and the only ones able to receive the direct address of God. Mary is the uncorrupted image of God, living according to God's original intention, as *"partner of the Absolute."* She is not removed from what should be ordinary experience; it is ordinary experience that now is removed from its original realization. Realizing authentic personhood remains an open possibility for all persons, who are free to assent to each invitation to grace. Each assent reforms the person to more closely image God.

Mary's solitude need not be seen as problematic in the sense of her being unattainably or unrealistically superior to every other woman, or every other person. Her solitude serves two figurative purposes: it reiteratively enacts "man's 'theological prehistory' " (*TOB* 18:3), the state of original innocence; and it anticipates the eschatological future. Mary is the realized possibility, and guarantee, that full personhood is possible for an exclusively human creature. Mary's solitude reprises and exceeds the original solitude of humankind: she alone is "Full of grace" and in her alone, virginity and physical maternity will meet. In Mary, the *"unique, exclusive, and unrepeatable relationship with God"* (*TOB* 6:2), which distinguished the first male and female, is fully operative. She intentionally lives her life in conformity with God's plan, fully and recognizably the image of God. She will only be alone until her spiritual fecundity multiplies.

Unity and Communion

Man's original unity is understood in two ways in the Genesis texts: the unity of person as a spirit-infused body, and the unity of man male-and-female. The unity of male and female "overcomes the frontier of solitude" (*TOB* 9:2) and also affirms all that constituted man in his solitude: self-consciousness of his distinction, and a desire to transcend his solitude by "opening toward and waiting for a 'communion of persons' " (*TOB* 9:2). This personal communion is a key dimension of the value expressed in God's assessment of all that he made: that it was "very good" (Gen 1:31). Included in this evaluation is the potentiality of man to transcend himself in love for the woman; each can live "for" the other (*TOB* 9:1).

The chronologically earlier creation text, the Yahwist, deals with the separate creation of woman (Gen 2:21–22). For contemporary readers, this poses a more contentious account of man's origins than the later account as the woman is formed after the creation of the man. As the man's solitude was deemed by God to be "not good" the woman's subsequent appearance can seem to suggest that she is the answer to the lonely man. If this is so, it would disastrously diminish her dignity as she would not be a subject desired in her own right, but only for how she could complete the man.[43]

John Paul's reading rejects reducing the woman in such a way. Starting from the proviso that the Genesis language is mythical, "an archaic way of expressing a deeper content" (*TOB* 8:2), John Paul sees in the Yahwist creation text the unfolding psychodrama of man's origin formulated as a dialogue between man and God. Man begins life as a literal earthling, created from the dust of the ground. That primordial, sexually undifferentiated man learns about himself first, in relation to God, and then in relation to the other creatures whom he resembles in having a body, but whom he exceeds in his personhood. Once he has formulated an interior understanding of himself as one longing for communion with his own kind, he is induced into a "sleep," which John Paul explicitly distances from any Freudian interpretation. John Paul sees the biblical author as having a theological intention to express "the *exclusiveness of God's action* in the creation of woman." Not only did the man have no conscious part in the woman's creation, his sleep is analogous to "a specific return to non-being" or "to the moment before creation, *in order that the solitary 'man' may by God's creative initiative re-emerge from that moment in his*

43. Loughlin, "Nuptial Mysteries," 183.

double unity as male and female" (*TOB* 8:3). John Paul sees God as *pacing* creation to the developmental stage of the man: "Creation takes place simultaneously, as it were, in two dimensions: the action of God-Yahweh, who creates, unfolds in correlation with the process of human consciousness" (*TOB* 8:2).

Although there is now sexual difference, John Paul sees the textual stress as falling upon the homogeneity of the two: she, like Adam, is an *I*, a subject "which is also personal and equally related to the situation of original solitude" (*TOB* 8:3). It is the homogeneity which is recognized with delight when Adam awakes and first sees the woman. She resembles the man in such a way that her sameness of being, but difference in body, is immediately apparent. Theirs is a complementary similarity better thought of as "exact correspondence" (*TOB* 8:4n16).

Helen Kraus's exploration of gender issues in the first four chapters of Genesis endorses this reading. She points to the woman and man sharing the same substance, expressed in the story as the woman being formed *from* the man's living tissue. This human couple are "closer than any other pair of creatures."[44] Neither, says Kraus, did the woman require a second infusion of divine breath in order to live. The same divine spiration enlivens them both. The man's instant recognition of the woman, "bone of my bones and flesh of my flesh" (Gen 2:23 NRSV), indicates that their unity forms the basis for understanding their bodily differences. "Bone," synecdochic for *being* and *flesh*, signifies a sharing of the same personhood that is detectable through their differing physical characteristics. The woman's humanity is recognized, and responded to, even before her femininity. The two are consubstantial and this grounds their difference. John Paul's avowal of the deep equality of the created subjects is redolent of a feminist hermeneutic. *Woman* here is not derivative or secondary to man-the-male, nor that which completes his privation. The human person is read as "two 'incarnations' of the same metaphysical solitude before God and the world—*two reciprocally completing ways of 'being a body' and at the same time of being human*" (*TOB* 10:1). Again, Kraus endorses John Paul's reading of the Hebrew text: that the woman is neither inferior nor derivative; that man and woman are consubstantial and so equal. It is only when the man knows that he has a perfect

44. Kraus, *Gender Issues*, 25.

companion that he speaks for the first time. He can now hear and be heard; understand and be understood. He now has a "dialogue partner."[45]

As transformative as this is, it does not express the full compass of the change that has taken place. More than a partnership, a new relationship has been formed. Genesis 2:24 speaks of the two becoming one flesh. Kraus notes that "those languages that distinguish between woman and wife (Latin and English), here use the latter matrimonial form."[46] Kraus again notes that Genesis 2:24 describes their commitment to each other first, and that this is prioritized over progeny. This newly possible spousal unity is, notes John Paul, one that "*derives from a choice*" ("a man leaves his father and mother and clings to his wife"). It presupposes a mature consciousness of one's own body, and its meaning: "*reciprocal enrichment*" (*TOB* 9:4). It is through this consciousness that "humanity forms itself anew as a communion of persons," which John Paul suggests constitutes a layer "deeper than the somatic structure as male and female" (*TOB* 9:5). Spousal unity rests on the foundation of man's original solitude, structured according to his self-determination and self-consciousness (*TOB* 10:4) and is situated within the context of the "communion of persons." Spousal sexual union expresses man's surpassing of the limit of his solitude and "This surpassing always implies . . . one takes upon oneself the solitude of the body of the second 'I' as one's own" (*TOB* 10:2). In this context, it is surely no accident that in the Yahwist text, the serpent deceives the woman when she is alone. Evil insinuates itself within the heart of first the woman, and then the man. Once admitted, evil comes between the primordial couple, straining not only their relationship, but the divine-creaturely one on which it was grounded. The infiltrator is an interloper who fractures spousal unity, resulting in chaos and disharmony.

Man's realization of his solitude in Genesis 2 precedes sexual differentiation, and John Paul sees in this the priority of the body as such; and that therefore "the meaning of original solitude . . . is substantially prior to the meaning of original unity" (*TOB* 8:1). Being human is also prior to being male or female: "Bodiliness and sexuality are not simply identical" (*TOB* 8:1). The *soma* is the manifestation of human personhood, as distinct from *sarx* (flesh). John Paul affirms the dignity of every human body, owing to its personhood. This complete correlation of dignity with

---

45. Kraus, *Gender Issues*, 25.

46. Kraus, *Gender Issues*, 26.

humanity includes those with chromosomal and/or hormonal abnormalities that render their biological sexual characteristics ambiguous
or indeterminate. The priority of the *soma* also releases space for those
whose bodies do not conform to normative sexual differentiation, such
as the intersexed. Human bodiliness construed as a value deeper than
sexual differentiation means that anyone whose biological sex is ambiguous is not deemed lesser in value. It means that to be male or female is
to experience the body in one or other particular modality but that if
this modality is indeterminate or damaged, that body is still expressive
of human personhood. The priority of the undifferentiated body may
have eschatological significance. According to the words of the Matthean
Jesus: "in the resurrection they neither marry nor are given in marriage"
(Matt 22:30). Sexual differentiation, although "constitutive for the person" (*TOB* 10:1) in this earthly life, may be ultimately provisional.

The Virgin Mary fits within the pope's exegetical scheme in regard
to her unity of person yet seems outside its scope in regard to spousal
unity. Although espoused to Joseph, the marriage had not been consummated. The dogma of Mary's perpetual virginity indicates that their ensu-
ing marital relationship did not include sexual relations. How, then, can
Mary and Joseph stand as a sign of conjugal unity?

Although their marriage was exceptional, John Paul devoted seven
of his Wednesday audiences in July and August 1996—a period outside
the *Theology of the Body* catecheses—to the theme of how the virginal
state is included within spousal unity. Either state is intended to be a sign
of the coming kingdom of God: the married couple in the way they live
together; the chaste virgin, or celibate, in the way he or she anticipates the
greater love and unity that is to come. How might this co-inherence of
virginity and spousal maternity be understood of the Virgin Mary? Mary
in her virgin state is asked at the Annunciation to consent to the divine
initiative, but her freely given *fiat* is structured according to a marriage
being contracted: Mary's consent is sought to join her life in a particular
and exclusive way with God's; she consents; her word of consent brings
into effect the thing consented to. As with the priestly words of eucharistic consecration, Mary's words "make a new reality out of an old reality."[47]
The virgin is now wife. Mary's word, united to God's, is fecund, align-
ing with God's original, creative "let it be." Mary's utterance ("may it be
done") fully images, in its earthly modality, God's own.

47. Turner, *Thomas Aquinas*, 254.

Nakedness without Shame

In Genesis 2:25, the man and the woman see each other naked. As yet in a state of innocence, this presents no difficulty for them. They see each other with a purity of vision which reprises, says John Paul, the way God beheld his creation, *seeing* that it was very good (Gen 1:31). This comprehensive vision encompasses, but exceeds, the surface data perceived by the eyes, and is only possible for those pure of heart. Mutually gazing upon each other, naked but not embarrassed, indicates the purity of original man. The body, as yet, "does not contain an inner break and antithesis between what is spiritual and what is sensible" (*TOB* 13:1). There is no cleft between the personhood of the subject and all that distinguishes the subject's body as sexual. That all this is discernible in the "concise, and at the same time suggestive" (*TOB* 13:1) formulation of Genesis 2:25 implies a poetic language register.

While Genesis 2:25 records the man and the woman seeing each other naked, yet being unashamed, Genesis 3:7 has them realizing their nakedness and making coverings for themselves. John Paul draws attention to the uniqueness of Genesis 2:25, the only biblical reference to morally upright nakedness. Numerous other biblical texts link nakedness to abjection, dishonor, and loss of dignity (*TOB* 16:3n27). The textual lead-up to Genesis 2:25 shows *man's* consciousness of his personal subjectivity; in the verse itself, male and female each experience the sexual distinctiveness of their bodies, but neither feel shame in the presence of the other. This is not because they did not recognize or know that they were naked (*TOB* 11:5). On the contrary, they saw each other's nakedness as a source of joy. Only after having broken the covenant by eating the fruit of the forbidden tree did they *then* become ashamed of being seen naked. There has been a crucial shift. The new situation they are now in brings with it "a new content and a new quality of the experience of the body" (*TOB* 11:4): shame, which John Paul therefore calls a "boundary" or "threshold" experience (*TOB* 11:4–5). The boundary put in place by God, and trespassed against, has not been overcome, it has multiplied, *nakedness* and *shame* now constituting new boundaries.

So as to probe this crucial shift in bodily meaning, John Paul looks to the *a priori* condition of original nakedness, devoting one entire audience to it (*TOB* 12). He had already spoken of original nakedness as constituting the "proximate context" of "the unity of the human being as male and female" (*TOB* 11:6). He discerns two dimensions of nakedness.

In one, the body's outward visibility mediates to man the realization of his distinctive creatureliness; the naked body mediates man's solitude. In the other, the naked body mediates awareness of, and capacity for, personal communion; the body mediates unity. This knowledge about the meaning of his body, which John Paul calls "the original innocence of 'knowledge'" (*TOB* 12:3) is gained from participation in the world. The Genesis story traces man's deepening self-knowledge, from the pole of non-identity with the animals, to that of immediate recognition of his own type: "flesh of my flesh."

Man's participation in the exterior world does not offer a full accounting of the nature of original nakedness, though. For this, John Paul turns to what he calls "The Inner Dimension of Vision" (*TOB* 12:4). The man and woman communicate through their "common union," which allows "both to reach and to express a reality that is proper and pertinent to the sphere of subjects-persons alone." What was evident from their visible, exterior participation in the world—that "the body *manifests* man" and "acts as an intermediary" that allows sexual communication— "*corresponds* [to] *the 'interior' fullness of the vision of man in God.*" This vision of God for man is that he will constitute God's own "image." John Paul sees in the text an important distinction concerning original nakedness. There is an "'*exterior*' *perception*"; that is, physical nakedness, and there is how man is in the *mind* of God; that is, ontological nakedness. Man's nakedness, says John Paul, is what he *is*, prior to his subsequent awareness of himself as naked.

Further scriptural support is given for the "nakedness" of man before God who "penetrates the creature" (*TOB* 12:4n22). The body—human matter—is thus understood to be, in some sense, porous or permeable. Such a body can be penetrated by, and permeated with, the Holy Spirit; it can host divinity. This allows a different perspective on Marian exceptionalism. Mary's unique gestational hosting of the incarnated divinity becomes not utterly inaccessible to the experience of everyone else. All persons are encouraged to respond to the Holy Spirit by requesting, and/or permitting personal ingression so that they, too, may host divinity. Notwithstanding Mary's singular hosting of The Word, each believer is tasked with interiorly gestating the Spirit, so realizing maternity in the spiritual order.

God's penetration of the person has a reciprocal dimension. Just as the naked man stands before God fully exposed and fully comprehended, so man comprehends himself only when exposed to the penetrating gaze of God. Man not only receives God's penetrating gaze, but analogically participates in it, penetrating his own opacity. The divine capacity to pervade and penetrate all things is associated with divine Wisdom. Man can share in this capacity by cultivating his interior vision. God's piercing insight confers insight. The strongest expression of divine-creaturely inter-penetration uses a gestational metaphor: God dwelling in the believer, and the believer in God (John 17:21). This graced state of mutual indwelling is only really possible, says Rowan Williams, when the creature foregoes any pretensions to self-sufficiency, as holiness and dependency are inseparable. This holy dependency constitutes our "nakedness before God as God."[48] When the original woman and man beheld each other, they exercised true insight into their shared nature, recognizing each one's capacity for "*interpersonal communication*" (*TOB* 12:5). Seeing beyond the surface, with true insight, is a participation in the pervasive purity of the divine, all-seeing Spirit. They are seeing each other "*more fully and clearly*" than through their eyesight (*TOB* 13:1).

Shame disrupts the "interior gaze" and is associated with "a specific limitation of vision through the eyes of the body" (*TOB* 13:1), which troubles, even threatens, personal intimacy. The distorted vision affects not only the morally culpable human agents, but the whole of the created order, attesting to the integration and ordered unity of creation. Levi-Strauss in his 1955 essay, "The Structural Study of Myth," notes that some myths use garments as a mediator between nature and culture. In the Yahwist creation myth, the first body coverings were fig-leaves stitched together; nature/life is now bound to culture/death. Not necessary for warmth or physical protection, they are concrete signs of alienation; self-protective body prophylactics, the purpose of which is to block and withhold. The serpent's lie, believed and acted upon, initiates a world of coverup. What had been morally neutral vegetal life is now co-opted as a sign of moral guilt and shame.

Until the late twentieth century, artistic portrayals of the Virgin Mary have dressed her very modestly, shying away from all but essential renderings of flesh, most usually just of the face and hands. Margaret Miles has noted how visual images of female nakedness in the West purported to reveal the moral nature of the woman depicted. Naked women were deemed "sensual, sinful, or threatening," as, for example, Eve, and

---

48. Williams, "Seal of Orthodoxy," 28.

Susanna.[49] Inversely, Mary's moral supremacy demanded visual modesty. There is a sense, though, in which nakedness more befits her nature, as she conforms to the original divine image. Under this revised visual scheme, Mary's physical nakedness would sign her exemplary moral nakedness. Unlike Adam and Eve, she has no need to clothe herself as she has nothing to hide. Having always trusted in God and the benevolence of God's vision, Mary has never sought to self-protectively withhold anything of herself. This psychic and spiritual nakedness associates Mary with divine Wisdom whose purity penetrates those hard of heart.[50] The Epistle to the Hebrews sees a reiterative nakedness as the *telos* of each person: "And before him, no creature is hidden, but all are naked and laid bare to the eyes of the one to whom we must render an account" (Heb 4:13).

The artistic portrayal of nakedness is a delicate issue owing to the tensions between its original innocent meaning and its subsequent debasement. Three of John Paul's catechetical audiences in 1981 (*TOB* 60–63) appear under an appendix heading: "The Ethos of the Body in Art and Media." In this short sub-series, the pope reflects on the difficulties of portraying the naked body in art so that its innate "*meaning of a gift* of the person to the person" (*TOB* 61:1) is retained. He identifies the central problem as being "a question about the human body as an object of culture" (*TOB* 60:3). The "very delicate problem" (*TOB* 61:1) is that in artistic portrayals, especially those of photography and film, "the human body loses that deeply subjective meaning of the gift and becomes an object destined for the knowledge of many" (*TOB* 61:1). The pope's contention resonates with the experience of Kate Moss. In an extended interview in which she reflected on her twenty-five-year career in fashion modelling, Moss disclosed her discomfort and distress at being photographed naked for work assignments while still a teenager. At the age of sixteen, told to model naked, she recalls: "So I'd lock myself in the toilet and cry and then come out and do it. I never felt very comfortable about it."[51] Of another work engagement, Moss further recalls: "I had a nervous breakdown when I was seventeen or eighteen. . . . It didn't feel like me at all. I felt really bad about straddling this buff guy. I didn't like it. I couldn't get out of bed for two weeks."[52]

49. Miles, *Carnal Knowing*, 120.

50. The Deutero-Canonical Wisdom of Solomon says of Wisdom: "Because of her pureness, she pervades and penetrates all things" (Wis 7:24, cited in *TOB* 12:4n22).

51. Fox, "Kate Moss," 146.

52. Fox, "Kate Moss," 148.

Nakedness in artistic representations *per se* is not rebuked in the *Theology of the Body*. John Paul explicitly praises some artworks of naked subjects for their capacity to lead the viewer "through the body to the whole personal mystery of man" (*TOB* 63:5). The pope had presided over the restoration of the Sistine Chapel (1979–1994) and approved the removal of loincloths which had been painted over some of the original nudes. In his 1994 homily at the celebratory Mass in the restored chapel, he had lauded the place as "the sanctuary of the theology of the human body." This elevated assessment may seem surprising as the loss of the pure gaze presents a problem on both sides of a work of art that depicts nudity: on the creative side, involving the intention of the artist; on the receptive side, involving how the work is looked at. Between this binary of artist and viewer sits the "model," a designator which has already signaled an eclipse of the sitter's agency and subjectivity. The ambivalence of nakedness in ecclesial settings, and attendant tensions concerning modesty and propriety, were highlighted in the controversy accompanying the installation of a small (eighteen-inch), commissioned, limewood sculpture, *Madonna and Child*, in an Anglican church, St Matthew's Westminster, in 2000. English sculptor, Guy Reid, then a practicing Anglican, explained the complete nakedness of the two figures as a visual reference to their being the new Adam and Eve.[53] The naked Christ-child was the less contentious, as it drew upon a seam in medieval and Renaissance art where Christ's nakedness signified his true humanity. While there is no such artistic precedent for depictions of the Virgin Mary, there is a fittingness in her nakedness as her body did not undergo "an inner break and antithesis" (*TOB* 13:1). In her, the spiritual and the sensible are seamlessly conjoined.

The Spousal Meaning of the Body

The foundational premise of the Genesis creation accounts is that man understands himself rightly only in so far as he sees himself as a creature created out of love. This proceeds from the logic that God assessed creation as "very good": goodness only proceeds from the good; the One who is good is Love, that is, God (*TOB* 13:3). The body given to its spouse in love manifests the "mystery of creation" (*TOB* 13:4): that the world was made as gift *for* man (male and female) who, as the image of God,

53. Boss, "Naked Madonna."

is the only creature able to understand the meaning of the gift. This gift relation is mutually reciprocal. Man both receives the world as gift and gives himself as gift to the world.

By virtue of the dual modalities of human embodiment, the gift relation can be experienced in interpersonal relations—most fully in a spousal relationship where each is able to "*exist in a relation of reciprocal gift*" (*TOB* 14:1). As the undifferentiated man's solitude was deemed "not good," the implication is that relationality—living with, or for, someone else—is a necessary good and is one marker of the content of the *imago Dei*. In a relationship of a unique type, spouses have the privilege and possibility of sharing in the creative act of God through spousal sexual union. Their union frees each spouse from "*the 'constraint' of his own body and his own sex*" (*TOB* 14:6). Spousal nakedness effectively signs this freedom from constraint. Citing the Vatican II document, *Gaudium et Spes* 24:3, that man is the only creature willed by God "for its own sake," John Paul II says of the spousal relationship that it is intended to manifest most fully that same "freedom of the gift" (*TOB* 15:2); each spouse is to relate in love to the other "for their own sake."[54]

The hermeneutic of gift runs so deep that the world is "irradiated" with love, present as the Holy Spirit (*TOB* 16:1). Man receives himself as that which he is: the image of God. His daily living is imbued with a transcendent dimension: man lives as himself but in this living, he communicates God's image to others. Even if he does not have progeny, his act of living fulfils his life's task: to multiply the divine image in the world. In man's original state, this imaging of God included spousal sexual union, as the spouses were in a state of innocence. This innocence was so radical that "*at its very roots, [it] excludes the shame of the body* in the relation between man and woman" (*TOB* 16:4). This innocence, in which the human heart is undefiled, could better be understood as "original righteousness" (*TOB* 16:4).

While the qualities of mutuality, givenness, and loving acceptance of the other carry their own appeal, other claims of John Paul's in relation to the spousal meaning of the body are more contentious. The pope ascribes essential characteristics to each of the sexes. Of Genesis

54. William Newton says that John Paul II either referenced or cited *Gaudium et Spes* 24:3 more than one hundred times in his papal writings. He had been heavily involved in the redaction of that Vatican II document, during which time its emphasis had shifted towards theological anthropology. See Newton, "John Paul II and *Gaudium et Spes* 22."

4:1, he says: "the one who knows is the man and the one who is known is the woman, the wife" (*TOB* 21:2), and later in the same section: "*the mystery of femininity manifests and reveals itself in its full depth through motherhood.*" The former seems to ascribe active cognition and agency to the man; passivity, receptivity, and objectivity to the woman. John Paul appears here to promote, as divinely intended, a hierarchical relation within the male-female distinction. The linkage of femininity and motherhood seems to resituate woman within the familial and domestic sphere; woman is apparently defined and circumscribed by the maternal realization of her female body. The universalist declamations of *TOB* 21:2 seem to preclude alternative manners of manifesting femininity. While sex-based differences are detectable throughout the body, and are not limited to chromosomal differentiation, (recent genetic research has determined that in excess of 6,500 gene expressions—approximately one third of the human genome—differ between man and woman),[55] identifying the content of such difference in terms of *masculinity* or *femininity* is problematic if one wishes to avoid sexual stereotyping. It is difficult to reconcile equality of sexual difference with relational equality where one sex is deemed to be, of its nature, the active agent and one the passive. Ironically, criticism of, or reticence in endorsing, John Paul's apparent sexual stereotyping, tends to proceed from a presumed binary hierarchy of value where *active-passive* has the value *desirable-undesirable*, giving a sublimated endorsement of masculine values over feminine.

John Paul contextualizes his statements of sexual essentialism, such as those above, within an analysis of "knowledge" as a biblical term and concept. He explains that knowing in the Bible signifies "concrete experience," not only intellectual knowledge (*TOB* 20:2n31). It is a term especially used of conjugal relations, but also of all sexual relations, including the illicit and the intentionally abstemious. To say of the first conjugal unity that Adam in that act "knew" his wife, is to equate the experience of their being "one flesh" with knowledge. The pope is careful to extend this knowledge, gleaned experientially, to the woman as well as the man. Although Genesis 4:1–2 speaks of the man's knowledge, John Paul argues that the nature of the act, their equality before God, and the mutuality of the hermeneutic of "gift" means that knowledge was also bestowed on each. It is not only that the woman "is given" to the man, but he is likewise

---

55. As reported by the Weizmann Institute, Rehovot, Israel, May 3, 2017. The report concerned the findings of Gershoni and Pietrokovski, "Landscape of Sex-Differential Transcriptome."

given to her (*TOB* 20:3–4); a reading of mutuality which mitigates the reservations indicated above about John Paul's essentialist understanding of sexual difference.

Conjugal union as a particular form of knowledge (which is not limited to the physical relation) is so developed in scripture that it comes to stand as an archetype of the union between God and his people.[56] It becomes integral to a literary tradition that culminates in Paul's application of it to Christ and the church in Ephesians 5. It stimulates the creative imagination, which generates further images based on the archetype. Unlike Platonic *eros* that yearned for a release from materiality towards the transcendent Beautiful, biblical knowledge shows no hostility to the physical (*TOB* 22:4n35). Rather, marriage is used in the book of Isaiah (Isa 62:5) as the supreme image of God's engagement with his people, where the metaphor of construction ("builder") gives way to that of conjugality, as it encompasses "rejoicing." The matrimonial metaphor segues into the metaphor of wine, possibly via associations of a wedding banquet, so linking and binding the construction metaphor (builder-creator) to an image of communal feasting, transformation, and the full and unrestricted outpouring of self for another, in love. The particular valences of committed love are so appealing that for some, they trump the language of fatherhood. Feminist theologian, Sallie McFague, is one who sees limitations in "parental images" for God, as these, she thinks, "cannot express mutuality, maturity, co-operation, responsibility, or reciprocity."[57]

John Paul grounds his assertion within the logic of the particular *gift* of the man to the woman and vice versa. Both human-as-male and human-as-female were equally willed and created for their own sakes. Man and woman come to a deepened understanding of each other's identity through the experience of self-donation: together, they are reconstituted

---

56. John Paul's use of "archetype" is in accord with C. G. Jung's usage: an a priori form that is filled with the content of experience. The archetypal form here is the mutual relation between the man and the woman, "a relation based on the binary and complementary realization of the human being in two sexes" (*TOB* 21:1n32).

57. McFague, *Metaphorical Theology*, 179. McFague's preferred alternative is "friendship." The image of friendship is used in the Bible, though rarely: directly of Abraham (Jas 2:23); comparatively of how God spoke with Moses (Exod 33:11) and provisionally of believers (John 15:14). The combined message of these usages is that being deemed God's friend is highly demanding; mutuality, maturity, and co-operation extending to readiness to lay down one's life for one's friends. Biblical friendship is a costly relationship but it lacks the sense of ineradicable belonging and binding, which the metaphor of family forcefully encapsulates.

as "one flesh." This act of self-donation confers "mutual self-realization" (*TOB* 21:3). John Paul sees a theological scriptural link between the prayer offered by the Johannine Christ that "that they may be one, as we are one" (John 17:22b NRSV) and an authentic union of creatures-as-gift. Christ's comparison maximally elevates the type of unity that his followers may hope for: differentiated persons who are bound together in a relationship of loving faithfulness and fecundity while keeping their personal integrity intact. Although specifically praying for believers, unity was one of the essential primal characteristics and that original "exemplary" union is included within Christ's intention (*TOB* 15:1n25).

In his pastoral *Letter of Pope John Paul II to Women* (1995), the pope spoke of the need for women to be included in employment and service outside the home in order that feminine perspectives be incorporated into wider society, where they could act as checks and balances against social and economic structures "organized solely according to the criteria of efficiency and productivity."[58] The themes of this letter continue those of *Mulieris Dignitatem* and harmonize with the themes developed more extensively in his *Theology of the Body*. The woman, he says, is especially predisposed by the experience of gestation to accept the other, and to meet others' needs.[59] Motherhood deepens and expands the *knowledge* experienced in spousal union as each now *"know each other reciprocally in the 'third,' originated by both"* (*TOB* 21:4). The woman stands before the man not only as spouse, but as mother; motherhood manifests and reveals what John Paul calls the *"the mystery of femininity"* (*TOB* 21:2).

While in some ways, marriage symbolism is readily comprehensible as a way to grasp what is meant by God's love for his people, there is also a complexity attached to it. At the Annunciation, the decisive moment of her spousal giving, Mary was aroused by the Spirit to respond to the Father which was then realized in the conception of the Son. Inevitably, one of the drawbacks of the Trinitarian language used here is what appears to be the gendering of God. Imaginatively, guided by the classical language, God is formulated as male to Mary's female. In consenting to her own participation in God's plan, Mary is fulfilling her own set of relations with each person of the Trinity, which can be formulated as: daughter of the One who sent, spouse of the One who is poured out, and mother of the One who is sent. It is the maternal relation, that relies

58. John Paul II, "Letter to Women" 4.
59. John Paul II, *MD* 18.

upon Mary's being female, which activates a corresponding *masculine* conception of God, as human generation requires maleness which Mary could not supply.

The union of wills between Mary and God at the Annunciation is life-generating. Here is the summit of restored relationship, which anticipates the *eschaton*, and reprises the original prototype of right relation established "in the beginning." Mary both reserves herself for the sake of the kingdom and spends herself in uniting with God's will. Noel Rowe's poem, "*Magnificat*: 1. Annunciation," recognizes and exploits the strong metaphoric linkage between the spousal and celibate aspects of Marian chastity.

Eros as a Theological Category

One contemporary scholar who has shown interest in retrieving the idea of *eros* as a theological category is Sarah Coakley. The central theme of her book, *God, Sexuality and the Self,* is how human desire indicates an embedded yearning for God, and what light this may shed on how best to construe sex and gender. On this account, humans long for others, perhaps for one especial, spousal other. This embedded desire to give and receive love is fundamental to humans imaging God. Persons long for relationship, or more profoundly, communion, with others because God—not through any lack in Godself—first longed for us, desiring that others share in the plenitude and perfection of divine love. *Desire* is, in this sense, ontologically God's, and only secondarily, man's, from which Coakley deduces that "*desire is more fundamental than 'sex.'*"[60]

In the exploration of this theme, Coakley looks to some patristic writers, notably Gregory of Nyssa (c. AD 335–395) and Augustine of Hippo (AD 354–430), each of whom is sensitive to the importance of sex and gender, although handling them differently. Gregory sees in Genesis 1:27, a "double" creation: man is initially non-physical and therefore, sexless; physicality, and attendant sexual differentiation occur only as the Fall becomes imminent. For Gregory, the general resurrection of the dead will see persons revert to the initial paradisal state of sexless, spiritual beings (recalling, perhaps, Jesus's words that none will marry at the resurrection, cited above). Eschatologically, persons will relate to God in feminine mode, as receivers of God's presence. In this sense, Gregory's

---

60. Coakley, *God, Sexuality, Self,* 10.

theology suggests the ongoing *gendering* of the human person. This analogical, or metaphorical, feminine gendering of humanity is complicated, says Coakley, by reading it alongside Gregory's late commentaries, where the sexual imagery is reversed: the soul reaches deep into the unknowable darkness of God, losing mental control; the human person, now gendered male, is released and received.

Coakley finds in her reading of Gregory a handling of sexual difference that avoids subordinating the female to the male, perhaps even leaning towards seeing ascetic superiority in the female. In what Coakley has dubbed the "paradox of 'equality and difference' "[61] concerning the sexes, where the former tends to overlook bodily difference; the latter to begin from it, Gregory's theology favors "equality." Augustine, on the other hand, is more insistent on bodily difference, so the need for the male to protect the female. *Female,* finds Augustine, is in some sense subordinate to, and dependent on, *male* (cf. 1 Cor 11:7) while nonetheless being spiritually and mentally equal. The idea of any loss of control, even noetic control, was highly fraught for Augustine, who had struggled unsuccessfully with sexual continence in his early life. Mastery of the self as the goal of the Christian life, and not yielding to ecstatic loss of control, has astringent valences for him. From his personal experience, Augustine sees the phallus as problematic in its resistance to regulation by the will, for which reason it is connected in his symbolic with disorder, confusion, and potentially exploitative danger for women. Sexual distinctions point to procreation, a good within marriage, but Augustine is wary of extolling the good of marital sexual relations outside of procreative intention.

Though their biographies were very different, Augustine and Gregory converge in finding the virginal state superior to the marital. For Augustine, intentional virginity short-circuits lust and guilt. For Gregory, married earlier in his life, sexual relations do not provoke such inner conflict. For him, virginity short-circuits death (all who are born will die; virginity breaks this cycle). Virginity therefore functions for Gregory as a sign of the celestial sphere in its impassibility, and in its modelling of the chaste intra-Trinitarian relations.

In their different ways, both Gregory and Augustine point to the possibilities and limits of extrapolating from human desire an image of divine-human relations. As Coakley is rightly aware, human desire is in need of constant purification. Its persistence, though, is a sign, or clue, of

---

61. Coakley, *God, Sexuality, Self,* 273.

the existence of a personal prototype, or source, in whom perfect desire is perfectly met. The only human possibility for replete satisfaction of desire is eschatological union with God, who is the *telos* of *eros*. As God is the source and destiny of desire, God is the proper standard against which all desires are measured. This conception of *eros* properly orients theology towards a sense of divine-human relations as a love story; an orientation that is coherent with the Incarnation—God's self-realization in human flesh—which made God present to be seen, heard, and touched. In Coakley's scheme, human beings are sexed on account of *desire*. So far, nothing in Coakley's theological exploration of *eros* would conflict with John Paul II's theological anthropology. Yet Coakley, in outlining three theological pathways she wished to avoid, identified one as "a high, authoritarian ecclesiastical Christian 'orthodoxy,' cut off from the 'sea' of lived religion by hierarchical avoidance or denial."[62] This orthodoxy she explicitly associates with John Paul II and Benedict XVI.

Phenomenology and Doctrinal Orthodoxy

Coakley shares with John Paul II an interest in phenomenology, but invokes it differently, seeming at times to oppose it to orthodoxy. Coakley's construal of *orthodoxy* separates her theology from that of the magisterium of the Roman Catholic Church, which teaches that it holds authoritative interpretations of doctrine. For Coakley, this would imply a self-understanding of *ownership*. Doctrine, though, says Coakley, cannot be possessed, nor, she implies, is its current interpretation necessarily complete, as there will always be more to know. The magisterium understands itself not to *possess* but to uphold doctrinal orthodoxy. Doctrine is held in trust, and while it may be said to unfold its meaning over time, it cannot, if it is true, substantively alter. *Truth* is public, freely-available to all, and not a restricted possession. Coakley and the two popes with whom she is not theologically in sympathy have different attitudes about doctrine and its place in the lived life. Coakley leans towards apophaticism, reluctant to speak definitively about doctrinal matters as she thinks in terms of journeying, which gives a different *view* as the journey progresses. The mysteries of the faith will, until the *eschaton*, remain imperfectly though progressively better known. John Paul II and Benedict

62. Coakley, *God, Sexuality, Self*, 71.

XVI lean towards cataphatic theology, seeing their theological roles as instructive.

Both John Paul II and Benedict XVI were concerned that the faithful, lay, and ordained, adhere consistently, both in public and in private, to formal church doctrine.[63] Coakley's characterization of these two popes as defensive towards the content of the faith is therefore uncontentious, as the magisterium has historically understood its function as preservative, not innovative. So seriously did John Paul II take this responsibility that in 1986, he initiated a major undertaking to enshrine dogmatic clarity by commissioning a panel, under the chairmanship of Joseph Ratzinger, to write a comprehensive catechism, systematizing and extensively summarizing church doctrine, which was promulgated in its original Latin form by John Paul II in 1992.[64] Coakley, in contrast, appears to distinguish doctrinal assent from orthodoxy, akin, in her scheme, to a separation of *theory*, and the *practicum* of daily living; between (possible) interior assent to those ideas, and the seeming impossibility of living by them.

A purported misalignment between doctrinal statements and phenomenology, sees Coakley wanting to affirm experience, perhaps even at the expense of inherited propositional claims, but without herself making any definitive theological statements. Her commitment is to doctrinal openness that is not restricted to formal articulations of belief. Alert observation of life is the vocation of the contemplative and artist and can enrich theological reflection. How such observations are made use of, becomes the issue. Problems arise if experience becomes a rationale for doctrinal revision. The well-worn metaphor of the pilgrim believer is recast by Coakley as pilgrim doctrine, *en route* to its final destination. The appeal of this way of thinking for some would be its readiness to accommodate differences in people's lives; the difficulty it presents is in suggesting a distinction between present orthodoxy and eschatological orthodoxy. This has major implications for evangelism. If orthodoxy is a process in this life of never arriving, then what is the status of the content of revelation, and on what basis could evangelism proceed? As there is no clear provision in Coakley's scheme to allow for a determination of authentic orthodoxy, there is a likelihood that orthodoxy would splinter into multiple, different doctrinal interpretations. Orthodoxy may then

63. See, for example, John Paul II, "Holy Mass In Phoenix Park."
64. See John Paul II, "*Fidei Depositum*."

even cease to be recognizably constant over time. This is suggested in Coakley's desire to rethink sex and gender.

Differences of Sex

Coakley would like to see purged what she refers to as the "*fallen* 'gender binary.'"[65] This means, for Coakley, the differing ways in which male and female are culturally circumscribed, including in Christian theological cultures: Eastern Christianity offers a type of de-sexed equality; Western tends towards female subordination. Coakley wants to navigate between the two, drawing upon the strengths of each: a corporeal equality of the sexes that accommodates the differences of the corpuses, while neither under- nor over-articulating those differences. In an effort to maintain openness about how gender may be expressed, she avoids the terms *masculine* and *feminine*, wanting to distance *gender* from biological sex. For this reason, she keeps the definitional boundary of *gender* deliberately minimalistic: "embodied difference."[66] This, though, poses its own problem. In dissociating *sex* from *gender*, so that no inherent relationship is suggested between the two, the basis of gendered *difference* falls away— different from what and in what ways? If *gender* is to be more than merely individuated difference, then it needs a connection with some ontological category. In her intentionally loose and unrestrictive construal of gender, Coakley hopes to minimize (erase?) attitudes toward sex and gender that she finds untenable, such as: female subordination; presumed stability of the gendered person; and gendered stereotyping. In the attempt, though, some other problematic conceptualizations are introduced: no intrinsic relationality signed in the differently-sexed bodies; no materiality on which gender difference is grounded; no linkage of the procreative possibilities of sex difference with the *imago Dei*.

In her effort to transcend the contemporary impasse in theological and secular thought between those for whom sex distinction is an essential trait of the person (such as John Paul II) and those for whom it is not, vigilance is needed so that neither the material body, nor the strength of metaphor, is unintentionally eclipsed. If one is prepared to accept, along with Coakley, that Freud's aphorism is better inverted; that is, that sex is about God, who endlessly pulsates in an ecstatic outpouring and

65. Coakley, *God, Sexuality, Self*, 57.
66. Coakley, *God, Sexuality, Self*, 55.

ingathering of intra-Trinitarian love, then *desire* needs to stay rooted in male-female *eros*. If not, then the characteristics that made it a uniquely apt metaphor for union with God (experiencing a loving encounter with real otherness, which can be mutually fashioned into a permanent community of love-in-unity, oriented toward begetting and nurturance) are sacrificed.

John Paul II, as the title of his theological anthropology indicates, reads sexual complementarity as speaking something profound about the nature of human beings, and about God's intention in making them that way. Sexual dimorphism structures human life around the interest of difference (male and female) and the comfort of sameness (human being). Accommodation of otherness is necessary in order that human quiddity is fully expressed, most strikingly so in the case of procreation. Sexual difference can also be distorted into sexual dominance and conflict, with women particularly vulnerable to bodily exploitation. Daniel Horan is among those who have criticized the construal of *complementarity* as *harmonious difference*, as he finds it obscures female subordination, and the lesser valuing of qualities deemed feminine.[67] John Paul II would implicitly share that criticism if he thought it had merit. He, though, sees the creation texts forestalling such concern, with their prioritizing giftedness, mutuality, and reciprocity in spousal relations. Such qualities are ordered to securing the equal dignity of both sexes. Equally importantly, and perhaps surprisingly, John Paul resists sociocultural essentialism that would equate the male with *separateness*; the female with *relatedness*. Rather, *relatedness* he finds, is an essential human quality, *a priori* of sexual differentiation. The person always *refers*, both to proximate origin (parents), and ultimate origin (God). Persons are ontologically relational.

John Paul does, though, imply a gendered social essentialism in his 1995 *Letter to Women*. He lauds the "*genius of women*" which he identifies as their willingness to serve and care for others, and their skill at doing so; relational gifts that can be nurtured and exercised not only within the family, but within the church and wider society. It is not strictly essentialist in that the relational qualities John Paul admires are not deemed to be essentially present in every woman, so much as markedly more pronounced, or more prevalent, in females. In this sense, they are presented as being *gendered* characteristics, grounded in the determinate givenness of sex. A notable aptitude for, or interest in, serving or caring for others

---

67. Horan, "Beyond Essentialism and Complementarity," 100–102.

could, on this account, be seen as a marker of *motherliness*, as the capacity for maternity, a byword for service and care, is inscribed only on the female body.

One of the criticisms levelled against sexual essentialism is that it prioritizes the general over the particular by assuming the universal presence of qualitative, identifiable sexual differences. That assumption is elusive of objective confirmation, with some science suggesting, contra, that the behavior and cognition style of any given subject does not consistently align with one sex type, or the other. Daphne Joel has found that: "having one brain/gender characteristic with the 'male' form is not a reliable predictor for the form of other brain/gender characteristics."[68] Joel's observation does, though, illustrate and confirm that knowledge in the natural sciences proceeds on the basis of identifying generalities to which organisms conform. Particularities are noted for how they conform to, or deviate from, the general. As Daniel Horan warns, over-emphasis on the particular "runs the risk of dissociating the human person from humanity as such."[69] Sexed bodies can be qualitatively described according to the presence of different properties: primary or secondary sex characteristics, gonads, chromosomes, or hormones. These characteristics usually fully align, forming the person as female or male. Exceptionally, in the cases of intersexed persons, alignment of genes, gonads, and genitals, is not fully realized.[70] The atypical configurations of sexual markers in these persons indicate that maleness or femaleness, while an expected norm, is not inevitable. Persons with indeterminate biological sex presentation complicate the ways in which sex interacts with gendered presentation, and with a psychological sense of the sexed self.

The Language of the Body

A key concept of John Paul's *Theology of the Body* is "the language of the body" to which he devotes fourteen of his 129 catecheses. Michael Waldstein's index entry for the phrase draws attention to the Polish of the pope's original text, noting that it refers to "words that are actually spoken rather than language in general." John Paul's rich metaphor encompasses

68. Joel, "Misconception of Brain and Gender," 3.

69. Horan, "Beyond Essentialism and Complementarity," 102.

70. Joel, "Misconception of Brain and Gender."

speech, actions, gestures, and deeds, while also implicating the person, as "language" is an expressive action of the speaking subject.

The philosophic underpinning for these papal reflections had been worked through in *The Acting Person*. Writing for an academic readership, the then Karol Wojtyła sought to undertake a systematic analysis of the relation between person and action, by analyzing the cognitive process that takes place when a person performs an action. The actor experiences himself both as subject (*I*) and object (*the me that I have to face*). He cognitively apprehends that he acts, that he is an "acting person," and in this apprehension, he is able to learn about himself, because in the experience of acting, the actor always experiences him- or herself. This relation between *person* and *action* allows for, and invites, self-reflection: man is an object for his own interpretation. Correct interpretation, leading to self-understanding, is, paradoxically, an event of self-transcendence.

Christian understanding is that the interior and the exterior life of the person should harmonize; thoughts and intentions should be consistent with deeds and actions, and all should cohere with the divine commands of scripture. Such persons are oriented towards God, their lives constituting a type of worship. Christian liturgical devotion and practice, more especially within the Roman Catholic and Eastern Orthodox traditions, also acknowledge the especial significance of liturgical language in orienting and shaping the person. The liturgical and scriptural language domains are ordered so as to form active disciples in the world. Those who worship worthily receive transformative words, and in the process, become agents of the foundational Word, in knowledge and in action.[71] *Action* is crucial for Wojtyła, because actions reveal the person (rather than presupposing the person); actor and action are in "dynamic interrelation."[72] A morally positive action effects personal fulfilment. Wojtyła deduces from this that there are two dimensions of any action: the external (an action is outwardly directed to some object in the world), and the internal (an action determines the actor's selfhood). The internal dimension means that, notwithstanding actions are performed in time, they are not fleeting; they perdure, leaving their trace within. Acting persons therefore acquire experiential knowledge not only of those objects to which their actions were directed, but also of themselves. Wojtyła expands upon this connection, drawing out its implications for devotional

71. Finch, "Rehabilitating Materiality," 626.

72. Wojtyła and Tymieniecka, *Acting Person*, 31.

practice: inner devotion outwardly practiced is personally fulfilling because the objective moral value of the devotee's action coheres with the inner person.

Language and Symbolic Thought

John Paul's use of *language* as a concept in his theological anthropology can be further clarified by considering language's relationship with symbol. In his enquiry into the origins of symbolic thought, social anthropologist, Alan Barnard, constructs a hypothesis that human language developed in order to accommodate symbolic thought. Barnard hypothesizes that the syntactic complexity of languages is directly correlated to the complexity of symbolic thought that is inherently social in nature.[73] Linguistic complexity, he suggests, developed in order to meet the demands of narrative, one of the chief characteristics of which is recursion: the embedding of sentences within sentences which requires changes in wordforms to make meaning clear. Recursion can be extremely complex and multilayered. Barnard uses an illustrative example of a myth that contained: five sentences within one; a quotation within a quotation; mythological characters who are not human but who behave as if they are; and a narrative as a whole that was built upon a metaphor. Barnard therefore argues that the complexity of language far exceeds what would be necessary for communication.[74] The reason for this, he suggests, is that symbolism lies at the heart of society and symbolism requires sophisticated, "full" language. Such language includes "non-communicative aspects" by which Barnard means "art forms [that exist] in their own right, such as mythology and other examples of narrative, and also poetry and song."[75]

Barnard's reasoning about the complexity of language speaks to Denys Turner's explication of Thomas Aquinas's anthropology. Barnard's claim that human language is predicated on the symbolic, indicates sophisticated human consciousness, as the symbolic can only develop after

73. Barnard states that symbolic thought can only develop after several stages of intentionality have developed in a person, from the primary stage of believing something, to the second-stage of "believing that someone else believes something." Religion seems to need fifth-level intentionality. See Barnard, *Genesis of Symbolic Thought*, 4–5.

74. Barnard is here narrowly defining *communication* as that which denotes.

75. Barnard, *Genesis of Symbolic Thought*, 6.

a multilayered, cognitive grasp of human consciousness has developed. Human social life relies upon the symbolic in order to articulate its complex narratives. On Barnard's hypothesis, symbolism is foundational to being human. Human language developed as it did to accommodate symbolic thought, but *meaning* is construed as something carried by the language; it is not something that inheres in the body that generates it. For Aquinas, rational human action forms the "narrative" or "plot" of a human life, which life can itself be recounted in narrative form. The human being is, on Aquinas's account, a unity of body and soul; neither can properly be thought of as separable from the other. Rather, matter (*body*) is fully infused with *soul* which, for Aquinas, borrowing an Aristotelian term, is the *form*, or "that which accounts for a thing's being alive in a certain kind of way."[76] Turner articulates the Thomist "methodological principle" as: matter has meaning.[77] The much later Cartesian view, by contrast, saw the self as the center of the subject's understanding of the world, and of God. Descartes upended the Thomistic ordering whereby God and self are known "from the standpoint of the world."[78] *Knowing* from one's immersion in the world coheres with the Genesis account: humans are embedded in a life-sustaining world, with which they interact and grow to know themselves, and their place within creation.

Human communication, whether expressed as gesture, word or deed, extends to every action of the person including, *inter alia*, meeting another's eyes; weeping; breathing.[79] It is owing to their particular embodiment, psychical and physical, that humans have the need and capacity for language. Denys Turner succinctly summarizes the Thomist anthropology informing John Paul's thinking: "For our bodies are how we are present to one another. Our bodies are how we speak to one another.

---

76. Turner, *Thomas Aquinas*, 60.

77. Turner, *Thomas Aquinas*, 237.

78. Turner, *Thomas Aquinas*, 56.

79. In his poem "Deaf Language," Les Murray speaks of the triple modality of language: the spoken-audible (negatively intimated in deaf); the written-visible (present in his poem's published text); and the gestural-felt (where felt can refer to interpreting the meaning of another's gesture). The gestural language of the deaf woman in his poem is likened to an occidental language, differently conceived of, which indicates the richness and diversity of the body's capacity for language. Expressive constraints can induce alternative, imaginative inventiveness. See Murray, *Subhuman Redneck Poems*, 80.

We might say, the human body is the human person's extension into language."[80]

John Paul's usage of the term, "language of the body," is not always obviously consistent throughout his *Theology of the Body*. He tends to mean that the language of the body is an act of the acting person, but he also suggests that the body, *qua* body, is a sign-system or language. This innate somatic expressiveness is owing to the *a priori* inscription by God of each person's meaning: being willed for his/her own sake to live in communion with God and others. This forms the ground of the "deep *order of the gift and of reciprocal self-giving*" (*TOB* 61:3) by which the body is constituted. The body itself is a dense sign along the lines of a symbol, icon or sacrament. The body visibly signifies and makes present the dignity of the person while also pointing beyond itself. It is therefore reasonable and accurate to say that "the body speaks us," telling what we are. The body is an epiphany of the person.

All persons are given knowledge of themselves by virtue of being embodied. This foundational experiential knowledge is deepened and expanded as their lives progress. John Paul devoted several audiences (*TOB* 20–23) to analyzing how the term *knowledge* is used in the Genesis accounts. Acknowledging the historic linguistic background, John Paul establishes in a footnote (*TOB* 20n31) that the Hebrew word translated into English as *knowledge* means something experienced in one's concrete existence, not just something assented to interiorly. *Knowledge* is something experienced in the body, not only something that exists disconnectedly in the mind. Such a hermeneutic honors the body in its totality. The Cartesian hermeneutic restricts its honors to the self's awareness of having abstract thoughts ("*cogito ergo sum*"). Such a hermeneutical standard minimizes or ignores significant areas of human acts and expressions, such as sensuality, intuition, and imagination, divorcing them from *intellect* or *thinking*. Anything outside that which the mind makes is apt to be viewed with suspicion.

Such an abstracted and restricted understanding of how the person is present to him- or herself is contrary to the Roman Catholic Church's doctrine and practice which centers around sacramental participatory rites. As Karl Rahner writes, in his explication of devotion to the Sacred Heart, there is an interconnectedness between thought and action.[81] It

---

80. Turner, *Thomas Aquinas*, 248.

81. Rahner, *Further Theology of the Spiritual Life*, 217–29.

is only in the worshipful action of devotional practice, he says, that one grasps truth: "here action is the only right way of knowing"; an insight applicable not only to devotional practices but to interpersonal relations. Rahner is making a case for the performative, participatory nature of knowing. This is the type of knowing that the Genesis creation texts present: every dimension of life provides fertile ground for gleaning self-knowledge, and knowledge beyond the self. It is a hermeneutical position shared with John Paul II, most notably in his proposition that conjugal sex, when all the proper circumstances are met, images God.

The term *knew* applied to conjugal sexual union occurs for the first time in Genesis 4:1–2 and "*raises* the conjugal relation of man and woman, that is, the fact that through the duality of sex they become 'one flesh,' *and brings it into the specific dimension of the persons*" (*TOB* 20:3). John Paul means that human sexual relations are not merely animalistic and instinctual. Sexual relations never restrict themselves to *sarx*. They reveal and involve the whole person—physical, affective, spiritual, mental—who is the acting subject. Every action, including every sexual action, is invested with a moral value that the acting subject experiences in the experience of acting. There is a whole depth of meaning to becoming "one flesh" (*TOB* 20:4). John Paul explicates this more fully in the same section: "Together, they thus become one single subject, as it were, of that act and that experience, although they remain two really distinct subjects in this unity." Neither one can know from the *inside* what the other is experiencing. In sexual union, male and female act as a concrete biological unit: male and female sexual gonads are the only organs of the body that contain a single, rather than a paired set of chromosomes.[82]

---

82. See Lee and George, *Body-Self Dualism*, 182.

4

Bodies of Words

Poems Marian and Maternal

THIS CHAPTER TURNS TO a different way of knowing, gleaned through the experience of reading poems. We may ask what knowledge poetry reading affords, and why poetry-reading may be a productive endeavor. If we begin from the foundational Judeo-Christian premise—that the world has been created, and is sustained, by God—then, as we come to know the world, we also come to know something of its Source. If the world is indicative of God, then the world is more than it appears to be; it is a sign-system, a vast network of signs. This meaning, or excess of significance, is only discernible by humankind. Persons and world exist in a relation of reciprocal mutuality: humankind, the world's beneficiary and recipient, is inclined towards knowing it; the world is ordered towards giving itself and being known. As something made and given, the world may analogously be regarded as a work of art. As such, it exerts a moral force upon those who encounter it, to respond to it. One way to respond is to add to the order of signs. Any of the visual or literary arts could answer, however there are several reasons for thinking a poem may answer best.

Firstly, a poem captures the sense of the two complementary metaphors used of divine *poiesis* in the Genesis creation accounts: God speaking something new into the void, and God fashioning something new from extant material. These two modalities are echoed and synthesized in literary poems: something new is spoken into the world using inherited, existing language. Secondly, poems lend themselves to different modes of transmission. They can exist in oral or written form, the latter making unsustainable a rigid boundary between the visual and literary arts. Two of the poems considered below, R. S. Thomas's "The Annunciation by Veneziano," and Les Murray's "Pietà once attributed to Cosme Tura," consciously exploit the visual arrangement of words on the page for poetic effect. Thirdly, poems interact differently with their audience than do the visual arts. Whether heard or read, words, the material of the artform, penetrate their recipients. A poem becomes an enacted presence in the act of utterance, becoming "corporeal and corporate—*incarnate*"; a descriptor Fergus Kerr used of sacramental liturgical prayer.[1] During either manner of its transmission, a poem participates in the fluid present; the *now* of its corporeal instantiation. A poem recited aloud becomes an agent of real-world change through the mediation of its orator. The oscillations of spoken words disturb the air, passing through the reader to anyone within auditory range.[2] In being spoken forth, poem and performer form a unity of the two in a performative analogue of John Paul II's "spousal unity." The performer's body mediates the work: poem vivified in the instrument of its realization. Supremely, a reader can become more than a poem's mediator, so fusing with it as to seem to become its very embodiment.

Additionally, a poem conforms to, and instantiates the characteristics thatJohn Paul II identified as being constitutive of personhood. John Paul's use of metaphors, of the body speaking its own language that can then be read, acknowledges a connection between *body* and *language*, where *body* equates with *text*. If the body can be thought of as a text, the most apposite would be, I suggest, a poem. The reasons for thinking so are that poems are open, not closed texts, which encourage, by their presence, interaction with others who read and contemplate them. Owing to the evocative and memorial aspects of poems, they embed others' voices within them. These voices form the background, context, and extension of the poem. Intra-textually, a poem's words are ordered to relationality. A poem, like a person, is sheer gift, fulfilling no utilitarian function. Its orientation is outward-facing, which can be parsed as other-centered; a poem is a response to something *out there* in the world. The *sine qua non* of a poem is to transcend its own limits, reaching out beyond itself.

---

1. Kerr, "Need for Philosophy in Theology Today," 253.

2. Plotinus (AD 204–270) noted that as spoken words disturb the air they fall into the category of meaningful action. See Markus, "St Augustine on Signs," 65.

This transcendent quality aligns it with theological enquiry, which is also concerned with *reaching beyond* to arrive at truth. A poem is the fruit of its writer having looked at some phenomenon that he or she wants to understand or feels she or he has been given to understand. It is an attempt to reveal some insight into a part which may have been overlooked or misunderstood, or to grasp how some part informs a whole. To write a poem is to try to see into the heart of a thing. Its adequacy—how far or not it succeeds—is up to its reader to decide. The poem does no more than present itself for consideration. Poetry writing is directly related to the Adamic naming of the animals, that "test" as John Paul called it, of authentic self-understanding. The very fact of naming attested to Adam's distinctive type of creatureliness, as only persons can generate abstract concepts ("names") to apply to things. The poet, and the theologian, each try to name things so that understanding can be shared. The practitioners in both disciplines aim to express truth. Speaking truth, the name correlating with the thing, is an offensive strike and defensive bastion against corrupt language usage. The honest use of language is a grace. Les Murray, in dedicating each of his poetry volumes, "To the glory of God," is doing more than piously gesturing to his faith. He is risking a reiterated, public declaration that his work is bound to a spiritual purpose. His dedication indicates his intention and reaches to the heart of his poetic vocation. God can only be glorified in truth; Murray's poems will only glorify God to the extent that they are truthful.

A series of poetry readings follows. Each poem was written in the second half of the twentieth century at a time of escalating cultural challenge, both secular and ecclesial, in the West. They are poems written in the leadup to, and aftermath of, Vatican II (1962–65) when the Roman Catholic Church reassessed its ecclesial identity and its relations with the wider world. The subject matter of each poem deals in some way with the motherhood of Mary. All except one deal with either her call to motherhood (Annunciation) or its tragic conclusion (*Pietà*). The one exception is Tric O'Heare's poem which engages critically with the Roman Catholic Church's handling of the Mary figure.

While all these poems deal with Mary, their subject does not predetermine what may be said of them theologically. The poems are a form of linguistic reflection, formed with the intention of opening out perception and, optimally, growing understanding. The readings are given as case studies of the claims made in this book for the importance of poetry, and of the maternal body. They are reflected upon theologically but approached agnostically. This open-ended approach does not commit in advance to a particular way of seeing, nor to arriving at a particular conclusion. The close textual analysis given to the poems gestures to the relevance of every aspect of a work of art, to the overall accomplishment.[3] The readings look at the poems in terms of literary criticism (form, linguistic devices, organization; the *body* of the poem) and also make associative connections to theological ideas, scripture, doctrine, practice, and authorial autobiographical material. This is an approach of observant engagement.

Annunciation poems

Edwin Muir, "The Annunciation"

The angel and the girl are met.
Earth was the only meeting place.
For the embodied never yet
Travelled beyond the shore of space.
The eternal spirits in freedom go.

See, they have come together, see,
While the destroying minutes flow,
Each reflects the other's face
Till heaven in hers and earth in his
Shine steady there. He's come to her
From far beyond the farthest star,
Feathered through time. Immediacy
Of strangest strangeness is the bliss
That from their limbs all movement takes.
Yet the increasing rapture brings
So great a wonder that it makes
Each feather tremble on his wings.

Outside the window footsteps fall
Into the ordinary day
And with the sun along the wall
Pursue their unreturning way.

---

3. See Jakobson, "Closing Statement."

Sound's perpetual roundabout
Rolls its numbered octaves out
And hoarsely grinds its battered tune.

But through the endless afternoon
These neither speak nor movement make,
But stare into their deepening trance
As if their gaze would never break.

Edwin Muir's lyric, "The Annunciation," was originally published late in his life, in the 1956 anthology, *One Foot in Eden*. It is a contemplation of the moment of the Incarnation portrayed as a state of ecstasy with a strong focus on the physical. While there is an angel, it is an angelic presence as embodied as the unnamed Mary's own: it has a face, it gazes, and it experiences bliss and rapture. The central conceit of the poem is that the reader is accompanied and directed by the narrator to "See . . . see." The urgency of the double imperative suggests both voyeuristic watchfulness, and a pedagogical instruction to look more searchingly than superficially so as to "see" with understanding. The word glances upon the range of differing types of sight: physical, imaginative, enhanced understanding (insight), the illumination of faith, the privileged visions of a seer, and vicarious sight through, for example, reading. The seemingly ordinary injunction to "See" is an invitation to see that which, in its totality, only the eye of God beheld: the Annunciation event. The Lucan gospel account, in as far as it is historically accurate, would have been reliant upon the historic Mary to have furnished the details. The poem is an extended invitation to see into and beyond what is usually available to sight. The imaginative cooperation with the scriptural account becomes a type of enhanced sight, the result of slowed-down reading.

An injunction to see also engages with aesthetic theory. Muir's is a quietly contemplative poem. Meyer Abrams, in his essay looking at the antecedents of late twentieth-century attitudes to art, identifies the "contemplative model" as dominant, and characterized by disinterested attention, "without reference to anything beyond its [the art work's] own bounds, and for its own sake."[4] The end of art, so this model holds, is to exist "for our disinterested contemplation." Abrams, mindful that this model, now taken for granted, once constituted a revolutionary

---

4. Abrams, "Kant and the Theology of Art," 152.

about-face in attitudes to art, traces the lineage of the change through the eighteenth century. The Earl of Shaftesbury wrote that the prototype for his espousal of disinterested contemplation was Christian as well as Platonic.[5] Contemplation without any self-interest or utilitarian intent is, says Abrams, theologically grounded in "the absorbed contemplation of a metaphysical absolute or deity whose perfection consists in being totally otherworldly, serenely self-contained, and self-sufficient." Muir seems to draw upon such theologically grounded theoretical aesthetics. His poem is structured as a double vision, the reader-viewer enjoined to contemplate the girl and the angel who are themselves lost in self-forgetful contemplation of each other. The poem gives itself as a window to be seen through, or a portal through which another dimension can be visually accessed, the skill of the poetic composition allowing the poetic subject to become the object of attention.

Muir's first stanza introduction to what follows, the poetic heart, places the event in the world: angel and girl are "met" and "Earth was the only meeting place." Muir is earthing the prototype of the picture he draws in words. This is not a spiritualized account of the Incarnation; not a case of the Word-made-flesh being made word again.[6] This is incarnation in the materiality of life seen and lived. Muir, in his autobiography, recalls the United Presbyterian Church he and his family attended in Orkney as being bare and austere: "It did not tell me by any outward sign that the Word had been made flesh."[7] Many years later, on a work assignment to Rome, he was struck by the contrasting approach to Christianity as evidenced in ecclesial art, architecture, and cultural behavior. He particularly mentions having been entranced by a small exterior domestic wall plaque of the Annunciation which would seem to have been the immediate inspiration for his poem. He describes the image showing girl and angel "as if they were overcome by love"; that they "gazed upon each other"; and that this representation of intense human love "seemed

5. Two other aesthetic models Abrams mentions, the "construction" model and the "contemplative" model, also seem to have ancient theological antecedents in the Genesis creation narratives. Abrams does not offer such a connection, but the earlier Genesis account is of the artisan God (construction). In the later account, God repeatedly pauses to attend to his creation, declared as "good" (contemplative).

6. Muir's poem "The Incarnate One" is his critical commentary upon Calvinist Protestantism, which he adjudges as having disincarnated Christ: "The Word made flesh is here made word again" (line 8); "the fleshless word" (line 22); "the abstract man" (line 28) (Muir, Selected Poems, 66).

7. Muir, Autobiography, 273.

the perfect earthly symbol of the love that passes understanding." He was much attracted to this earthiness, which in his childhood island would have been thought "a sort of blasphemy, perhaps even an indecency."

Muir's poem closely follows this description. He avoids denominationally contentious terminology such as *virgin* in talking of Mary and presents her and her angelic visitor as young lovers. The direction of travel has been from "beyond the shore of space" to Earth; to the realm of the "embodied" ones. Muir's metaphoric connection between space and the seashore transfers the place of liminality where land meets sea to the "place" where planet meets vast void. By the poem's penultimate line, the *deep* of "deepening trance" has reprised the metaphor of the sea, making their locked look of love an allegorical cosmic meeting place between spheres terrestrial and celestial; a wholeness enacting the hoped-for reunion of creation. The comfortable harmony with modernity of the second line, "Earth was the only meeting place," becomes by its stanza's end the provoking chords of ancient story; Earth inhabited not only by physical beings but by "The eternal spirits." Earth, as with the Orkney Island Muir was born into and raised on, is now "a place where there was no great distinction between the ordinary and the fabulous."[8]

It is the unabashed holding gaze between the two that has effected the transfer of the earthly into the heavenly, and vice versa: "heaven in hers and earth in his." Mutuality is so much the dominant register of the encounter that it is this quality which secures the sense of Mary's *fiat* that is not articulated. Muir's Mary is one equal in dignity to the angel, with an equal status as subject as registered by the repeated use of the genitive plural: "their limbs," "their deepening trance," "their gaze." There is no sense of hierarchy, nor is Mary overawed as in, for example, Elizabeth Jennings's imagining of the event. Muir's poem avoids a structure of potential dominance and submission. Mary is not the recipient of any imperatives. Muir adumbrates a quietly intense eroticism in the meeting. In rapt contemplation of each other, speech is disengaged, each finding the suspenseful tension one of "bliss" and "increasing rapture." Although the reader is expressly not to assume sexual consummation, as this bliss is "strangest strangeness" which "from their limbs all movement takes,"[9]

8. Jennings, "Uses of Allegory," 149.

9. Abrams cites Plotinus, who wrote of the contemplation of Absolute Beauty that it entailed a surrender of the self: "The soul's peace, outside of evil . . . here is immune. . . . He is become the Unity . . . no movement now, no passion" (Abrams, "Kant and the Theology of Art," 168). It is a passage that could readily be ascribed to Muir's poem.

there is nevertheless a discreet hint of coital climax in the trembling of each angelic feather. The allusion is reinforced by its placement. The climactic line being the stanza's last, the stanza break immediately following functions as a postcoital deliverance, or bliss. When read aloud, the sound qualities of the aspirated *hs* ("He's come to her") and *fs* ("From far beyond the farthest star / Feathered . . . ") with their exhaled air, mimic in sensuous fashion the exhaled breath of the Holy Spirit now breathed out into the womb-world.

Even within this blissful encounter, there is the immediate intimation of darkness and difficulty. Entering the world means entering the constraints of time, a theme Muir returns to repeatedly in his poems. Here is where "the destroying minutes flow," the entrapping linearity of time further suggested in the footsteps that "Pursue their unreturning way." They, in turn, find their context within "Sound's perpetual roundabout." In these two images, Muir has implicated the whole of humanity, whether time is conceived of according to a phallic, linear trajectory, or to a feminized circularity. Time's tyranny, whether of the inexorably passing, or of the repetitively futile, is conquerable, though. While the "unreturning" footsteps do move away, holiness passed by unawares, Muir's use of "footsteps fall" works to suggest how the world has been restructured. The use of "fall" entails a mental return to Eden, from whence all footsteps are *fallen*. The footsteps sound "Outside," though. Inside the room, womb of the world, time is suspended as what has fallen into this room is the angelic representative of eternity. The retreating footsteps, immaterial trace of human presence, are registered at the very moment when God realizes himself as material Presence. Now the extemporal world is nested within the temporal world of "destroying minutes" and the "Outside," thereby redeeming it from within. Muir further complicates this relationship. The stanza dealing with the "Outside" is placed between the stanzas dealing with the protagonists in the room where history is being restructured by eternity. By the final stanza, time has become eternity in anticipatory inauguration of the eschaton: "the endless afternoon." The relation between time and eternity as expressed within the poem's stanzaic structure is that of a holding within or a mutual "enfolding";[10] a notably maternal image.

The normality of the "ordinary day" into which the footsteps sound suffers in comparison with the silent intensity that has preceded it. Within that inner room, life pulses; each line one of four iambs, the pulse of a

10. Malcolm Guite uses this word to describe how reason and imagination, two ways of knowing, are "mutually enfolded" (*Faith, Hope, and Poetry*, 12).

heartbeat. The strong propulsion is reigned in with "Shine steady there." The two monosyllabic words steady the line which, while also one of four iambs, needs for the sense that the intonational stress fall equally upon each word. The stop midline and the altered spoken rhythm mean form enacts content; movement halted to a steady presence. The contrast between the inside space of the second stanza and "Outside" of the third is registered in the altered rhythm. In a display of rhythmic dexterity, Muir echoes the sense of the outside's fallen ordinariness by altering the pulse of the lines to trochees whose long-to-short reverses the short-to-long of the preceding iambs. In this realm of damage ("battered tune") and non-advancement ("perpetual roundabout"), the ordinary and the fallen have become conflated. Owing to the Incarnation, though, ordinariness has been reconfigured to that originally envisaged by the Creator. A redeemed and expanded sense of ordinariness upends any modern skeptical gloss on the dogma of the virginal conception: it is the fallen, reduced expectations of what constitutes ordinariness that needs reconfiguring. To reject the possibility of God's extraordinary intervention in the world through Mary is to persist in a reduced vision that confuses ordinariness with only the rational and the scientific, allowing no room for the possibilities of a dream-like, mystical "trance" of love. The inauguration of a restored, enhanced ordinariness is signaled by the initially separate realms of heaven ("angel") and earth ("girl") being conjoined as "These" by the poem's end.

Muir challenges the preoccupations of modernity: objectivity, scientific enquiry, and materiality. Music according to this scheme can only be accounted for inadequately as "numbered octaves." Modernity's systematic analysis cannot render a full account of the poetry of music (nor of words). The damaged instruments of a lapsed creation are antitheses of the silent absorbed couple. In the poem, it is the mythical world that invites and sustains reader interest; its strangeness not wholly unfamiliar as it images the strange fascination of romantic love. It is the "Outside" that is the distraction. This pattern follows that of the Matthean Jesus who, when twice questioned by the Pharisees about marriage practices, declined to answer according to their terms of current practice, instead redirecting them to the Genesis creation myth, a move which iterates that echoed in Muir's poem: from the "Outside" of the ordinary world to the inside of God's, or from the prosaic to the poetic. John Paul II also follows this move, beginning his theological anthropology with the myth (*TOB* 1–4) read as the key by which the contemporary social world is unlocked. Muir's own autobiography consciously followed a similar path. He wrote of trying to locate one's individual life ("story") within a larger more transcendent frame ("fable"), even calling the first version of his autobiography, published in 1940, *The Story and the Fable*.

This approach directs Muir's treatment of the Annunciation. Luke's gospel gives the only scriptural details of the event. Their inclusion attests to his interest in the "story" of this part of Mary's life as this knowledge reveals what it is to be human before God. It is this revelatory inner truth that Muir would call "fable," as distinct from what he calls the "dry legend" of outer facts, such as one's appearance or routine life.[11] In his poem, although he presents the encounter as one of romantic love, he has no interest in the usual motifs of the genre, such as eulogizing the beloved's features or particular qualities. On the contrary, Muir is taken with the quality of recognition and appreciation between "girl" and "angel" and what this will mean in terms of reshaping the fable of man. In not naming her or identifying her by any of her honorific titles, she becomes any young woman in the throes of romantic love. The noun also has historic pedigree as one of the few details about the legend of the historic Mary that could be stated with a degree of probability: that she may have been very young at the time of the Annunciation. In first-century Judea, girls tended to be betrothed at puberty, which may have meant around the age of twelve.[12] If this were so, then irrespective of whether her body had reached the menarche, she would have been considered by most to be in the transitional state between girlhood and womanhood. In this hinterland, she would culturally have been under the protection and authority of a man, making her personal and individual encounter all the more striking. Within Muir's poem, her girlhood suggests the liminality of the teen years where romantic love can be experienced with heady intensity. The locked gaze of love, anticipatory of (or memorial of) the holding gaze of mother and newborn, is so irresistible that the angel foregoes his freedom to leave. The final line captures the single -sighted intensity of focus upon the face of the beloved, each participant eager to prolong beholding, unable to see the other enough. The locked gaze will necessarily be broken when the angel goes, but the relationship has been established as one founded on authentic reciprocal love which implies enduring faithfulness. The interlocked gaze is an immediately recognizable image of

11. Muir, *Autobiography*, xii.

12. A minimum age (between twelve and thirteen years) for a girl's betrothal was later established by rabbinic decree. See McDonnell, "Feminist Mariologies," 537.

creaturely love, (here analogical of divine creaturely love), but it is more than this. As with a kiss, the interlocked gaze is simultaneously sign, signifier and signified. Implicit is the equality in dignity of the participants. Love is in this sense, non-hierarchical. Image (creature) and original (angel mediating divinity) are restored to perfect register, communicating through the intense silence of their mutual delight.

Noel Rowe, "Magnificat: 1. Annunciation"

The angel did not draw attention to himself.
He came in. So quietly I could hear

my blood beating on the shore of absolute
beauty. There was fear, yes, but also

faith among familiar things:
light, just letting go the wooden chair,

the breeze, at the doorway, waiting to come in
where, at the table, I prepared a meal,

my knife cutting through the hard skin
of vegetable, hitting wood, and the noise

outside of children playing with their dog,
throwing him a bone. Then all these sounds

dropped out of hearing. The breeze
drew back, let silence come in first,

and my heart, my heart, was wanting him,
reaching out, and taking hold of smooth-muscled fire.

And it was done. I heard the children laugh
and saw the dog catch the scarred bone.

Australian poet Noel Rowe (1951–2007) published his suite of five "Magnificat" poems in his first full-length poetry collection, *Next to Nothing*, in 2004. Under the rubric "Magnificat," he sequences the key events of Jesus's life: Annunciation, Visitation, Nativity, Crucifixion, and Resurrection, from the imagined perspective of his mother. The meta-title serves to link the joyful and the sorrowful events within the attitude of trustful praise and steadfastness shown by Mary in Luke's gospel. In their earliest published version, in *Wings and Fire* (1984), Rowe, then a Marist priest, stated in the preface that his reason for writing the suite was to answer modern nostalgia for a sense of the transcendent. Rowe, contra, suggests modernity's loss is of a sense of immanence. He wrote the poems to "set up a dialogue between the presence of Mary in the gospels and her presence, 'hidden and as it were unknown' in the modern world."[13]

Rowe sought to realize this aim by anchoring his poems in the mundane details of ordinary life, and foregrounding Mary's presence and voice. The first of these methods is uncontentious. A sense of immanence is restored by Rowe's inclusion of sensible details: the play of light on the chair, the cutting of vegetables for a meal, the sounds of children playing. Rowe's Mary displays sensory awareness that codes spiritual sensitivity. She registers the subtle alterations of her immediate environment such as the attenuation of the light "just letting go the wooden chair," but Rowe's deployment of the motifs of light, wind, and silence do more than de-mythologize the event. Mary's sensitivity is directed to the natural signs that manifest the presence of God in scripture: light, wind, and silence. The light's movement marked as a gesture of release subtly signals the movement not only of sun but of Son. The courteous and restrained "breeze . . . waiting to come in" is the self-effacing Spirit of God who "drew back" to "let silence come in first." This is the One who makes known the Son (cf. *CCC* 687). It is because of Mary's receptivity to the subtle presence of the Spirit that she is able to discern the presence of the living "silence," the paradoxical manifestation of the Word, the utterance of God. Having God's Presence signaled in mundane earthly life liberates and elevates ordinary life, the vehicle through which divine immanence is disclosed. Daily life can be saturated with God.

The second of Rowe's methods, the poetic conceit of giving Mary the narrator's voice, is more problematic. While the device uses the spare biblical account to advantage, exploiting the latitude it leaves for imaginative infilling of its narrative gaps, it opens up political difficulties associated with sex and gender. In presenting all the words of the poem as ostensibly

13. Rowe, *Wings and Fire*.

Mary's, Rowe is open to a charge of sexual imperialism because he is a male purporting to speak not only on behalf of, but as, a woman. Rowe's strategy to redress the masculine bias of Christian scripture and tradition by making Mary the interpreter of her own life, is open to a charge of continuing the appropriation of women's stories by men.

Rowe himself was not oblivious to such a possible charge. In a critical essay first published in 2007, Rowe tackles the question of the relationship between story, author, and ethics.[14] He argues that it can still be "considered honorable to write on behalf of others" as imaginative empathy used to fashion a character always leaves space that acknowledges such empathy as analogical, a "something like,"[15] "not an exercise in complete identification." In terms of sexual politics, he is not attempting to pass as a woman, as he is not making a claim to be one, nor attempting to conceal his maleness. His imaginative empathy whereby he affects to speak in the first person as another is a mental and emotional effort to inhabit another's perspective without claiming to have erased the distance between that other and himself as writer. Rowe's position here echoes that of John Paul II regarding the construal of the *imago Dei*: that an image is not the thing itself but indicative of similarity. As Mary is considered the image of complete humanity and the model of discipleship, identifying with her through imaginative empathy is a possibility for any of the faithful, irrespective of sex. Rowe's own measure is whether any literary analogy is "imaginatively captivating, credible and satisfying," so providing a critical standard by which to evaluate his own analogical identification with Mary.

Rowe attempts to strengthen the sense of Mary's agency by way of a risky strategy of depriving her of direct speech. While her articulation of willing acceptance of God's intention has been expunged in this, the final version of his poem, the poem and its presentation of Mary is considerably strengthened in the process. The poem loses the bathos of his earlier version ("I said, 'Yes'")[16] and gains for the Mary character a sense of the fullness of meaning and longing that words seem inadequate to express. Karl Rahner has perceptively understood this as the incompleteness of human words: each word "is always, as it were, floating upon a deeper

---

14. Rowe, "Will This Be Your Poem, or Mine?"

15. Rowe quotes here from "Speaking as a Woman," a paper delivered by Philip Martin at the 1985 conference of the Association for the Study of Australian Literature.

16. Rowe, *Wings and Fire*, 8.

level of meaning which cannot be communicated."[17] Rowe has her *fiat* communicated through the desire of her heart, the *locus classicus* of the soul. This gives poetic expression to gospel strands where it is the desire of the heart that God discerns and judges (cf. John 2:25). John Paul II makes the heart's desire the subject of several of his *TOB* audiences (cf. *TOB* 45:2). It is the *heart* that prompts personal choices and actions.[18] The heart acts as metaphor for hidden desires and emotions. It is in a sense both *vessel* that contains the emotions, and the organ that indicates and shapes the overall health of the organism. The desire of the heart, hidden to all except God, is metonymic of the person. Inner desires map a person's value system, which in turn governs relationships with others and with God. This understanding informs the Sermon on the Mount, referred to in scores of John Paul II's *TOB* audiences.[19]

Rowe's decision to highlight Mary's heart draws upon the rich gospel associations between the inner and the outer person, or the spirit and the flesh, all of which is transparent to God. In reimagining Mary's consent as the passionate desire of the heart, her assent is relocated to her innermost personhood. This is an intensely intimate union of creature and Creator; which Rowe's suggestively erotic analogy makes clear. The analogical relationship between erotic desire and desire for God is seldom invoked in association with Mary. This move lightens the load of her cathected modesty, aided by his transference of humility from the poetic Marian domain to the angelic. The panting repetition of "my heart, my heart" (cf. Ps 42:1) ardently "wanting him" constitutes her assent. The present participles that follow give a strong sense of her agency: "wanting," "reaching out," "taking hold" and strongly articulate the embodied nature of Mary's assent. Rowe's suggestion of God's fiery Presence as phallus is less a flirtation with pagan ideas than an invocation of the God of Israel appearing as a burning bush and a pillar of fire. It also draws upon the use of *knowledge* in Old Testament texts when speaking of the relations between God and His people, where *knowledge* draws upon what John Paul II calls "the

---

17. Rahner, *Further Theology of the Spiritual Life*, 224.

18. Susan Sered wrote of a cohort of Kurdish Jewish women living in Israel, aged fifty-eight to ninety, who were questioned about their religious observance. While they had kept kosher and attended ritual baths when younger, they now viewed religion as "a matter of belief in God, of having a 'clean heart'" (Sered, *Women as Ritual Experts*, 79).

19. The Sermon on the Mount is mentioned one hundred fifty-five times in *TOB* (Waldstein, "Index," 718).

very poverty of the language [from which] there seems to arise a specific depth of meaning" (*TOB* 20:2; cf. Hos 2:22; Ezek 16:62). In having Mary's assent constituted both by her "wanting him" and her "taking hold," Rowe is uniting the Western church's focus on Mary's being and the Eastern church's commitment to her action, as equally determinative of her unique status.[20] Rowe's image draws upon the biblical seam that identifies God as lover, most notably in the Song of Solomon.[21] Rowe's deceptively simple presentation of Mary is not as straightforward as it seems. Here is Mary who, in her relation to God, is virgin, bride, wife, and mother.[22] Rowe has reimagined the *fiat* so that it is no longer heteronomous of submission, with a Mary meekly obedient. Here, *obedience* is closer to its Latin root of hearing, and making appropriate response, rather than following instructions from another.[23]

The astonishing series of transformations that the Annunciation triggers are veiled in simple syntax and spare couplets. The known "familiar things" once transformed, are knowable in a different way. Mary's mundane "I prepared a meal" is transformed into a metaphor for the gestation of Jesus, food of the faithful. The symbolic weight now attached to "hitting wood" is that of Calvary; Mary "at the table" becomes the proto priest of the Eucharist. The narrative simplicity belies the layered transformations in progress: raw ingredients into meal; maternal flesh into fetal flesh; Christic flesh into eucharistic sustenance. This is liturgical "ordinary time" made extraordinary through the irruption of the eternal God into the temporal order: the entry of God's "silence," Mary's response, and the conception take place in the interval between the toss

20. Aaron Riches sees John Paul II's ecumenical interest in the Eastern Orthodox traditions, together with his earlier phenomenology, as helping to move the Latin Church towards a more positive construal of Marian virtue in her fiat. Wojtyła had sought to show how the person is a unity of "being" (the Latin emphasis) and "act" (the Eastern emphasis). See Riches, "Deconstructing the Linearity of Grace," 182–83.

21. The canticle expresses the passion of God for his people. It was influential in the lives of Jews and Christians in the Middle Ages. Arthur Green thinks it constituted "the heart of revelation" for Rabbi Akiva, traditionally credited with including the book in the canon early in the second century (Green, "Shekhinah," 3).

22. MarilynLavin looks at how the biblical literary allegory of the sacred lover crossed over into visual representations, reaching its zenith in the High Middle Ages in Europe, with images of Mary and the risen Jesus entwined in a lovers' embrace. Two such examples are the fresco in the mother church of the Franciscans in Assisi, painted by Cimabue (c. 1272–1280), and the "Stella Altarpiece," painted in the early 1300s. See Lavin, "Stella Altarpiece."

23. Sell, "Magnificat as a Model for Ministry," 36.

and catch of a bone to a dog. As a framing image, it encompasses salvation history: the consequences of the original fall from grace ("scarred"), the instigation of redemption ("caught"), and the gospel pericope of the Syro-Phoenician woman ("dog"),[24] so fully loading the ordinary with a sense of dense immanence.

Elizabeth Jennings, "The Annunciation"

Nothing will ease the pain to come
Though now she sits in ecstasy
And lets it have its way with her.
The angel's shadow in the room
Is lightly lifted as if he
Had never terrified her there.

The furniture again returns
To its old simple state. She can
Take comfort from the things she knows
Though in her heart new loving burns
Something she never gave to man
Or god before, and this god grows

Most like a man. She wonders how
To pray at all, what thanks to give
And whom to give them to. "Alone
To all men's eyes I now must go"
She thinks, "And by myself must live
With a strange child that is my own."

So from her ecstasy she moves
And turns to human things at last
(Announcing angels set aside).
It is a human child she loves
Though a god stirs beneath her breast
And great salvations grip her side.

24. Cf. Mark 7:24–30.

Elizabeth Jennings's 1958 treatment of the Annunciation also deals with it as a mystical event of union with God but unlike Muir, Jennings probes the difficulties that piety glides over and challenges any easy assumptions concerning Mary's encounter. The assertive opening, "Nothing will ease the pain to come," resituates the event as one of high stakes, which exacted a price of suffering from Mary. Provocatively, it introduces, while not committing to, the idea of natal pain, strongly echoed in the poem's final line, "And great salvations grip her side." The *sensus fidelium* is that Mary was free from labor pains that had entered the world as a result of mankind's fall from grace. It is a challenging opening as it makes central the negatives and darkness usually absent from, or obscured by, the joy of Christ's conception. The following two lines follow a tradition in the writings of Western mystics of expressing mystical experience in the images of profane love, following the biblical precedent of the Song of Songs. Jennings firmly resists romantic expression or conceptions that would ignore difficulties and ambivalences. The intimation of sexual ecstasy is expressed in a troubling passive voice: "lets it have its way with her." The referent of "it" is not articulated, which allows for the unknowability of the encounter with God who is neither male nor female. The use of a now historic colloquial idiom used to mean *fornication* retains a problematic strain within the language, though, that the neuter pronoun does not eclipse. The ecstatic moment is repositioned so as to be secondary to the initial line of negation. At the summit of "Something" happening, Jennings places "Nothing" over it. Jennings seems to be consciously avoiding a shortcoming she perceived in Albert Camus, which she later touched upon in her book of critical analysis: "for Camus ecstasy was almost always another name for escape or self-deception."[25] Jennings, contra Camus, has ecstasy as momentary ("now") and as that from which she imagines Mary needing to "Take comfort" and to move "from"; any idea of *escape* being reversed.

Jennings's treatment of Mary's passivity shows the negative aspect of a Marian piety which overly articulates her docility, reducing her agency to that of passive compliance.[26] She pursues this line of thinking with the image of "The angel's shadow" made sinister in light of the following,

25. Jennings, *Every Changing Shape*, 15.

26. Mary's consent is stated positively in the chapter devoted to her in *Lumen Gentium*: "Rightly, therefore the holy Fathers see Mary not merely as a passive instrument in the hands of God but as freely co-operating in the work of human salvation through faith and obedience" (*LG* 56).

"as if he / Had never terrified her there." The angelic attempt to mitigate his behavior "as if" it had been other than it was, introduces a worrying implication of possible deception. While *terror* can refer to proper awe in God's Presence,[27] its use here implies fearfulness made especially troubling by the male gendering of the angel. Submissive almost to the point of erasure, Jennings's presentation of the Annunciation hovers around notions of entrapment that militates against Marian free consent. The angelic "shadow" alludes to the "overshadowing" of Mary in Luke 1:35, itself a literary allusion to the cloud that covered the tent of meeting and the glory of the Lord that filled the tabernacle (Exod 40:34). Jennings reworks the *overshadowing* into one of intimidating dominance.[28]

Jennings keeps her focus resolutely on Mary. The newness of the Annunciation she locates within Mary herself: "in her heart new loving burns"; an image which internalizes the Mosaic burning bush. This is the new "Something," suggesting both a thing newly called into being through this new encounter, and something already present but called forth from Mary's depths. This image modifies what seemed to be the assurances in the preceding lines: "again returns," "old simple state," and "comfort from the things she knows." *Return* for the person is an illusion, hence it is "The furniture" and "the things" that can be restored as they do not live nor change. The thing she has given for the first time causes her to probe her relationship with God (How? What? Who?) and to ponder her future. Jennings presses the strangeness of the event: God's manifestation paradoxically rendering Mary unable to pray; all prior certainties are removed. Her induction into new fervor accompanies induction into alienation ("Alone"). Mary's imagining bypasses any mention of Joseph, reiterating her sense of solitude: "by myself must live." This solitude carries its own dark ambivalence in her exposure "To all men's eyes," linking with, and continuing, the unsettling associations from the first stanza. The mystical union she experienced inaugurates the *missio Dei*, visible in her developing pregnancy; Jennings foregrounds the element of public

27. See Jennings's discussion of a poem by Gerard Manley Hopkins, where she distinguishes the "terror of awe" from "craven fear" (Jennings, *Every Changing Shape*, 103).

28. The association of "overshadowing" with sinister implications is a reading strongly influenced by culture. In the Northern hemishpere, it may be interpreted as darkly threatening but, as Elizabeth Johnson notes, within a Middle Eastern context of punishing heat and sun, it implies restorative respite (Johnson, *Truly Our Sister*, 252).

display usually absent from annunciation accounts that focus on the intimacy of the domestic and private.

The linkage of "strange child" with "my own" implicates Mary's maternal relationship, and by extension, all such mother-child relations; the child being both of the mother and different from her. Mary's motherhood is characterized as an uncomfortable encounter with otherness. The "strange child" will need to be explored and decoded, his meaning not easily accessible. The recognition of an alien quality points to the distance existing between all persons, each one standing alone before God, even when within intimate and loving human relationships. It also implies a linkage of strangeness and the mother. The identification of oddity is not selectively focused outward toward the child but shows Mary's concomitant self-awareness: that she, as mother, is implicated in her child's strangeness. Motherhood entails an encounter with one's own self as other, suggesting its capacity to open the maternal self to greater depths of self-knowledge. Such strangeness is weighed against the commonplace which provides the ballast to the "ecstasy." Within the daily world, the supernatural is parenthesized, just as are the "Announcing angels." Jennings's handling of the Annunciation rejects pious romanticizing, which detracts from its real human dimension. The divine who is unknown and unknowable is not apostrophized but rendered as an unconfirmed myth, so the lowercase "god" and the use of the indefinite article. With divinity sidelined, Mary as representative of humanity is "hungry both for certainty and for safety."[29] It is the humanity of mother and son that occupies Jennings. Shadowiness is the governing motif of the poem. In her later appreciative essay on Edwin Muir's poetry, Jennings writes of "the shadow side of his verse, a darkness that can never be entirely cast off. His work is affirmative, yes, but there are no easy answers in it."[30] These are words that could just as aptly constitute a self-assessment.

Bruce Dawe, "Mary and the Angel"

for Helen Gould

When Mary had attained her fifteenth year
she went with her parents (i.e. her mother)
to see Dr Gabriel, the high-school gynaecologist,

29. Jennings, *Every Changing Shape*, 18.
30. Jennings, *Every Changing Shape*, 153.

and sat reading *Spaceways* in his dove-grey waiting-room,
until in the fullness of time she was called.

And Dr Gabriel rose from his desk and said,
Well, aren't you the lucky girl to now have such
an all-round future beautifully planned?

And when Mary looked up at his thoroughly professional
face, his fluffy beard, the hands like wings,
the diplomas on the wall and the portrait of his wife
and children in a garden, she was troubled in herself
and said, What is it
makes you think I'm lucky?

And Dr Gabriel answered, Because you shall experience through
                                              tubal ligation

an inconceivable joy which shall liberate your body
from the bondage of your gender.

And Mary said to Gabriel, But what if later
I should choose to take a partner?

And Dr Gabriel answered, Then you shall be given
hormones to encourage
superovulation,
and a no-risk laparoscopy, and your ovum will be placed
in a little petri dish for your spouse to fertilise.
And we shall then evaluate the three healthy embryos
for genetic abnormalities, to be frozen and then stored.
And after the study, the travelling, the career,
should you decide on
the option of a baby, the embryo of your choice
shall be transferred to you—or, should you prefer it,
to a specified breeder woman . . .

And Mary sat there, her head dumbly bowed,
and tried very hard
to imagine happiness.

Bruce Dawe's 1980s reworking of the Annunciation is a bleak parody. In his presentation of an impoverished and reversed encounter, Dawe prosecutes contemporary misuse of language and its effect on conceptions of personhood. The Lucan lowly annunciate becomes in Dawe's poem, the annunciate brought low. Structured around an imagined dialogue between Mary and a Gabriel recast as "the high-school gynaecologist," Dawe observes each one's differing relationship with language.

Significantly, "Dr Gabriel" opens with a rhetorical question which neither expects nor seeks an answer. Dawe, as with Muir, uses "girl" of Mary but to different effect. The doctor's vocative, "the lucky girl," a parody of the angelic salutation, depersonalizes Mary, reducing "grace" to "chance," and signals an attitude of paternalism. The definite article mimics the singularity of her namesake, but her specificity is then undermined as the article modifies a generic noun. "Girl" here plays against Mary's gynecological maturity. Her physical maturity is inferred from her visit to the gynecologist, yet she is subject to the authority and decisions of others, unable to determine her future and vulnerable to the manipulations and desires of others in the liminal state between clearly designated girlhood and womanhood. The invocation of luck has immediate resonance for Australian readers of Donald Horne's *The Lucky Country*. The title of Horne's book passed into common parlance but in doing so, shed the ironic bite of the original. Horne's title is taken from the opening line of the book's final chapter: "Australia is a lucky country run mainly by second-rate people who share its luck."[31] The allusion directed to Mary now appears with an ironic twist and a covert denigration.

In contrast "the girl" asks two questions which are open-ended and signal a sincere attempt to glean understanding and engage in dialogue. She tries to interrogate the assumptions of the doctor ("What is it / makes you think I'm lucky?") in a reversal of Socratic dialogue. Rather than the master feigning ignorance in order to prompt students into formulating answers, Mary as enquiring student seeks answers from one "thoroughly professional" who is quick with practiced answers that are delivered as a series of unselfconscious ironies: the black pun of "inconceivable joy," the nihilism of "tubal ligation," the falsetto "liberate your body" and the perversity of envisaging her sex as "bondage." Each alleged descriptor and claim amounts to an unspeaking of the body's language. The answers

31. Horne, *Lucky Country*, 209.

she is given sketch an inverted scheme of values where fortune is equated with disabling her body's fertility so as to avoid any [un]lucky pregnancy. Not only does this treat natural gynecological maturation as pathological, it is a direct inversion of the recurrent biblical motif where the fertility of God's people is equated with blessing; infertility with curse.

The doctor's language domain contrasts unfavorably with Mary's. He is blasé in using jargon ("superovulation," "laparoscopy") and resorts to journalese ("placed in a little petri dish," "frozen and then stored"). This message of the technical usurpation of conception is delivered casually, glossing over potential difficulties, such as the risk to maternal health of inducing "superovulation." The interpolation of a third party into the generative union of Mary and her hypothetical spouse is not only undisclosed but implied not to exist with the claim that the ovum will wait "for your spouse to fertilize." In illogical and covert double-speak, any resultant embryo is simultaneously described as "healthy" and subject to investigation for "genetic abnormalities," the fate of embryos who fail evaluation not raised. The doctor's language conforms to the type of political speech sharply criticized in George Orwell's 1946 essay, "Politics and the English Language," being that of "euphemism, question-begging and sheer cloudy vagueness."[32] The adjectival modifiers "no-risk," "little," "healthy" resonate with positive associations designed to forestall closer critical enquiry. This is language used to circumvent questioning and to thwart communication. Orwell sees such political speech indicating a speaker's "reduced state of consciousness." This is signaled in the poem by the metastatic narration of the doctor (his fourfold use of "and"), indicating speech made without conscious awareness of, nor interest in, its own shortcomings. Such political speech, said Orwell, is used in "the defense of the indefensible."[33]

In the doctor's language world, words not only do not reliably mean what they say, they mean the opposite. The sterilized body hailed as "liberation," critically invokes the Women's Liberation Movement of second-wave feminism. The word choice doubly misleads as the tubal ligation eliminates, possibly permanently, any future elected pregnancy, negating any idea of freedom. A future pregnancy attempt may rely upon a commissioned surrogate; hers the true "bondage." Hers is the unspoken and anonymous servitude that supports techno maternity. "Liberation"

---

32. Orwell, "Politics and the English Language," 115.
33. Orwell, "Politics and the English Language," 114.

and "bondage" are also the keywords of extremist political propaganda that Dawe balances with the touchstone words of capitalism: "option," "choice," and "prefer." The latter are political palliatives suggesting they serve a program of freedom. It is, though, a faux freedom operating upon the fault lines of class, nationhood and economics. The historian and sociologist, Naomi Pfeffer has pointed out that the governing body of the UK's licensed fertility clinics, the "Human Fertilisation and Embryology Authority" (HFEA), allows a so-called "egg-sharing" scheme where women undergoing IVF are offered substantial financial reductions on the cost of their treatment if they agree to "donate" some of their eggs. An egg, though, cannot be "shared" and a financial inducement nullifies the freedom of a gift.[34] Furthermore, as demand for eggs in the UK by subfertile women far outstrips supply, IVF tourism to Eastern Europe and the Far East has grown; most eggs are sourced from women in developing or transitional economies with weak regulation, weak civil societies, corruption, and restricted access to healthcare. The physical manifestations of the body's health and developmental stage, which constitute the silent speech of the body, become an unreliable indicator in this scheme: amenorrhea now indicates not sexual immaturity, nor pregnancy, nor menopause, nor real pathology, but intentional curtailment of the body's potential to conceive.

The language scheme used by the doctor, within which Mary is expected to operate, dominates by imposing control over both nature and vocabulary. Here, natural procreation is usurped; God's sovereignty over procreation, displaced.[35] Here "planned" is promoted as the highest good. In an embedded inconsistency, the doctor's advocacy for planning contradicts his reference to "luck." The elision of planning with luck distances the doctor's advocacy from the Christian vision, which is of a providential deity who actively intends (plans) for each person's life, the person then being free to cooperate with the divine intention. Planning without reference to, and inclusion of, God is the hallmark of sin. The imposition of a self-generated plan has implications for language. Poets consciously plan their poems, shaping language, choosing, honing, and revising their words. This does not, though, give a full account of poetic creation which is craft but also art; a summoning and also a

34. Pfeffer, "Older Mothers."

35. In each act of non-contracepted sexual relations, neither party has control over whether or not conception takes place, notwithstanding that they are taking part in activity ordered towards procreation. See Lee and George, *Body-Self Dualism*, 193.

finding. Words are not only fashioned, they are waited for, discerned, recognized, and received, so, *inter alia*, Les Murray's "dreaming mind";[36] C. S. Lewis of writing his Narnia stories, "Everything began with images," which prompted him to "keep quiet and watch and they will begin joining themselves up";[37] Glyn Maxwell saying a poem can contain "words you didn't expect, echoes you couldn't foresee, matter you never chose."[38] All are expressing a sense of participating in something beyond themselves and their own conscious planning.

The poem's Gabriel is outside these mysterious bounds of poetry. The humanist scheme of the doctor is signaled by the suggestions of, but dissonances from, the gospel story. The troubling displacement of "hands like wings"; the Spirit trivialized to a residual allusion in the "dove-grey waiting-room" from whence the girl is called to a consulting room where, ironically, she will not be consulted but disregarded. This misconceived, Cartesian dystopic annunciation bypasses the heart of its meaning: freely-given consent. Her assumed *fiat* is not a participation in God's new creation but denial of it and resistance to it. The control, which is allegedly hers, as seen in the thrice repeated "you" ("you shall be given," "should you decide," "should you prefer it") is a reductive and misdirected echo of the Hebraic superlative expressed as a threefold repetition. Power relations are inverted in the poem, the primordial power of giving birth now usurped by the controlling (male) power of specialist medical knowledge; man's reliance upon woman to give birth is now woman's reliance upon man so she does not. Here is privation of word, deed and body.

Dawe's poem is notable for situating his Mary within her social context, in contrast to the usual preoccupation with her personal holiness which can seem to bypass her formative religious inheritance. The broader social program is indicated in the (State?) provision of a high school gynecologist, of her mother accompanying her there (although she is little more than a cipher), and of Mary's own slippage into the values of the world of which she is a part. Significantly, Dawe has Mary enquire about a future "partner" rather than husband; her language choice already subtly signaling her absorption of the subliminal text of her social environment. Equally significantly, the doctor avoids talk of

36. Murray, "Embodiment and Incarnation."

37. Lewis, "On Three Ways of Writing for Children," 41.

38. Maxwell, *On Poetry*, 126.

a husband, instead opting for the gender-free "spouse." Mary is named by the narrator, but not by the doctor. As naming is linked with attentive personalized care, her non-naming deprives her of dignity. John Paul II expounded upon dignity as a value intrinsic to the human person in twenty-eight of his Wednesday *TOB* audiences. Mary is linked with the indignity of the nameless "breeder woman." The reductive terminology evokes the imaginings of mid-twentieth-century science fiction, an example of which Mary has been reading in the waiting room. *Spaceways* was a children's annual published in London and distributed throughout the British Empire. The characters were based upon toys sold in Woolworths stores, those stores being the primary distributors of the comics. Dawe implies similarly interrelated commercial interests between those parties invested in promoting teenaged contraceptive practice. Science fiction hailed science as the harbinger of progress where *progress* was seen in materialist terms, not to mention being cosmically imperialistic. The poem's Gabriel is the messenger of such "scientism." The language of scientific procedures and conclusions are inadequate to encompass human experience as the nature of such language is to eliminate the "individual personality, purpose, passion, drama, and value" of the human subject.[39]

Dawe's free verse form facilitates the loose conversational style of the protagonists; its abandonment of the discipline of a more formal poetic form coaleses with the social practices of which he is critical. His use of a wide range of language registers: archaic/mock biblical ("When Mary had attained her fifteenth year," "in the fullness of time," "What is it makes you . . . ?"); rhetorical ("aren't you the lucky girl . . . ?"); metastatic (the doctor's four-time usage of "and"); and informal (the arch use of the abbreviation "i.e.") collates all language types, implying the contemporary corruption of all linguistic expression. By the poem's end, Mary has no words of her own, effectively rendered linguistically sterile. Her muteness ("dumbly") displaces the expected "humbly" of Christian piety and connects her with the animal world that cannot transcend itself in word.[40] She resists being misplaced in this way ("tried very hard"), struggling to retain her personhood. It is an unequal struggle in a social context bereft of grace where, in ironic reversal, instead of ushering in the Word, Mary is unable to generate any. The language world that has defeated her is the antithesis of language that is open and generative; that is, poetic language.

---

39. Abrams, "Language and Methods of Humanism," 98.

40. Rahner, *Theology of the Spiritual Life*, 302.

It is no coincidence that the doctor advocates infertility as his language world is non-generative. This (non) consultation amounts to an opposition of word worlds, between, on the one hand, that which, in Rahner's poetical phrase "render[s] a single thing translucent to the infinity of all reality," and on the other, that which would "delimit and isolate."[41] As representative of the poetic language realm, Mary's imaginative capacity, signaled by the "what if?" of her second question, has stalled by poem's end; the glimmer of hope offered by her trying to "imagine" extinguished by the past tense and defeated outcome.

Poems are open to the unexpected but hoped -for possibilities of words; to a shared creative relationship between author, reader, and critic. Counterintuitively, Dawe is one among many poets who have attested to a sense that the words they seek find them; that in some sense they are not the sole authors of their own creations.[42] Dawe expresses a conviction that a writer's language choice is necessarily "intuitive," implying how this should foster a sense of authorial humility: "instinctual nature . . . should act as a corrective to any belief that the author knows best." Dawe seems to have seen in this humility not only a check against possible artistic hubris, but an organic link to the openness of the artistic calling: "I do not know the answers, and see my role being limited to the exploration of the questions."[43] Such exploration does not foreclose critical interrogation, nor prosecution of contemporary practices, and the assumptions on which they rest. Just as the relationships within the poem have collapsed (mother an ineffective, silent, and overlooked chaperone of her daughter; doctor inauthentically speaking secular politics rather than medicine; the paradigm of relational intimacy, motherhood, no longer covenantal but contractual) so too have words. The "tubal ligation" cauterizes words themselves; the conduits of transmission are severed, so that communication becomes impossible. Words can no longer be conceived; imagination is arrested, and articulation gripped by seizure. Possibilities for the world implode as the chosen mother of the Word becomes unable to deliver any.

41. Rahner, *Theology of the Spiritual Life*, 295.

42. Clive James, contra Dawe, says that a poem is made, not found, but he also allows for what Dryden called a "hit," or felicitous phrase, that comes unbidden. James also expressed a sense of a poet needing patience and discernment; that the poet must "wait for it [the poem] to speak" (James, *Poetry Notebook*, 57, 132, 207).

43. Dawe, "Australian Poets in Profile," 242.

Overview of Annunciation Poems

Muir's Annunciation poem enacts an argument in defense of poetry as a different way of seeing. *Sight* as the governing conceit speaks to its being the prime metaphor for *knowledge*. In his poem, what is seen is what could not be seen other than as it is, through his poem. What the poem leads its reader to see is the value of the unhurried gaze that *takes in* the other, speaking to the pleasingly ingressive nature of sight when it is focused by love. This subtle endorsement of the poet's vocation makes a claim not foreign to the tradition. Pope Leo the Great (c. AD 400–461) gave a nascent papal endorsement of the imagination as a potential spiritual and devotional aid in his Sermon 26, saying of the Annunciation that, on contemplating Mary's conversation with the angel and her conception by the Holy Spirit, that memory is stirred but also our interior *eyes*.[44]

When sight is concentrated, it can absorb speech, as in Muir's poem, which builds an image of silent, mutual contemplation. Muir's image resonates with Sarah Coakley's advocacy of contemplative prayer as a resource for systematic theology; such silent prayer acting as a balance to systematizing attempts at mastery. Silence of this kind can open up possibilities for other voices to both speak and be heard. In Muir's poem, the silence of the contemplative couple enacts a Heideggerian approach to poetry as that which shows the unsayable while showing that it can "never be fully brought to language."[45]

Muir's poetic vision anticipates by some two decades the importance John Paul II attached to mutuality in male-female relations. In Muir's imagined scene, the issue of authority, in the sense of enforced domination or control, recedes to the point of irrelevance. He configures *authority* according to Sarah Coakley's description of "non-coercive divine power."[46] This then allows him to present Mary's obedience from a different perspective. He does not abandon magisterial teaching of her obedience and humility but emphasizes that it is an outgrowth of love, which desires the other's best interest. When that other is God, the lover secures her own best interest incidentally while seeking that which God seeks.

Rowe's poem also draws upon *eros* as that which can direct to God and be turned to God. His strategy of using overtly sexual imagery when

44. Gambero, *Mary and the Fathers of the Church*, 308.
45. Strhan, "Religious Language as Poetry," 928.
46. Coakley, *Powers and Submissions*, 5.

the subject is the Annunciation is an especially risky one. It succeeds, though, in constructing an image that avoids the type of sexual hierarchy that compromises mutuality. It succeeds, too, in presenting a Marian figure that is receptive but not passive, so establishing relational reciprocity.

In keeping with his stated aim of reclaiming the disclosive power of immanence, Rowe's poem opens up an implied contrast between the ultimate transcendent event—God's Incarnation—and a contemporary worldview that he thought had lost faith in the possibility that ordinary life could be meaningful. His poem attempts to restore faith in the value of the mundane present; to open minds and hearts to the possibility of finding poetry in ordinariness; of reclaiming an imaginative eye. Rowe presents his poetically transformed vision through the suggestiveness of the ordinary (wood, table, meal, bone, breeze). These simple objects become, in his poem, evocative signs, so becoming the very means of their own transcendence.

Jennings's poem is more overtly concerned with authority, in particular the question of heteronomy and the implications of this for personal freedom. Informed by a darker consciousness of what passivity and obedience can mean for a woman where the relational or social power dynamic is exaggeratedly skewed against her, Jennings's Mary teeters on the brink of being subsumed by Transcendence, in the presence of which her immanence appears dangerously powerless. Jennings's poem grasps the potential for the Annunciation to be read as sexually exploitative, viewing the gospel reading from an unfamiliar, uncomfortable, perspective. For similar reasons, Sarah Coakley does not see the Lucan Annunciation as providing the possibility of a feminist reading. She, like Jennings, reads in it themes of fear, humility, and submission.[47] While Jennings reads fear as a negative affective state, a well-developed biblical thread also positively associates "fear of the Lord" with wisdom (see Prov 9:10).[48] Jennings's poem, though, evokes disquiet. Damaging humility that devalues the self has been identified in some feminist discourse as more likely in women than in men, possibly as women have wielded less political and economic power.[49] Humility's true meaning—having a modest assessment of self in relation to others—is, though, a necessary virtue for harmonious

47. Coakley, *Powers and Submissions*, 60.

48. Reiterated in Ps 111:10; Job 28:28, among others.

49. See Ruether, *Sexism and God-Talk*.

personal and civic relations. Jennings's poem refuses an easy account of salvation's beginning, suggesting instead its costliness to the mother.

Dawe's poem offers a critical appraisal of the currency of words in his post-Christian dystopia. If words are understood to be morally neutral attempts to express concepts, then the person who uses them is excused from moral accountability. If, instead, words are understood to be an expression of the mind's judgement, then the speaker is held morally accountable. The former understanding has the speaker held captive by the world; the latter secures the speaker's freedom to form mental judgements about all that is encountered in the world. This freedom ensures each person's moral accountability for linguistic, and other, choices.[50] Dawe's doctor is therefore morally accountable for his self-identification with a political scheme founded upon a distaste for the feminine potential of motherhood, and a determination to shut down female fertility as soon as it has physiologically matured.

Dawe's poetic world displays the consequences of abandoning a pattern of thinking that is governed by Truth as the origin and standard of all that is. This alternative vision enthrones man (here, specifically *male*) as the manufacturer of life; an inverted vision that fails to generate a W/ word in Mary, the woman who enthrones God, not self. The doctor's words enact the distinction between expression (here, *choice*) and what is expressed (here, *determinism*), his words obfuscating the distinction.[51] The moral neutrality of determinism rejects freedom and responsibility.[52] Dawe's presentation shows how a key tenet of the Aristotelian and Classical traditions—that the practice of virtue leads to happiness—can be rendered null within a civil context that opposes happiness to virtue. Dawe evokes the social landscape of a "New Cartesianism"[53] which reverses the direction of the relationship between technology and persons, hailing technology as the paradigmatic good. His poem presents the consequences to the person when *self* is conceived of as an independent actor whose interior state is all. The resultant loss for the subject is not only a relationship with the exterior world, but harmonious integration with one's own body.

50. See Markus, "St. Augustine on Signs," 80–81.

51. Carpenter, *Theo-Poetics*, 125.

52. See Hill, *After the Natural Law*, 196–200.

53. Kerr, "Need for Philosophy in Theology Today," 258. Kerr attributes the term's coinage to John McDowell.

Pietà poems

R. S. Thomas, "Pietà"

Always the same hills
Crowd the horizon,
Remote witnesses
Of the still scene.

And in the foreground
The tall Cross,
Sombre, untenanted,
Aches for the Body
That is back in the cradle
Of a maid's arms.

Images of the *Pietà* are artistic fictions: imaginative creations of an extra-biblical scene. They nevertheless resonate with truthfulness, have a satisfying emotional register, and provide narrative cohesion. The *Pietà* completes the circle of Jesus's earthly life, placing him back in the arms of his mother. It is an image of the costliness of love; pain inscribed on both the subjects. The all-encompassing pain extends to the whole body: physical, spiritual and emotional. Intense somatic pain eradicates a person's capacity to speak and erases personal agency. Incapacitated, pain speaks the person, who utters involuntary cries and groans. This reversion to a state "anterior to language"[54] obliterates the volition, agency, and power of the sufferer. Such deconstruction of the person is the *raison d'être* of torture.

This coalescence within the *Pietà* motif of suffering, trauma, closure, and the annihilation of language made it a uniquely apt subject for exploration by the Welsh poet and ordained Anglican, R. S. Thomas. At the time of the poem's composition, Thomas had been much preoccupied with the demise of the Welsh language. Published in 1966 within a collection of the same name, academic M. Wynn Thomas sees the "pathos of this linguistic crisis" evident throughout the collection.[55] The choice of book title makes a dramatic and inflationary connection between the loss of the Welsh language and the death of the foundational Word,

---

54. Scarry, *Body in Pain*, 4, 49.
55. Thomas, *Serial Obsessive*, 88.

intimating the former to be a cultural apocalypse that strikes at, or strikes out, identity.

The poem is notable for its unusual handling of the identities of the *dramatis personae*, neither of whom is directly present to the reader-viewer. Thomas's is a curiously disembodied *Pietà*. Eschewing the suffering bodies, Thomas instead foregrounds the "untenanted" cross of Protestantism. The real flesh-and-blood bodies of son ("the Body") and mother ("a maid's arms") are only alluded to. Anthropomorphized, Thomas's cross "Aches for the Body": dead wood paradoxically alive to the meaning of Christ's body. The yearning discomfort attributed to the cross operates ambiguously, suggesting both the amorous and the maternal. Viewed as the latter, the attributes "untenanted" and "Aches" read as displacements of the *postpartum* and laboring mother. Wood rendered sensate is a mirror image of the gospel strand that exhorts believers to *die* in order for Christ to live within them. This ongoing, interior spiritual transformation sees the disciple more fully conformed to Christ, hence the Pauline oxymoron, "dying is gain" (Phil 1:21).

The chiasmus that transfers inertness to the fleshly mother, whose arms are "a cradle," and animates the inert cross, is a poetic strategy that not only anchors the poem but shapes it as a cross. While this arresting rearrangement is consonant with Christian theological understanding of the cross event as reordering history, it is unsettling in its near total disregard of the mother. That Thomas gives the Holy Mother, embodiment of religious duty faithfully performed, and costly maternal loyalty, only the briefest allusion may, in part, be attributable to an Anglican attenuation (or absence) of Marian devotion, but biographical considerations also seem relevant. Barry Morgan relates that Thomas had felt smothered by maternal love and only at the end of his life came to think that he had judged his mother too harshly.[56] This seems significant for the poem's unusual contrast between the *adult* cross ("tall," "Sombre") and the son, now returned to childhood ("back in the cradle") in the dependency of death. While "cradle" echoes Jesus's nativity at this occasion of new birth, it also uncomfortably infantilizes the grown son. The use of the indefinite article in denoting Mary, who is unnamed, possibly implies an unattractive instrumental attitude to her. While "maid" is technically correct to denote Mary's virginity, its use here suggests ambivalence to Mary as mother. Western painterly convention often portrays the older

56. Morgan, "Kyffin Williams and R. S. Thomas."

Mary as maiden-like in youthful beauty. Thomas's usage connects with the motif, common in medieval popular piety, of Mary as the true spouse of Jesus. The cradling arms are ambivalently suggestive of a mother or lover. Mary had historically been construed as Jesus's spouse, the metaphor confirming her as the true believer, and hence, the true church.[57] Having spoken of his own mother as having been possessive,[58] Thomas saves the poetic Jesus from this fate by giving him into the arms of a mother whose youth he implies. *Mother* is subtly transfigured into *lover*, in a maneuver that assumes her to be of the non-possessive variety. Morgan cites two other Thomas scholars, Elaine Shepherd and M. Wynn Thomas, as each seeing in Thomas's poetic responses to paintings an erotic sensibility which, they surmise, may have been suppressed in the poet's life;[59] an observation which seems apposite in this context.

Thomas's poem lends itself to being read in the light of those original characteristics, *solitude* and *communion*. The sense of solitude is especially acute both within the generic subject—son alone in death, mother alone in living grief—and in Thomas's unusual handling of it. The focus of the poem is the cross ("in the foreground"). Empathetic to the suffering victim it has lately supported, it is humanized with sensuous insatiability; desire not spent, even after the Word has climaxed. This is no mere instrument in the Passion drama. Its contact with Christ's body has been transformative, bestowing it with dignity, and elevating it to almost human consciousness. Its voice has become pluralistic, expressing not only its own desire to recover the lost Christ, but absorbing Christ's yearning cry of dereliction to the Father (Matt 27:46). Christ's desolate sense of abandonment gives voice to the realization of ultimate loss: the self cut off from any and every relationship. It anticipates the cry of the person standing in radical solitude before God after death. The adjective, "Remote," marks a sense of psychic distance that during personal crises can isolate the sufferer from others. The cross may long for Christ, but re-establishment of communion is, for it, impossible. It stands, as does Mary

---

57. Marina Warner surveys use of the motif, inherited by Christianity from Judasim, of the faithful community portrayed as God's bride. In the West, this motif became identified with the Virgin Mary. Warner locates stirrings of devotion to "Our Lady" as "sweetheart" in the tenth century. Influenced by the ardency of Bernard of Clairvaux for Mary in the twelfth century, it became a widespread and popular devotion. See Warner, *Alone of All Her Sex*, 30, 122.

58. Thomas, *Serial Obsessive*, 123.

59. Morgan, "Kyffin Williams and R. S. Thomas," 8–13.

in paintings of the scene, immobilized in heartache. Relationships within the world of the poem are fatally ruptured or unable to be realized, communion longed-for but denied: the relationship between witnessing and being a hill; the relationship between insensate wood that silently "feels"; the relationship between the comfort "Of a maid's arms" and being dead.

Thomas's *oeuvre* is characterized by a sense of solitude which can seem to thwart the communion he desires. Richard McLauchlan sees Thomas's poetry as marked by "Holy Saturday theology"[60] which takes seriously the silence of the day between Crucifixion and Resurrection. The motivation is not to evade the difficulties posed by "suffering, silence and absence," but, by allowing a Holy Saturday theology "to stretch itself in new directions," to allow that "It challenges, unsettles and problematizes religious language and concepts."[61] Christianity must contend with a foundational religious figure who is, in the usually accepted sense, not there. It is only with the Resurrection event that this absence is understood as a transformed kind of presence hidden from sight in the invisible presence of the Spirit, located within persons and within the consecrated bread and wine. In one sense though, this is not what believers see. What is seen is emptiness—the cross "untenanted"—and, as with Thomas's poetic cross, what may be felt is unfulfilled longing and loneliness. McLauchlan sees the poetic medium as particularly suited to engaging the reader with both God's absence and presence:

> In the formation of a poem, where rhythm, enjambment and caesurae are integral to what the poet is saying, the spaces between words and the points at which lines end become crucial. The poet says something in the very act of forcing the reader to stop and breathe. The silence, implied by the boundaries that the poems set up as they "stop short" of God, becomes a form of revelation as it witnesses to the fundamental freedom of God from the confines of human language. (981)

The hills as "Remote witnesses" usurp the women who, in the synoptic accounts, stood at a distance from the cross (Matt 27:55; Luke 23:49). Thomas had been witness to change in Wales he did not welcome, and perhaps felt himself to be remote in his linguistic isolation (although he learnt to speak Welsh, and wrote prose in it, he did not ever feel able

---

60. McLauchlan, "R. S. Thomas," 976.
61. McLauchlan, "R. S. Thomas," 978.

to express himself poetically in it),[62] and in his quarrel with the seemingly inexorable advance of the English language in Wales. This sidelining of the real witnesses seems to express something of Thomas's concern that the [Welsh] hills may be all that is left "the same" once the local language has disappeared and so changed all else. The hills suggest the comfort of stability, permanence, and reliability ("Always the same"). Thomas disallows much sense of reassurance by their presence, though. Instead, he destabilizes their chief characteristic, immobility, by transferring to them the jostling associations of "Crowd," intensifying associations of movement by using it as a transitive verb.

Thomas exploits the ambivalences latent in seemingly incontestable phrases and simple syntax. This is so in his opening line where "Always the same hills" could imply comfortable recognition of the visual formula adopted in artistic depictions of the scene but could as easily imply a certain weary detachment: *same* in the sense of formulaic and unimaginative. The latter is consonant with Thomas's own personal feelings of "dislocation and displacement" even from that part of Wales he had made his home at the time of the poem's composition.[63] Repeated sameness can blunt appreciation and imply stagnancy. The repeated rituals of the church, structured according to the liturgical year, are deemed to be meaningful, rather than mechanically familiar, as reception of them can continually cast up new understandings and initiate the congregant more fully into what they disclose. Repetition of actions also improves and reinforces agility in performance of them, and it is repetition that engenders cognitive familiarity that strengthens recall. The opening line, then, raises questions of memory and memorial enactment: what they are, how they function, and how reliable they are. The sameness of the hills, as of the Christian salvation story, indicates a continuous present, which is the tense used throughout the poem. The poem is therefore realizing in its own timelessness a small something of the excess of the cross which, although an historic event of a particular time and place, exceeds its own historic realization. The sameness of the background hills, or of any of the story's other elements, provides reassurance that the story has been rightly remembered, the narrative faithfully transmitted. The narrative motifs have become ritualized through continual repetition and it is this that both transmits and establishes right memory.

62. Morgan, *Strangely Orthodox*, 11.
63. Thomas, *Serial Obsessive*, 90.

Similar ambiguity inheres to the following "still scene." Stillness suggests both a serenity in which there is space to absorb, consider and grow in understanding, and the shocked stillness immediately after trauma; the arrest of energy, movement and the activity of life. There is a still surface-calm to Thomas's poem, dominated as it is with sibilant sounds, but this sits above the sense of dense compression of meaning; Thomas's usual spare style pressed to its editorial limit. The phrase carries resonances of the painting genre *still life*, which, through the presence of objects left behind, alludes to the absent people who have used them and who may again return, although not in this field, in this painting. This simultaneous presentation of presence and absence has also been noted by Richard McLauchlan as being characteristic of Thomas's "Holy Saturday theology." The image also has a temporal meaning: the "still scene" is still current, available through the communal memory of the faithful and their central liturgical event, the Eucharist. This temporal dimension connects it with "Remote," which, when considered in relation to the Eucharist, prompts consideration of ecclesial memorial enactments. The public sacramental repetition of the liturgical words and actions ensures that the ritual is held in common by all the faithful and keeps it open to constant inspection; its public openness is its defense against idiosyncratic personal distortions and changes. It is upon the foundational memory of the initial contemporary witnesses, upon which the gospel account relies, that the faith now relies. Current adherents of the Christian faith who attest to the truth-claims of the story have inherited the memory from others. They can claim to be "witnesses," although not present at the historic event, even though "Remote" as the distant hills, as the event of the cross is not solipsistic, enclosed upon itself. Christology interprets Christ as the manifestation of the *Always-the-Same-One*, so his person and actions continue to be available in the present in a strongly memorial way. The "still scene" is still current, available through the communal memory of the faithful, present in scripture, preaching and the sacraments.

The extreme leanness of Thomas's poetic style, realized in this *Pietà*, seems an outgrowth of a certain chariness about embodiment, perhaps reflecting ambivalence towards the maternal. His *Pietà* is a lament for the Word laid to rest. Yearning for a loved presence that has passed away could be seen as the *leitmotiv* of the poem, Thomas having made Christ's words of abandonment his own. This cross is substitutionary, but within the context of Thomas's poem, it substitutes for the human, the bodily and the maternal. The linguistic crisis of the cross becomes, in Thomas's hands, a maternal crisis. The personal voice of his poetry was embodied in an encroaching language, foisted on him by a mother resented for this, and personal reasons. His *de facto* mother tongue is not the language he "Ached" for. The usual study of embodied pain and grief that the *Pietà* evokes becomes instead a landscape poem allowing a quiet but intense detached meditation. His poem is a delicate cameo whose smallness of scale and tendency to silence paradoxically marks the greatest language event of all. He chooses to render poetically the very moment when God's Word *cannot* speak. Thomas does not presume to speak for the now-silent God but contemplates instead the scene of dereliction.

James McAuley, "Pietà"

A year ago you came
Early into the light.
You lived a day and night,
Then died; no-one to blame.

Once only, with one hand,
Your mother in farewell
Touched you. I cannot tell,
I cannot understand

A thing so dark and deep,
So physical a loss:
One touch, and that was all

She had of you to keep.
Clean wounds, but terrible,
Are those made with the Cross.

James McAuley's "Pietà," composed and published in 1963, while lengthier than Thomas's, is also compact. The discipline of the sonnet form restrains the expansive sentiment; its association with love poetry speaking to the content. The dense compactness is further reduced in this curtal sonnet form, compression of vast meaning into small scale echoing the physical size and truncated lifespan of the child. Contrary to Thomas's, McAuley's focus is closely upon the mother. Emotional intensity is gleaned from the particular circumstances of this *Pietà*: the death of a one-day-old neonate, and associating it through the title with the archetypal image of maternal suffering. The connection McAuley makes between the contemporary scene and the low point of the Christian story has precedent. It is common artistic practice to use live models to pose as Mary and Jesus in visual presentations of the subject. By this association, he suggests the poetic mother and child both model, and inherit a relationship with, their prototypes. Neither protagonist is named in the poem. Identity is established via second- and third-person pronouns, so making relationship the crux of the poem.

The poem is addressed to the dead neonate, the narrative enacting the kind of familial story-telling that informs and shapes the autobiographical identity of young children. Invoking the deceased as addressee situates the poem between tentative hope that the child continues to live in some way beyond biological death (the hope of Christian faith) and an agnostic position concerning *hope* where the direct address is an arresting literary device. The poem inclines to the former as the poetic memorial purports to be written one year after the death, the time when, in the Roman Catholic Church, a memorial Mass for the departed is traditionally requested. The "Early into the light" denoting premature birth (the cause of premature death) can, by the poem's end, be reread more hopefully: immediate and unhindered progression into divine light; the hoped-for *telos* of earthly life now reached. There is no premature closure upon the pain and struggle of the event, though, as the associations of hope with "light" are overshadowed with the following "night," "dark," "loss," and "wounds." Dark following light reverses creation. Light, and its attendant associations with revelatory knowledge, is stalked and overtaken by dark ignorance and ineffable mystery.

With the essential outline of the narrative given, the second quatrain turns attention to the mother. The epic proportion of her small gesture is marked by the stately, weighty pulse and the rhythmic allusions to the Elohist creation narrative: "a day and a night" and "dark and deep." While this contextualizes even the degeneration of infant death within the creative generativity of God, it also implies the contrast between creation's original goodness, with its ordered scheme unfolding in timely manner, and the disordered entropy of the world that poet, reader and protagonist now inhabit. The Genesis story narrates the physical manifestation of God's creative speech-act that is echoed in human generation. The divine resonances are immediately disturbed, though, by the dual linkage with its opposite: the numbness of bereavement.

Loss as a theme extends to the nature of words themselves. At the heart of McAuley's poem lies a paradox: that the mode of his memorial relies upon the shaping of words, yet words are stretched to their limit, struggling to express the barely expressible. Having reported the farewell touch of the mother, negative expressions of incapacity follow: "I cannot tell / I cannot understand." Words and understanding chase themselves in a futile exegetical circle: articulation aids the process of understanding, but the necessary words are elusive prior to some comprehension of what it is the poet would express. Words hover on the edge of inarticulacy, failing to offer more than the imprecision of "A thing" for what has happened. The very capacity of words to act as witnesses is threatened if words are incapable of telling; existence threatening to collapse into a story never told. The depth and scale of meaning threatens to exceed the communicative capacity of words which are strained under intense pressure. In a critical analysis of McAuley's poetry, fellow poet and critic, Noel Rowe, sees in the "connection between 'farewell' and 'I cannot tell' a farewell to language, a despair of making meaning."[64] The material loss is not only "So physical" but verbal as well. This calls into question the very viability of the poetic vocation. However, although words themselves teeter on the brink of defeat, the poem by its very existence refuses to concede the failure of language. Words struggle to authentically express the real, but they are not abandoned. McAuley succeeds in marshalling words that attempt to tell, so averting that which Charles Taylor, in *A Secular Age,* has identified as the primary fear of the present secular age: the death of language.[65] The power of language is offset in McAuley's poem by a simultaneous awareness of the fragility of language; that words can lose their resonance, and so their revelatory potential.

The languages of poetic expression and of bodily gesture each tremble with the loads they labor to bear. The pressing solitude of the mother, and the uniqueness of the passing life, exert an almost unsustainable pressure on vocabulary, reliant on repetition ("Once only, with one hand"; "One touch") to communicate emotional *extremis,* amounting to a verbal stammer; words stalling in the presence of self-donating love.[66] The na-

64. Rowe, "Possibility of Despair," 30.

65. Taylor, *Secular Age,* 759.

66. Against reductive claims about the capacity for human language to speak meaningfully about God, Karl Rahner affirms theology's capacity to so speak, "even if it stammers in the attempt to do this" (*Science and Christian Faith,* 111).

ture of singularity means that it struggles to support synonyms, but here, words fumble when faced with the impregnable authority of uniqueness: the existence of *this* child and *this* mother at *this* time; each reiteration marking the multiple modes of uniqueness. The weight of feeling attached to oneness, within the context already alluded to of the Genesis creation story, recalls the weight of solitariness registered by Adam in the Yahwist account where, in naming the animals, he understands himself to be essentially alone within creation (Gen 2:19–20). The mother's "One touch" recalls the hemorrhaging woman in the Matthean gospel (Matt 14:36), an ambivalent allusion as that woman's faithful touch brought her bodily healing; this woman's touch seals a death.

The poem sets up a triad of viewing relationships—mother of child, narrator of them both, and reader of all three—each onlooker moved by what is seen. McAuley's watchful attention to the mother's touch invokes the relational nature of sight. This is the interest of Stephen Pattison in his book, *Seeing Things,* where he argues for the reintegration of sight with the other senses; a concept he calls "haptic vision."[67] This integrated approach alters the understanding of *sight.* No longer associated with a distant, detached, rational observer, Pattison reclaims sight's powerful affectivity: "an intimate, visceral experience that touches and moves." Touch allied to sight provides confirmation of what we see, as with the Apostle Thomas's insistence upon feeling the wounds of Christ. In Pattison's summary of the three core ways of conceptualizing sight: as perceptual experience, social practice, and discursive construct, it is the latter which threads its way through McAuley's poem; sight giving rise to, as per Pattison's thesis, "metaphors, images and constructs that shape thought and thinking." The sight of the mother and her doomed child recalls the natal scene of the Virgin and Jesus, now transposed to the foot of the cross; metaphors of birth and death coalesce in the superimposed images of the imagination.

The sight of the touch the poem directs our intense gaze to, is one saturated with meaning, both for the immediate participants, and for those who participate less directly, by seeing. All bodies have a tactile sense that provides the metaphor by which we understand how emotions are *felt.* In the confluence of mother, dying newborn, and their tactile bond, is a universally understood emotional register that needs no translation. The body, and what it feels physically and emotionally, is

67. Pattison, *Seeing Things.*

that which keeps us open, or attuned, to our existence; bodily sensibility is, in David Levin's words, "a mode of knowledge anterior to science, but not for that reason . . . necessarily inferior or 'confused.'"[68] The poem's existence attests to the possibility of being touched by another's pain, activating a *communio* of suffering: the mother's physical touch emotionally touching the poet-observer, who then writes in the hope of touching the reader's heart with some truth of the maternal body.

The poem is careful to distinguish the modalities of this felt sense, wanting to give primary emotional weight to the gravity of the loss experienced by the mother. To that end, the narrator practices self-effacement by not using of himself a personal pronoun. A respectful distance is maintained between narrator and mother. The latter touches the inner reaches of mystery ("so dark and deep"); the image resonant with associations of female embodiment and of the incomprehensibility of God, in a way not accessible to the narrator who "cannot tell," who "cannot understand." The pathos of the poem is deepened by knowing the biographical circumstances of its composition. McAuley and his wife experienced the death at one-day-old of their sixth child, a son, sixth months before the publication of the poem.[69] McAuley's care to preserve the distinction between the suffering mother and the paternal narrator is an act of humility that surrenders primacy to the mother's experience and acknowledges that it is not transferable across the sex divide. No attempt is made to colonize her experience nor assimilate it into something parental as attested by the line accents twice falling upon "cannot." The poem's emotional foundation is the commonality of the human experience of love and loss (the presence of the "ones" now inviting thoughts of unity) while honoring the distinctively male and female embodiment of it. McAuley's poem is never presumptive; the reader is given an opening or glimpse into an intimate moment which speaks for itself in the space the poem cleared. The poem becomes more than its words. It is McAuley's own gesture of farewell to his son, and of the admiring awe he feels for his wife.

McAuley as poet, and the narrator's voice he constructs, make "a kind of withdrawal," which Rowan Williams, in the published book of his 2005 Clark Lectures, maintains is essential for all artists.[70] He means by this that the original object that provoked the artist must be accorded a

68. Levin, *Body's Recollection of Being*, 49–50.

69. Pybus, *Devil and James McAuley*, 204.

70. Williams, *Grace and Necessity*, 161.

respect and following from this, any artistic response will require "letting the work develop in its own logic, its own space," an assessment invoking a strongly maternal-gestational image. Williams sees artistic endeavor as implying something *other* in the world; an elusive excess that the artist senses, and tries to respond to. What his imagination produces is, says Williams, "not a self-contained mental construct but a vision that escapes control . . . a *dimensional* existence." Williams here is giving some account of a sense that artistic product is neither an act of domination nor of imitation. The artist is neither oligarch nor mimic but is obedient to some depth in the world, which depth "exists in relation to more than your [the artist's] will and purpose." McAuley himself records a similar sense in the text of his 1975 lecture, "The Rhetoric of Australian Poetry," where he said of the series of small nature poems he was then writing, that they "are a quite unexpected thing for me to find myself doing. I can say that I decided to do them and also that I found myself doing them."[71]

Williams notes, in *Grace and Necessity*, a convergence between theological thinking and artistic endeavors; in particular, that art helps understanding of creation. The Christian understanding of the world's creation is rooted in a Trinitarian conception of God: the Father generating the Son who is both "utterly continuous" and "utterly other," wholly drawn from the Father and wholly a representation of the Father.[72] Reflecting upon this, Williams says that what is central to "making other" is "dispossession, disinterested love," which is the logic behind talk of the artist's "withdrawal." McAuley adheres to these artistic requirements in this poem. He looks with eyes that notice a lot and perceive even more. His choice of title is an explicit indicator both of dispossession, and of consciously relating to another depth of existence. His poem is wholly drawn from his life and is represented so that it stands apart from his personal artistic endeavor, and from his personal biography. He transforms his personal loss into an act of creative *poiesis*, transposing loss into gift. McAuley fashions the poem so that it can become a Christic sign of contradiction for the reader where, in the death of an innocent, God, who is Love and Life, can be discerned. In personal correspondence to fellow poet A. D. Hope, McAuley wrote of how the grief shared with his wife drew them closer together and became profoundly life-affirming:

71. McAuley, *Poetry, Essays, and Personal Commentary*, 115–16.
72. Williams, *Grace and Necessity*, 161.

"The loss became an occasion of extraordinary opening up of sealed off depths."[73]

McAuley's detached narrator-viewer focuses on the mother's act of attachment and the piercing handicap of her being able to use only one hand instead of the expected full maternal embrace. In the touch is embedded loss. There is also another dimension suggested through the separation and maternal solitude. The laying on of hands is one of the mediations of the Christian sacraments used in the rite of ordination and the prayer for healing and wholeness. The mother's touch suggests a sacramental communion expanding and complementing the action of the individual by linking the mother with the presence and mediation of the (mother) church. The central image and founding event of the church, the cross, is invoked in the last two lines.

McAuley structures the final lines so that the expected third quatrain is reduced to a tercet, the line reduction realizing in its own mode the central line: "So physical a loss." What would have been the quatrain's final line, "She had of you to keep," slips down to become the first line of a second tercet, adding itself to what would have been the expected final couplet. This is a second physical realization within the lineation of the word sense. The enjambment of the line end: "that was all" and the next line: "She had of you to keep," has travelled not only to the following line but across a blank white void. Her personal memorial of her child is now lodged beside the cross, the place where Christian faith sees life astonishingly springing from the site of death. The ambivalence of the cross is retained in the metaphoric field of "wounds" and "terrible," and their associations of knife, blade, and sword further alluding to the Matthean words of Jesus: "I have not come to bring peace, but a sword" (Matt 10:34B NRSV). Hope is embedded here, too, as in the preceding line in the gospel, the disciples have been exhorted to be unafraid, even in dying, as contrary to appearances, they will live on. The cross's capacity to wound is for the purpose of the salvation, or purification, of souls. Its capacity to wound is at one with its capacity to bring transformative healing. The tonal shift occurring with "Clean wounds" carries associations of holiness, wholesomeness, hygiene, and purity. These are wounds from which it is possible to make a sound recovery. This surgical action of God is manifest in the poem where the poet-surgeon exposes what is ordinarily hidden from sight. The cross as scalpel both opens up a greater

73. McAuley cited in Pybus, *Devil and James McAuley*, 204.

depth of sight via exposure and detachment, and implies postsurgical closure, so the cross as stumbling block which closes understanding. This is not the cross as an abstract idea of renewal. It actively accompanies and carries with it the love and pain of *this* mother, her particularity of suffering honored as she and her experience are lodged under the protective defensive bastion ("keep") of the cross.

McAuley's struggle with the fearful fragility of language has been reclaimed as an ultimate good, part of that creation which God declared "good." Our contingent language marks us off as different from, and dependent upon, the fullness of language who is God. Our *telos,* though, has begun: our contingent selves and language already taken up with God's creative Word into the Incarnation.

Les Murray, "Pietà Once Attributed to Cosme Tura"

This is the nadir of the story.

His mother's hairpiece, her *sheitel,*
is torn away, her own cropped hair looks burnt.
She had said the first Mass
and made Godhead a fact
which his strangeness had kept proving,
but what of that is still true
now, with his limp weight at her knee?
Her arms open, and withdraw,
and come back. That first eucharist
she could have been stoned to death for
is still alive in her body.

Les Murray's *Pietà* poem is a response to a painting of the subject by the early Renaissance Venetian painter, Cosme Tura (1430–1465). The painting is a springboard from which Murray ponders connections between *story* and *fact,* and the language used to express them. Murray's opening declaration: "This is the nadir of the story," a complete sentence of simple syntax, purports to give a straightforward proposition, however Murray subtly disrupts any implied certainty. The demonstrative pronoun ("This") does not function as a substitute for something already referred to but refers to what follows in the poem; to *that.* Murray's opening line has therefore introduced the structure of metaphor (*this is that*), ambiguating the apparent straightforwardness. The relationship between the terms of a metaphor invokes simultaneously similarity and difference. It also introduces consideration of perspectival shifts as metaphor rearranges the reader's view of both subject and vehicle. The reader-viewer's capacity to see, with the eyes of the mind, imagination, or spirit, is expanded.

That Murray is aware of perspectival associations is indicated by his use of "nadir," the etymology of which reveals its Arab origins. The historic Semitic origin of the word intimates the way the past lives on in the present; of the hidden associations of words which do not only straightforwardly speak in any given present but carry over into their articulation layers of the silenced words (and ideas and history) that have shaped them. One such silencing in the church, Murray's poem suggests, concerns Mary's Jewish identity. Originally meaning *opposite*, "nadir" was adopted by cosmology to mean that point that stands in opposition to the zenith and came from there to mean the lowest point of anything: place, time, or story. All three of those low points are evoked in Murray's poem. The word's poetic resonances include not only locational depression (here, cross tamped into earth) but of gravity, the cosmic force that attracts all Earth dwellers towards the surface of the planet. The dead Christ operates symbolically as its own cosmic force, pushing down the upward trajectory of Christ's ministry, which now appears to have been only a temporary elevation. Here is language itself brought low, the Word upon which all others depend, lifeless; word and body a synthesis of dead *corpus*.

The introduction of perspectival awareness is a reminder of the gap that can exist between the apparent and the actual. In the context of historic realities, even more so, heavenly ones, this implies a necessary reserve in speaking, as human sight is always limited by its vantage point of place and time. Perspective informs the background narrative field of the poem. According to the synoptic gospel accounts of the Crucifixion, a darkened sky immediately followed it (Matt 27:45; Mark 15:33; Luke 23:44).[74] If this were the result of a solar eclipse, its perceptible extent

74. As per the gospels, the Crucifixion took place on the day of Preparation for the Passover memorial, which begins each year on the fourteenth day of the lunar month of Nisan. Two dates towards the end of Christ's life would have met these criteria, the most favored being April 3, AD 33. The Markan gospel notes the three hours of darkness at Christ's death, offering no explanation. One family of Lucan papyri appends an explanation of a solar eclipse. As Passover occurs at the time of the full moon, a solar eclipse would not have then been possible. See Humphreys and Waddington, "Astronomy and the Date of the Crucifixion."

would be dependent upon a viewer's vantage point on Earth. It would only be perceptible within a certain latitude. What appears to be the case—and effectively is so—that the sun is occluded, is itself an optical illusion where the alignment of moon and sun makes the spheres appear to be the same size. Murray's preoccupation with the apparent and the factual is present in "looks" in line three, a verb that could either carry an unambiguous meaning, (this is how her hair looks), or an idiomatic one, (this is how her hair *seems* to look).

Having declared what follows to be the lowest point, the spatial framing of the first line acts in conjunction with the meaning. The follow-ing *line* is missing, blanked out. The reader must negotiate this breach, travelling down the page; the meaning of *nadir* enacted in the reading process. The regress of the story's movement by way of anti-Semitism, dis-rupting "strangeness," and death, unexpectedly turns at the penultimate line with the phrasal verb, "could have been stoned to death." That Mary was not stoned to death is inferred from the maternal figure: "is still alive in her body." The poem therefore ends by recasting what seemed to be the nadir as something else instead, perhaps even zenith—her son who is "eucharist" is "alive" within the body of his believing mother. A further ambivalence of the phrasal verb's use ("could have been") points in a dif-ferent direction. Murray's probing of the Roman Catholic Church's bar on women bearing priestly office, which seemed to imply his sympathy with reform, is unsettled as the words of a phrasal verb adhere to invari-ant (*received, traditional*) word order.

Murray's Pietà poem was first published in a collection, *Poems the Size of Photographs* (2002). Informing his poem appears to be the mid-twentieth-century biblical studies project, the so-called "third search" for the historical Jesus, aimed at seeing Jesus within his Jewish context. Murray extends this quest to his mother. The European medieval headdress she wears in Tura's painting is called a "*sheitel*," the head-covering of an Orthodox Jewish woman. The word resituates Mary within her Jewish lineage, challenging the effect of ecclesial enculturation of her, including church-commissioned art, which expunged her Jewish identity.[75] Mary of the church was elevated as external downward pressure forced out Mary of Zion. The disarray of her headdress ("torn away") now reads as an act of anti-Semitic violence. Her exposed hair that "looks burnt" incriminates

---

75. Piu-Lan Kwok argues that images of an "Aryan Christ," disseminated by Eu-ropean missionaries, contributed to "the oppression of the 'the other' living inside Europe—the Jews" ("Engendering Christ," 256).

European culture, including the church, in Jewish persecution which, in the early modern period, included occupational and residency restrictions, expulsions, scapegoating, and burning alive (as, for example, in Strasbourg in 1348); a lineage of persecution culminating in the *Shoah.* The relationship Murray establishes between "*sheitel*" and "cropped hair" reforges her dual identity within Israel and the church, and each to the other, as religious Christian women also cropped and covered their hair. Murray's poetic practice coalesces with Vatican II's reorientation towards the Jews. Formally repudiating the church's part in discriminatory abuses of the past, the conciliar document, "*Nostra Aetate:* Declaration on the Relation of the Church to Non-Christian Religions," states: "the Jews should not be spoken of as rejected or accursed" and that the church "deplores all hatreds, persecutions, displays of anti-Semitism levelled at any time or from any source against the Jews" (*NA* 4).

While Murray's inclusion of Mary's Judaism aligns with the church's favorable perspectival shift towards the Jews, he pushes beyond conformity to the magisterium in the next line, intimating that a further shift may result from reconsidering what the Incarnation implies. He opens up this contentious field by enacting in words just such a surprising imaginative shift in perspective: "She had said the first Mass." Deliberately anachronistic, the later formalized rite ("Mass") is returned to the originating person who is Mary. Confecting Christ's body and showing it forth before the assembly is the sacerdotal function of the priest in the Roman Catholic Church. This eucharistic sacrament is interpreted with a strongly sacrificial character. This sacrifice, though, was made possible by the Incarnation. As Murray has already invoked an historical consciousness in his lines about the headdress, they carry over to influence consideration of Mary's historic role in God's-becoming-flesh. At the Annunciation, the Blessed Sacrament of the Mass materialized within Mary's body. Her maternal body can therefore be thought of as sacramental in that it made visible the invisible, and her body has an inherent relationship with what she represents (Mary as *mother* represents the one of whom she is mother). As it was through her body that Christ was given to the world, she confects, carries and bears forth Christ in a unique manner. Mary is therefore the one able to say in a singular, especial and concrete way the Christic and priestly words of institution: "This is my body, given for you."

This connection was explored early in the church. One of the early Marian titles was "Virgin Priest," the origin of which may lie in poetic expressions used by the early Greek homilists.[76] In calling Mary's conception of Christ "That first eucharist," Murray both connects her pregnancy with the primary sacrament of the church and preserves a sense of its difference with the lower-case *e*. In intimating a difference, Murray appears to be simultaneously asserting Mary's priesthood but not unambiguously proposing it as support for calls for reform of church practice. The position of the magisterium is that Mary's priesthood is an instance of the priesthood into which all Christian believers are admitted, rather than indicating her ordination into the priestly order of the few from which her sex invalidates her. John Paul II, in response to persistent requests for this sexual exclusivity to be altered, declared unambiguously in his Apostolic Letter of 1994, *Ordinatio Sacerdotalis* (On Reserving Priestly Ordination to Men Alone), that "the Church has not in any way the right to confer priestly ordination on women and that this judgment is to be definitively held by all the faithful of the Church" (*OS* 4). Speaking as Supreme Pontiff, John Paul's words are intended to allow no degree of latitude in interpretation, so precluding further expressions of dissent. It is a statement disallowing disputation of this as *fact*. Murray's use of the lower-case *e* distances the originating event (figured as the Incarnation, rather than the supper in the upper room recorded in the gospels) from its subsequent formalization in liturgical practice and theological reflection, where it is given an uppercase *E*. Murray's concerns here seem twofold: to acknowledge a difference between the two e/Eucharists where difference may blur the distinction but not efface it, and to reclaim what should be the unity of church doctrine, liturgical practice, and scripture, where one is not posited over the other.

Murray's interest in language, and its relationship with the people who use it, is indicated in the phrase, "made Godhead a fact." The phrase conjures associations of Wittgensteinian philosophical thinking about how language works.[77] If language is not best thought of as being strictly

76. Tina Beattie writes of René Laurentin's 1950s doctoral thesis that, in his study of historical and theological writings, he found persistent recurrence of the idea of Mary's priesthood in the Patristic period. See Beattie, *God's Mother, Eve's Advocate*, 198–202.

77. Ludwig Wittgenstein, in his *Tractatus Logico-Philosophicus* (1921), saw language as logic-based and picturing the world. The world language described was one of independent facts that only gleaned value from the connections they had with other facts. These connections between facts were not intrinsic to the things themselves. This view of language could not accommodate ethics or aesthetics. For a discussion of this, see Wallace, "Empty Plenum."

logical and abstract, disconnected from the people who use it, the alternative version becomes one that begins instead with how daily language operates; a version that allows for what David Foster Wallace has memorably called, the "near-Nixonian trickiness of ordinary language."[78] Language that tries to denote closely and directly its referent is the language of containment, (as in John Paul's *Ordinatio Sacerdotalis*), rather than language that *breaks open* in a way that reconfigures perceived certainties. Murray's phrase also alludes to the Athanasian Creed which speaks of the unity of Christ, perfect God and perfect man; a unity that is owing not to God's being changed into flesh, but to the assumption of Christ's humanity into God.[79] This elevation of humanity is not a question of its being accounted *as if* it were of God, but is a real theosis. C. S. Lewis sees the Athanasian creedal formula as analogous to his own concept of "transposition," by which he means an attempt to account for the relation between things natural and things accounted as spiritual.[80] If, says Lewis, the transposition of human into divine is only approached "from the lower medium," error is the result, as such a critic will see "all the facts but not the meaning."

Murray's poem probes the nature of the relationship between the "fact" of Godhead in Christ, which Christianity proclaims, and how that understanding becomes traumatically threatened when Christ is dead: "what of that is still true / now, with his limp weight at her knee?" Murray seems here to be suggesting the fissure Lewis identifies between *fact* and *meaning*.[81] Christ's death apparently annihilates the meaning that some saw inhering in his person. Facticity *per se* cannot encompass all that is reality nor offer an account of it (*meaning*). The place of death is just the place where this tension is most poignantly realized: the fact of death undoes what was the fact of life and presses the possibility of meaning. Death appears to annihilate all facts, even the fact of life. The *fact* of Christ's death presses the possibility that the *fact* of Christ's divinity was not fact at all. The *Pietà* is the image of this crisis. In the lacuna created by Christ's death, belief in the potentiality of words to express

78. Wallace, "Empty Plenum," 109.

79. The Athanasian Creed was used in church liturgy from the sixth century. By alluding to it in the poem, Murray is drawing together doctrine and praxis.

80. "Transposition" was first delivered as a sermon in 1944 and first published in the current augmented form in 1962. See Lewis, "Transposition."

81. See also Jones, "Art and Sacrament," 170.

truth falters, as the foundational Word has apparently been permanently and disastrously silenced.

The exactitude of the poem's title, striving for academic precision, is seen by the poem's end to have furthered the questions raised in the verse. Certainties of artistic attribution can be over-turned as further evidence becomes available. The title implies the poem's question: "what of that is still true / now . . . ?" What was once believed to be the case: that Cosme Tura was the artist of a particular painting, is, so the title implies, no longer believed to be so. An artistic canon is always subject to revision. Some *facts* occlude others (the actual painter of the piece; the priestly mother, Mary). Within Murray's poetic exploration, it therefore remains a possibility that the Roman Catholic Church's position on the relationship of women to the priesthood could be modified. Murray's poem, from its opening presentation of spatial perspective introduced in the term "nadir," through its consideration of the relationship between myth and fact within ecclesial history, to the central question about truth and certainty, to the final line concerning the nature of the Eucharist and the body, is a reflection upon how we arrive at a truthful vision; a vision of comprehensive scope that neither distorts, exaggerates, minimizes nor omits.

Tric O'Heare, "Madonna of the Dry Country"

This time
they've put Mary in a 44-gallon drum
hacked down the middle
A tabernacle of galvanized ribs
to hold her in

She tells herself she has perfect balance
The world's a chipped beach ball
still under her gripping marble feet
Here in a backyard reclaimed from desert
she crushes the snake without looking down

When the faithful come, she sees
her ancient son hologrammed in their eyes
One minute baby, the next a corpse

and remembers the knowing brat
with the future encoded in his blood

Every year has a shooting season
when, tiring of ducks, men shoot at her
because she is there and once was beautiful
Their bullets have sheared away breasts,
nose, lips, elbow, the arch of her neck

Pared back to a suggestion in the rock,
she recites her own rosary
and prays her son will truly come back
to release her from a mantle
that webs her arms to her sides

Often she dreams he has come back
and is holding her in his torn and bloodied arms
but when dawn comes, working dogs
stretch awake and test their chains
She knows simply the story's not yet done

Some days she just weeps
People hurry down roads
in plumes of dust
to be sobered or cured
by the sight of a mute woman crying

Touched by their simplicity
she invokes her wayward son
to do something
Mary's thoughts are luminous
but her tongue is tethered

Tric O'Heare uses the attrition of the figure of the Virgin Mary to explore themes resonant with John Paul's concerns: subjectivity and freedom, relationship to the sacred, giftedness, and loss of communion. First published in her 2003 collection, *Tender Hammers*, "Madonna of the Dry Country," looks at the inability of the Mary figure to speak to ecclesial or secular culture owing to the religious climate which had generated and sustained the image no longer being dominant or widely understood. Present in the poem as a religious statue of the Immaculate Conception, there are still those for whom she is a recognizable sign that is responded to, ("the faithful"), although for others, ("men"), her significance as a sign has been almost entirely erased. She also suffers from the implied failure of her cultural transference from southern European Roman Catholic culture, registered within the poem's title ("Madonna"), to the desert of inland Australia. She is referred to within the poem only by her Anglicized personal name. Through disrupting the convention of naming, O'Heare is raising the question of personal subjectivity and its possible occlusion through archetypal renaming. By linking the archetypal title with the established informal descriptor, ("Dry Country"), the modifying effects of spatial and cultural migration are raised, along with the possible loss of meaning; re-location possibly resulting in dis-location. The poetic voice indicates the loss of the image's intelligibility in the new continent by use of a doubly incongruous metaphor ("beach ball") for the spheroid on which she stands.

The governing conceit of the poem is that Mary is a conscious subject, but this is far from straightforwardly so. The poetic speaker purports to speak on behalf of the personal subject, Mary. Unlike Noel Rowe's poetic voice which speaks as Mary in the first-person, O'Heare's Mary is present as a voice only in a secondary way through the third-person pronouns used of her. O'Heare's poetic voice interposes itself as a mediating third between Mary and the anonymous "they" of line two, and between Mary and the reader. Mary's subjectivity is inferred by the reader. She has an inner life of thought and feeling imputed to her—she "remembers," "prays," "dreams," "knows"—but is unable to make utterance. Her only exteriorization is the tears she sometimes weeps although how the reader is to construe these tears, given the complexity of imputed subjectivity, is unclear: Literal tears? Imagined? Miraculous? The responses of the remnant faithful to her weeping show a naïf "simplicity" that bypasses the difficulties of subjectivity, or perhaps, as hinted at with their "hologrammed" eyes, they mistake real subjectivity for sophisticated counterfeit. Her tears are the last vestige of her residual freedom. This is not the only ambivalence regarding subjectivity in the poem. The *I* who is the poetic voice is not simply a fiction. It does exist but only in and through the poem. It is a metaphor of presence, as is the reader—*you*—who may never materialize.

The only freedom of the personal subject remains her interior life but, as with her imputed subjectivity, this, too, is ambivalent. Restrained within "a 44-gallon drum," a travesty of the tabernacle, whose "galvanised ribs" associate her with the creation of Eve from the rib of the sleeping Adam, Mary retains none of the original associations of the mobility of the curtained tent of the ark of the covenant.[82] The tabernacle within Roman Catholic churches is the privileged housing of the pyx containing the consecrated host which was, until Vatican II, routinely placed centrally on the altar in the place of highest honor. Mary now shares with her son the experience of being shut away and de-centered from the church. Her residual association with maternal protection is also upended. While Helen Kraus says of the Hebrew word for *rib* that it has "an extensive semantic domain, much of it relating to structural support and associated with the Temple or altars; 'rib,' 'side,' 'corner,' 'beam,' even 'chamber,'"[83] the metaphoric continuity is disturbed in the poem where the rhythmic expansion of fleshly ribs within a living body is transmuted to rigidly inflexible ribs that effectively sign *rigor mortis*.

O'Heare implies this current mute state of Mary has had a long gestation. The poem opens in the middle of the present action, establishing contemporariness: "This time," which also locates it within a continuous history of which it is a part. This earlier history is indicated spatially by the introductory white space that constitutes most of the first *line*; the whiteness performing the blanking-out of Mary from her own discourse. O'Heare's use of the white space is a political gesture that refuses the erasure of particular histories, as those unrecorded histories have contributed to the shaping of the recorded present. It also situates the current abuse this Mary suffers within a hinted-at past although the non-specificity of "they" leaves open the question of culpability while the action of the poem strongly implies "they" are men. As these are the first words that open the poem, their unusual end-placement is a call to accountability: "This time" associates the present action with its historic antecedents and impugns those who continue the negative heritage.

This sense of negative temporality is implicitly linked with the type of statuary O'Heare's Mary is, and how this is misconstrued. David Jones has argued in his essay, "Art and Sacrament," that man's sign-making is an inherently sacred activity that also points to man's being involved in some

---

82. For these associations, see Barker, *Mother*, 266.

83. Kraus, *Gender Issues*, 24.

way with never-endingness. Signs, Jones says, are constituted by their significance of "some 'reality,' so of something 'good,' so of something that is 'sacred.'"[84] This means, he explains, that art is an inherently "religious" activity where the etymology of *religio* is key: that which binds or secures, as in a ligament that supports an organ. What it binds is man to God, a binding which "secures a freedom [of man] to function."[85] It is, on Jones's account, this distinctive type of sign-making that signals man's elevated position within creation, as only humans have the "unique title, poeta."[86] Jones explains that his definition of art is not making any comment about the kind of art, or the uses to which it is put, or to the intention of the artist. Jones has a broad understanding of what constitutes *ars* and when illustrating his analysis of it, uses a birthday cake as an example. It conforms to his definition of art, as it is a thing made gratuitously as an explicit sign which is shown forth to re-present and recall something significant (*x*'s birthday) with the "full intention to make this making thus."[87] Accordingly, O'Heare's Mary statue meets the requirements of Jones's definition of art. She is not, though, treated as art, one of the indicators of which is her thwarted involvement with the divine eternal. The numerous time indicators ("This time," "One minute," "the future," Every year," "Often," "dawn," "Some days") anchor her within the created temporal order, offering her no sense of its possible transcendence through a concomitant participation within eternity. She dwells in secular time unmarked by religious observance. Canvassing all time options, she searches for release which she fails to find; time imprisoning her as effectively as her own mantle, or the drum in which she stands.

The treatment of O'Heare's Mary amounts to the undoing of *ars*, an anti-poeisis or negative deconstruction at work. Regressively unmade as she is used as target practice: "sheared away breasts, / nose, lips, elbow, the arch of her neck," her distorted and reduced form makes her ever less recognizable as a re-presentation of any woman, much less one whose particular artistic form had been intended to direct veneration to the Holy Mother. She is no longer shown forth but held in, and soon she will no longer be recognizable as *ars* at all, as she is "Pared back to a suggestion in the rock"; a punning metaphor of her reduced presence

---

84. Jones, "Art and Sacrament," 157.
85. Jones, "Art and Sacrament," 158.
86. Jones, "Art and Sacrament," 149.
87. Jones, "Art and Sacrament," 164.

in Peter's church. This deconstruction activates a double metaphor of silencing prompted by the implicit double entendre: artistic fashioning (*articulation*) of Mary, the one who cannot speak/articulate, is reversed; articulated form rendered inarticulate. The bullets unsay the image; man the hastener of entropy, unleashing chaos over order in an inversion of creation. Engaged in an anti-*poiesis* that neither orders nor makes sense, it is no co-incidence that these men do not speak. If art is the binding to God to secure the freedom of man's making, that freedom has been so abused as to inhibit and bind the woman's body: Mary's tongue "tethered" and arms webbed. As this form is one endorsed and promulgated by statues installed within Roman Catholic churches and shrines, it constitutes O'Heare's critique of the church which has chosen to represent her in this way. The Roman Catholic Church on this reading becomes a negative binding by men which makes expressive freedom for women impossible. This extends to her "wayward son," object of her dreams, who fails to materialize, or in any way facilitate her emancipation.

Mary registers an equivocal example of human *poeisis*: "her ancient son hologrammed" on the eyes of the faithful. Here is real organic matter ("their eyes") that appears to be a sign referring beyond itself. It is, though, only a mimicry of presence and self-transcendence. A hologram plays with perspectival shifts by making dual images appear when either it, or the viewer, slightly changes position. The apparently three-dimensional image is a trick of light, recorded photographically. *Hologram*, a compound word meaning *whole writing*, is misleading as a descriptor. The holographic image is not *whole* but an incomplete, two-dimensional representation. Similarly misleading is the apparent mobility of the images which are, in reality, a series of stacked static ones. It has the status of the false image; misleadingly, rather than illuminatingly, similar. Mary's son is not present within these believers. His image rests upon the surface of their eyes. He is just an inert image of a person not really present, a trick of the light. Light's association with comprehension ends the poem where the "luminous" thoughts of Mary have no way of shining forth as they cannot be articulated with her "tethered" tongue. It is a reversed annunciation motif, her comprehending light (*comprehension* here in the sense not of cognitive grasp, but of recognition) unable to enlighten others; a word/Word unable to emanate from her. She is trapped in a confinement that will not deliver.

Within her intended devotional context, in church or shrine, the statue constituted part of the shared fabric of a religious community.

Community, though, is here undone: men pitted against the archetypal
woman; "the faithful" a disparate remnant; son absent from mother. Part
of the communal disruption of the faithful post Vatican II was marked
by changes within church furnishings. Chapter 7 of the Vatican II document, "*Sacrosanctum Concilium:* Constitution on the Sacred Liturgy," is
devoted to "Sacred Art and Furnishings," and enjoins bishops "to ensure
that works of art . . . which offend true religious sense either by depraved
forms or through lack of artistic merit or because of mediocrity or pre-
tense, be kept well away from the house of God and from other sacred
places,"[88] and that images intended for veneration "should be restricted
in number."[89] Many pieces of devotional statuary, notably those of the
Virgin Mary, were subsequently removed from parochial churches. According to David Jones, though, the standing of art is not determined by
its aesthetic quality or the skill of its making; perfection does not make
something a sign.[90] On Jones's account, *Sacrosanctum Concilium* and the
disposals it led to, misunderstood the distinction between *ars* and aesthetics. Real-world disposal of Marian statuary is negatively related to the
poetic shooting of her; each act relates to her as artefact rather than as
art. That this statue "once was beautiful" may signal that it qualified not
only as devotional object, but as art. Rowan Williams sees a relationship
to transcendence as being the distinguishing quality of beauty, which is:
"transparent to what is always present in the real, that is the overflow of
presence which generates joy."[91] Beauty to be perceived, though, needs a
sensitive beholder who completes the "performative circle."[92] This Mary
is not attended to as a gateway to something deeper, so is left in solipsistic
recitation of "her own rosary." Beauty triggers her desecration ("because
she is there and once was beautiful"), drawing upon the historic associations of abusers who blame their victims and disregard their personhood,
effectively corralling them with animals, as here: ("tiring of ducks, men
shoot at her").

   Having lost the means of self-expression and self-determination,
Mary is unable to be a gift for another. She is the exhausted image, so
marooned and self-referential that "She tells herself" in a parody of

88. *SC* 124.
89. *SC* 125.
90. Jones, "Art and Sacrament," 156.
91. Williams, *Grace and Necessity*, 14.
92. Hart, *Between Image and Word*, 83.

self-creation or self-portrait. O'Heare's presentation of Mary radically rejects any social or ecclesial linking of "maternal suffering and the ability to speak."[93] Making feminine speech contingent upon sufficient somatic suffering embeds an unethical incentive for male abuse and female collusion. Additionally, speech purportedly won at the price of suffering may be honored more in theory than in practice. Weeping, for O'Heare's Mary, is the only power she retains to transform others. Those who hurry past are "sobered or cured" by seeing her weep. Her tears are ambiguous and recall the central motif of Les Murray's poem, "An Absolutely Ordinary Rainbow," of passers-by reacting to the sight of an old man silently weeping in the middle of the day in a city center. In the poem, Murray draws a connection between tears and gift, both of which may be either received, returned, or refused by others, depending on how they read the tears. No explanation is given in either poem for their shedding. O'Heare is apparently linking her *Mater Dolorosa* figure with Murray's Christic male figure. Each presents the communicative affect and effect of tears which express an interior state of the weeper, while also interpreting those who witness them. Mary's tears also function within the poem as a residual possibility of fertility although the moisture of her tears is unequal to the task of greening the desert land, or hydrating the aridity of men's desires. A desert occludes its capacity to sustain human life and demands that those who would live in it garner, preserve and transmit its knowledge inter-generationally. It is land that must be respected and cannot be hurried. It takes patience to discover its knowledge, a characteristic it shares with art and poetry. A desert encompasses seemingly incompatible qualities, not unlike a metaphor. Its dual aspects are displayed in the Bible where *desert* signs positive spiritual possibilities of purification and strengthened inner vision (Hos 2:14; Matt 4:1–11), and of curse (Gen 3:19). The desert threatens to reclaim man, undoing him, returning him to dust.

O'Heare's Mary is linked with her imagined son in an unending cycle of violence which figures in her dreams of his "torn and bloodied arms." Blood both testifies to his victimhood and is the reason for it ("the future encoded in his blood"). As his blood came from his mother, she is incriminated as the cause of his suffering.[94] An image of a reversed

93. Bruzelius, "Mother's Pain, Mother's Voice," 228.

94. As death is the inevitable end of each life, women are not only life-bearers but also pall-bearers: those they deliver, journey towards death. Julia Kristeva makes explicit this connection—and personally appropriates it—in recording her own experience of new motherhood (*SM* 173).

Pietà, her son's comforting arms are ephemeral, the stuff of her dream, evaporating "when dawn comes" and "working dogs / stretch awake."[95]

John Paul II contrasts the respect for another's subjectivity, which characterizes receiving another in authentic love, with the objectification of the person whose body is viewed with lust. In the latter, the body is reduced to a "terrain of appropriation" (*TOB* 32:6). It is an apposite image to apply to this poem where Mary is presented as the violated gift (cf. *TOB* 61:4) and even the desert in which she stands has been appropriated ("backyard reclaimed from dust"). Her literal breakage betokens not life springing forth, as in symbolic and metaphoric breakage, but the reduction of the subject as "an object within our system of understanding."[96]

Overview of Pietà Poems

The *Pietà* is the Annunciation's counterpart and poetic completion: *counterpart* because it inversely images *absence* as the visibility of death, where the Annunciation had imaged *presence* as the invisibility of conception; *completion* because it completes Christ's handing over of himself to Mary at the Annunciation, inaugurating what *Lumen Gentium* calls the "indissoluble link" connecting Mary and her son.[97] If sons, though, have to psychologically and emotionally separate from their mothers in order to form themselves as men, then this image is unsettling, disturbing the purported finality of that developmental theory.[98] It provokes a disequilibrium in the viewer with the overthrowing of the expected order of generational death. Its resonance as an image is perhaps attributable to its fusion of specific immanence (*this* mother, *this* son) and typological transcendence (*any* mother, *any* son).

The *Pietà* supplements the gospel passion narrative by providing a visual motif of the inter-relatedness of life and death, suffering and love. Elizabeth Sewell explores the insight of German-language poet, Rainer Maria Rilke (1875–1926), for whom a partnership between love and death was not the contradiction it seemed. According to Rilke, when death is isolated from love, it becomes depersonalized, cheap, and wasted; when

95. Seemingly, a biblical literary allusion: "For dogs are all around me; a company of evildoers encircles me" (Ps 22:16 NRSV).

96. Paul, "Metaphor and Exegesis," 391.

97. *LG* 53

98. Chodorow cited in DeLamater and Hyde, "Essentialism vs. Social Constructivism," 13.

united, love transforms death into something rich, personal, and purposeful.[99] Viewed exteriorly, Jesus's death seems to meet Rilke's criteria for a death isolated from love, hence futile. The *Pietà* image, though, is a shorthand summary of this death's rich meaning; a visual repudiation of its futility. Mary's faithful presence, from a temporal perspective, retrieves this death's meaningful possibilities. The *Pietà* image oscillates between the two modes of death it presents (physical and psychic-emotional) and the two modes of love (filial and maternal). It encapsulates the frozen tensions of grief while transcribing an endless dynamic of chiastic love-in-sacrifice. McAuley draws upon this classic portrayal of the *Pietà* in his poem.

Suffering is always a particular, according to whichever measure one applies—severity, type, length of time endured, possibility of reprieve. It cannot be deputed to another, and this particularity is honored in McAuley's poem. The poem's narrator (imputed as male) submits to his unknowing, and to the mystery of suffering. He acknowledges that he cannot "know" the mother's suffering, except from outside, as an observer. In humility, the narrator rests within that aporia. The suffering of Mary at the Crucifixion has been interpreted as a displacement of natal suffering, which tradition teaches she did not experience.[100] The Crucifixion is therefore her alternative labor, her suffering a task which cannot be performed by another on her behalf. It is this non-transferability and particularity that confirms it as a personal event.

The implications of the particularity of suffering is broadened in Les Murray's poem to the Jewish communal body, represented by Mary. The longitudinal suffering of Mary's people is an objective reality which has, at various times in history, been obfuscated, enabled, or dismissed. Murray's poem looks at the intractability of the perspectival challenge, at the limits that bound our seeing. Murray's poem presents the tensions that can pertain between objective reality (*fact*) and interpretation (*perspective*). If the same reality can be apprehended differently, according to one's sightline, then humility is a necessary accompaniment to knowledge. This check nuances and strengthens the caution against a neo-Cartesian prioritizing of mind over matter. Murray's poem is a reminder that, as

99. Sewell, *Human Metaphor*, 170.

100. Among the early attestations of a pain-free delivery: Gregory of Nyssa, Augustine, John Damascene, Justin Martyr, Irenaeus. Some interpreters have seen it as prophetically indicated in Isaiah 66:7.

he is aware, "there are always more sides to a thing."[101] It is the exclusive, divine prerogative to see all perspectives of a given, at once.

The typological Mary in the *Pietà* image functions not only as mother but as spouse; typology which is strongly implied in Thomas's poem. Viewing Jesus and Mary as types, theologian, Kenneth Howell, sees the Christic-Marian bond as restoring the lost male-female unity of the two, (understood as pertaining to all male-female relations, not only spousal ones).[102] R. S. Thomas's poem overtly evokes this restoration, but also subverts it, by disincarnating his *Pietà*. In declining to display the bodies of the participants, Thomas is resisting their presentation as objects within a picture plane, more concerned with the evocative poetic possibilities of their absence. His handling of the subject does retain a sense of the graced nature of the material world. He achieves this not so much by transferring subjectivity to things (although the cross is anthropomorphized) as acknowledging materiality's orientation to the common eschatological end of creation.

Tric O'Heare's poem does not present a *Pietà*-type, but it is concerned with suffering and signage. A vandalized Marian devotional statue is the sign around which she arranges her consideration of certain hermeneutic and linguistic principles. Devotional statues are material mediators. Justifying the continued veneration of such figures and images, the Council of Trent (XXV, second decree, 1563) explained that the faithful could legitimately venerate devotional images of Jesus, Mary, and the saints, as whoever honored their images was referred beyond the representation to the image's prototype. The Marian figure in O'Heare's poem is a distressed sign, her presence being steadily obliterated by those who neither value, nor understand, her. The value of the Marian statue as religious, cultural artefact is read against her status as a material object of no monetary value. Once her sign-status has been obscured, either deliberately, or negligently, she gradually reverts to unrealized potentiality ("dust"). The poem is an encapsulation of the attenuated power of the Marian devotional sign and, possibly, of Mary's own personal sign-status within the church and wider society. O'Heare's poem implies that attenuated Mariology redounds negatively upon the sign-status of real women.

Effective signs rely upon a shared vocabulary and grammar between sign-maker, sign, and receiver. O'Heare's poem plays different types of

101. Murray, "Trade in Images," 347.
102. Howell, "Mary's Bodily Participation," 222.

imaginative productions against each other: the Marian devotional object (*art* in Jones's terms); her imagined interior voice; her poetic presentation. O'Heare presents the *Madonna* as an ecclesial abstraction which is ironically present as mere materiality. *Body* is the categorical ground that shapes O'Heare's poem: the hazy background of the implied body ecclesial of the hierarchy; the dispossessed body ecclesial of the remnant lay faithful; the sex-stereotypic body of violent males; and the female body gendered according to a schema of absence—of agency, of action, of possibility.

5

Towards a New Mariology

A Theology of Mary's Maternal Body

Make me a meteor, / Or else a metaphor
—ELIZABETH JENNINGS, "CLARIFY"

MARY'S BODY HAS BEEN attenuated in the Catholic imaginary, reduced in visual images to hands, face, and occasionally, until discouraged at the Council of Trent, her breast. To attend to Mary's obstetric body is to look to that which is naturally hidden from view and that which ecclesial officialdom would have strenuously kept hidden. It was this body, though, that grew the physical body of Christ. In order that the ecclesial body of Christ may grow in understanding by contemplating the poetics of Mary's maternal body, I look now for a way through the impasse between honoring Marian modesty, and contemplating her in her bodily totality. To that end, I look below at the several metaphoric terms (virgin, bride, and mother) said to indicate the ways Mary relates to God, and how these may offer a way through.

Western- and Eastern-rite churches see Mary's perpetual virginity as a sign of her holiness, of her being set apart for God. Her reservation is understood to be the form of her self-giving to God for the furtherance of his will (which is furthering the *kingdom* of her son). In this sense, virginity and marriage are not contradictory opposites, but signs that converge, pointing to the total self-gift of the spouses, each to each (God is deemed to be the *spouse* of consecrated virgins). *Virginity* is a boundary-marker that, once crossed, effects a permanent change in *knowledge*, which is negatively signed in the woman's body (perforated hymen) and in language use (no longer denoted *virgin*). Virginal spouses, upon their marriage, give to each other that which has never been given before, intending that the inaugurated sexual relationship will continue to be exercised exclusively between them. This is consistent with the nature of their relationship: to give oneself fully to another in the totality of one's personhood, is necessarily to be sexually exclusive. To act otherwise would negate the completeness of the gift by withdrawing, or reserving, some of oneself, and conferring it on a third party.

One of the chief metaphors for the church is the *bride* of Christ. Mary is honored as the first and chief member of the church, having been appointed by the dying Christ as mother of the faithful. Mary is therefore not only *virgin* but *bride* and *mother*. A bride is a liminal figure, standing in anticipation at a threshold. Mary is reserved for God, as signed by her perpetual sexual chastity (*virgin*), which is also consistent with her liminal status as *bride*. Scripture and tradition, though, also ascribe marital status to Mary. This bride is already spouse, as confirmed by the birth of her son. Mary, virgin bride, espoused to the Holy Spirit, is fecundated by that Spirit.[1] Although she did not experience human sexual relations, her body is nevertheless a *married* body.[2] The moment of her assent at the Annunciation is the moment she is conjoined with God in the unique act of unitive communion that results in her pregnancy. That moment of total self-giving is analogous to the human spousal relation. The personal communion effected between Mary and the Holy Spirit is definitively transformative in a way analogous to virginal first married sexual congress. If *eros* is indeed that which points to God, a persistent thread in Christian mysticism and a theme taken up, as already seen, by Sarah Coakley, then the Annunciation may be read as a mystical erotic experience in which mysticism does not bypass the body, as evidenced by her conception of her son.[3] Mary articulates her confidence in the

---

1. See Leo XIII, "*Divinum Illud Munus*" 14.

2. For discussion of Tertullian's logic that Christ's birth caused his mother to change from virgin to wife, see Willemien, "Christ's Birth of a Virgin."

3. *Eros* is a motif used in Solomon's Song of Songs and by Origen, Gregory of Nyssa, Bernard of Clairvaux, and St. John of the Cross (Coakley, *God, Sexuality, Self*, 344).

eschatological transformation to be wrought by the reign of God by joy-
fully declaiming the Magnificat in Luke's gospel account, anticipating the
beatitude of those pure in heart, who will see God (Matt 5:8; cf. 1 John 2;
1 Cor 13:12).

If desire for God is proportionate to holiness, then, as *Theotokos*,
Mary would be expected to instantiate maximal yearning for God. Luke's
gospel affirms, in the angelic salutation ("Full of grace"), that Mary had
been given the graces necessary to fulfil her unique calling. An experience of intense longing to join to another, giving of self without reserve,
is analogous to the spousal relation. Within that relation, spousal coitus
points to that which the completed sex act was intended to be: a sign of
the unique nature of the marital relationship, which both expresses, and
forms, the bonds of love. In the sex act, the husband and wife become
a single subject, acting as an organic unit.[4] These acts are in continuity
with the emotional and spiritual unity they already have formed. Spousal
sexual acts embody marital communion.[5] Spousal coitus, effecting a real
unity of persons, is also a sign that points beyond itself to the plenitude
that awaits the faithful: real union with the divine. Sarah Coakley sees
such an attitude interestingly developed in the theology of Gregory of
Nyssa. Coakley notes his positive attitude towards virtuous sex acts, as
contributory to a person's ascent to God, as they can give, through the
heightened experience of physical love, a foretaste, or introit into eventual
eschatological fulfilment. As persons increase in holiness, they are progressively transformed; *eros is* purified and redirected to God, in whom it
"finds its truer meaning."[6] The Annunciation can be read as Mary's experiencing such an eschatological quality of sublimed sexual union. Mary's
obstetric body bears the signs of both her reservation to God, and her
unique, divine communion. To reclaim the poetics of Mary's womanly
body is to "flesh out" a fuller understanding of what John Paul calls the
body's language. It is further desirable as an act of resistance to what has
been a religious cultural bifurcation in attitude to Mary which (properly)
valorizes her exceptional holiness while regrettably minimizing and cir-
cumscribing her body in which that holiness was manifest. Mary freely
gave all of herself to God, including her obstetric materiality, in order that
God could reside as a material person by first residing within her.

4. Lee and George, *Body-Self Dualism*, 182.

5. Lee and George, *Body-Self Dualism*, 210.

6. Coakley, "Eschatological Body," 67, 69. Sexual dimorphism is, in Gregory's
theory, something which serves a heuristic purpose but is ultimately outgrown.

Flowing

Sacrifice

Blood is a major biblical motif. Included in the proto-historic narrative of the post-diluvian world is God's renewal of his blessing upon humanity and his expansion of permissible food sources to include every non-human moving thing. This expansion is modified by a divine proscription against the eating of animal or avian blood as blood is "its life" (Gen 9:4 NRSV). The proscription, to be honored by mankind, functions so as to reserve life to God. The later Levitical laws explicate the role of blood within the liturgical life of the Israelites where it is to be reserved as an offering of atonement (Lev 17:11). The priestly sacrificial system of Israel is to be ordered around bloodletting. The bloodshed of women during menses and *postpartum* needed to be accounted for within this system of sacrificial blood atonement in such a way so as not to challenge or confuse the meaning of the cultic offering.

Levitical laws proscribed the presence of menstruating women anywhere within sacred space. Within the Second Temple, this included even the outer Court of the Gentiles.[7] The particular circumstances of the issuance determined the period of her exclusion. Regular menses precluded her for up to fourteen days; *postpartum* lochia invalidated her for forty days if she gave birth to a son, eighty days if to a daughter. Newborn sons were circumcised on the eighth day of life when they were deemed to be "ritually neutral," before which time they were ritually unclean owing to their proximity to the maternal blood loss during birth.[8] The presence of bleeding women within sacred architectural space was apparently deemed defilement. The logic of argument and symbolization is not structured as a simple dialectic, though.

Joan Branham points out that the antipathy between female reproductive blood and liturgical sacrificial blood seems to have arisen less from their polar opposition (profane versus sacred) and more from their kinship in purifying and bestowing life. The twelfth chapter of the book of Leviticus lists the exclusions pertaining to parturient women; verse two deeming her to be "ceremonially unclean seven days; as at the time of her menstruation" if she gave birth to a son. The next thirty-three days are described in verse four as "her time of blood purification." The time

7. Branham, "Bloody Women and Bloody Spaces," 16.
8. Glick, *Marked in Your Flesh*, 21.

periods are doubled for a daughter. Branham attributes this extension to the mother's having "redoubled life-bearing potential." Following her prescribed time of purification, the mother is to have a burnt offering and a sin offering made by the priest, after which "she shall be clean from her flow of blood" (Lev 12:7 NRSV). This requirement appears to posit the relationship that Branham disavows, as the animal blood within the cultus cleanses the parturient from exposure to her own blood flow. This seemingly clear interpretation is, however, not sustainable.

Branham notes that the same root in the Hebrew word for *purify* pertains to both reproductive and sacrificial blood. Animal blood from sin offerings is sprinkled by the High Priest at Yom Kippur over the mercy seat in the Holy of Holies, and upon the horns of the altar "to cleanse it and hallow it" (Lev 16:19 NRSV). This latter is intriguing, as sacrificial blood on one especially designated day is deemed to be supra-cleansing, even of previously shed, purifying cultic blood. Janet Soskice upholds the view that the Israelite purity laws governing female blood loss had "nothing to do with sinfulness and a great deal to do with holiness—the holiness of birth and blood and life."[9] Margaret Barker also notes that "in temple symbolism, blood was life," citing the explicit connection made in Leviticus 17:11 between blood, life, and atonement.[10] The life that is rightly God's cannot be seen to have a symbolic rival in the blood of the bleeding woman. *Prima facie*, the woman's blood would seem superior to that of the animal or avian sacrificial victim, as humans are the pinnacle of creation. Furthermore, her blood is shed for the purpose, potential or actual, of life-giving, rather than life-taking. A closer consideration of the distinctions between the different types of blood sheds light upon why they each give such different readings.

The ritual blood being animal or avian distinguished and distanced the ancient cult of Israel from alien cults that demanded human sacrifice. Its purpose was to reinstate right relations with God where the determinant of the whole sacrificial system—what constitutes an acceptable offering, including how, when and where it is to be offered—is understood to be God himself via the mediation of the Mosaic law. As blood is a substance reserved to God, the sacrificial spilling of it inscribes a structure of God claiming what is his own: lifeblood returning to life-source via the communal actions of the sacrificial priesthood. The blood of the sacrifice

9. Soskice, "Blood and Defilement," 340.

10. Barker, "Atonement," 5.

is only secondarily animal or avian; primarily, it is God's. The Israelite sacrifices were premised upon a *top-down* initiation, having been commanded by God, in order to activate a *top-down* blessing, from God to his people. This structure removes any arbitrariness concerning sacrifice. It is not a structure of at best, parallel lines, one of ascent and hopefully, one of descending blessing, but that of a circle or parabola, where the offering of the people via their priests is caught up in a tripartite movement of descent-ascent-descent, beginning and ending with God. Just as the sacrificial blood was primarily God's, so is the sacrifice *the people's* only in a secondary sense. The various sacrifices were a form of reparation or freewill offering to God, which God himself had ordained. Performing the sacrifices according to the divine prescriptions was an act of obedience, which the community trusted would result in divine blessing.

Womanly reproductive blood loss, by contrast, is non-volitional. This crucial distinction carries over into the early Christian church where actual and symbolic discontinuity is seen in the contemporary account of the martyrdoms of the Christian women, Perpetua and Felicitas, the latter of whom was martyred following the birth of her daughter. A careful distinction is made between the bloods of childbirth and martyrdom; the latter deemed superior and purifying because volitional.[11] The blood of fertility is kept symbolically separate from the blood of purification. This is the key to understanding the gendered reading of the blood of martyrdom. Perpetua's father appeals to her to abandon the faith, and so avoid martyrdom, and hence prove herself a good daughter. He and she agree that martyr's blood is masculine by virtue of being voluntarily shed, an interpretation also seen in Tertullian. Distinctions between the bloods of male and female are present in the Levitical laws. Burnt offerings, the most common type, had to be of a male animal (Lev 1:3,10), whereas offerings of "well-being" could be either male or female (Lev 3:1, 6). The picture is further complicated in that sin offerings for unintentional breaches were to be male if offered for "a ruler" (Lev 4:22–23 NRSV); female if offered for "anyone of the ordinary people" (Lev 4:27–28 NRSV). For all who had trespassed against the law, once made aware of the offence, an offering of a female animal was to be made (Lev 5:6).

What this breakdown makes clear is that the purported scheme of animal or avian sacrificial blood versus female reproductive blood misses the typological sex distinctions within the sacrificial blood system. Sex

11. Leyerle, "Blood is Seed," 36–7.

distinctions according to this system are acknowledged, and observation of their difference is mandated. The system suggests a sex-specific difference in meaning pertaining to the sacrificial victims. The community standing of the one who sins, along with the circumstances of the sin committed, determine what type of blood is demanded in reparation by God (see, for example, Lev 4:22–3). The crucial macro separations appear to have been between animal versus human blood loss, controlled versus uncontrolled bloodletting, and sacrificial versus fertile blood flow. The principle of unity of the Israelites of the temple is the shedding of blood in the mandated fashion. The chief symbolic focus seems to be upon *God's* blood being what establishes and maintains filiation. For this reason, the naturally occurring bloodline through the fertile woman needs to be kept remote, lest, in Tina's Beattie's phrase, there be any "symbolic confusion."[12]

Sustenance

Within this paradigm, it is easy to see how the Virgin Mary would have posed a sensitive problem. Female menstruants and parturients were forbidden anywhere within the temple precinct and required a time of purification before readmittance to the sacred space, yet Mary at the Annunciation had the sacred presence within her very body, anchored within her bloody endometrium. The symbolic problem becomes this: if Mary's body is figured as a living temple with God's holy presence within, then the Levitical laws appear to have been scandalously contravened. Unease with this conundrum is present within early Christian non-canonical literature, as Joan Branham notes. She cites the *Protevangelium of James* which narrated Mary's childhood spent within the temple precinct and the priestly decision to remove her, aged twelve, the approximate age of the onset of menses, by betrothing her to Joseph.

The gospels give few details about Mary. The age at which she conceived is not mentioned but has traditionally been thought to have been when she was a very young woman. Speculation about her physical condition entails considerations of the Levitical laws and her scripturally attested-to virginity. If she had already reached menarche, her body

12. Beattie, *Woman*, 119. Beattie acknowledges it would be problematic were a woman to act as a sacrificial priest. The woman's involuntary blood-letting would, she says, introduce "chaos." Such disorder she sees as linked to cultural ideas of impurity, founded upon things being "out of place."

would have been through a cycle of ritual uncleanness, which seems to compromise its fittingness as a *temple* of God's presence and to preclude an extensive notion of virginity; that is, of its signing the untouched, full integrity of the body. Leyerle, though, notes that virginity as a state of "sexual restraint" is consistent with the thrust of the Levitical laws governing sexual behavior (Lev 18). He further notes that Tertullian and Rabbi Matia see blood as a figure for righteous deeds, particularly those involving restraint. Virginity chosen as a way of life is also sacrificial.[13] Mary as a young virgin would be able to figure as a pure and living sacred space, where her blood is rendered acceptable through the proleptically effective blood of the personified paschal lamb she carries. This metaphor can be further developed so that Mary is the necessary vehicle (in a strictly non-utilitarian way) for the sustaining blood of Christ. As blood is liquid tissue, it relies upon a symbiotic relationship with containment in order to function as sustenance for the body. This metaphor of beneficent enclosure when applied to Mary's relationship with the blood of Christ is satisfying in several ways. It supports the physical property of blood's fluidity which is always contained within vessels that facilitate its movement ("mission") around the body; it expresses that "indissoluble link" (*LG* 53) between Mary and her son ("mutuality" and "relationality"); and it preserves the distinction between them. This latter is consistent with the mandated observation of sexually distinct bloods, operative in the ancient cult.

The deeper distinction is between Mary as wholly creature and Jesus as human and divine. As with bestial blood and human blood that superficially resemble each other, the bloods are crucially distinctive. Mary as the vessel of the sacred blood has obvious applicability as regards her eucharistic role: she is the mother of the eucharistic body, the same body in different modality as the fleshly body she gestated and brought to birth. She contains and presents to the faithful the sacred blood within the body of her son. Thought of metaphorically, Mary is the eucharistic chalice.[14] This notion of Marian containment is unique in its mode (she is the one mother of the one son; the one chalice of the one Holy Eucharist). This uniqueness, though, also contains sorority. Each of the faithful is called

13. Brant Pitre argues that Mary's response to the angel at the Annunciation: "How can this be, since I am a virgin?" (Luke 1:34 NRSV), indicates not only her present state but also her intended future state. Pitre, *Jewish Roots of Mary*, 106.

14. A more usual early-Christian theme understood Mary as the ark of the covenant. See Pitre, *Jewish Roots of Mary*, 64–65.

to become a vessel of Christ and, through faithfully being one, is progressively transformed into the person who is the content of the vessel.

Cleansing

While blood is known to transport waste products to elimination destinations within the body, talk of its *cleansing* quality, particularly when applied to Jesus's blood, appears strongly counterintuitive. When spilt, blood stains, is highly visible, and difficult to expunge. It shares an important metaphoric quality with language: neither blood spilled, nor words spoken can be retracted. They are spent only once. They change things.

The symbolic ambivalence of blood, traceable in the scriptural textual handling of it, has been observed in recent liturgical practice. Andrew Casad had noted a puzzling anomaly: the reluctance of participants at Mass to communicate through the Precious Blood; a number Casad had observed on one occasion to be fewer than one fifth.[15] This observation led him to examine the symbolic connection between blood, sex, and the Eucharist. Casad drew upon Foucault's *History of Sexuality* (1978) the main thesis of which is that blood had functioned symbolically for the aristocracy, in Casad's words, as "the locus of authority and legitimacy," but that such symbolic associations had been displaced by sex as the bourgeoisie's chief symbolic discourse. For the ruling class, legitimacy was traced in bloodlines and sociopolitical authority measured in one's ability to spill blood (in executions and wars), or refrain from so doing, as for example, in the granting of reprieves and stays of execution. The symbolism of blood as connected with sociopolitical power, signed by the violent spilling of blood, allegedly lost its symbolic power once it was replaced by the power dynamic associated with sex, interpreted broadly as life in all its aspects, signed in healthy bodies, individual and social. Casad argues that the same secular factors which effected a change in blood's signification affected the ecclesial symbolics of Christ's blood, causing the majority of contemporary communicants to eschew its reception.

Foucault had argued in *Discipline and Punish* (1975) that changes in penal regimens away from public, corporal punishments that inflicted pain or took life, towards those which sought to discipline the mind of the offender, had paralleled the move away from blood as the dominant social symbolic. Just as the new penal codes sought to change criminal

15. Casad, "Blood, Sex, and the Eucharist," 313.

behaviors so that they conformed to social behavioral norms, so in an analogous way did attitudes towards, and practices of, sexuality change. As with regimes of discipline and punishment, so with sexuality, which became the new object of knowledge; the new body-discipline moved punishment away from the public sphere into the private.

Casad finds Foucault's thesis convincing as a meta-account of the reason for minimal uptake of the eucharistic blood. While it may convince as far as it links the gradual removal of public blood-shedding from Western European countries with a concomitant diminution of blood's symbolic power, it leaves open whether, or to what extent, blood-shed still features as a mechanism of political control. That the new regimen advanced by Foucault seeks to govern its citizens' lives through encouraging their observance of body-discipline, suggests its power may have been driven down, but not out.

Blood has not, I would argue, lost its symbolic valence so much as had it sublimated. While blood is no longer used as a tool of control in the West by legitimate sociopolitical authorities, it remains present in a sublimated way in state concern for, and promotion of, contracepted (*safe*) sex and associated abortion practices. This new scheme builds upon the transfer of bloodshed from public visibility to restricted privacy. Onetime preoccupation with aristocratic blood lineage had involved a sublimation of *sex* for *blood* as the *right* sex would secure for one's family lineage the right (*clean*) blood. Foucault's proposition of sexuality replacing bloodlines as the new object of power may have, as Casad thinks, broad merit, but there has not been a clear-cut substitution of the one for the other. If, on this reading, sex is sublimated within *blood*, then the eucharistic blood may well occasion a symbolic crisis, owing to its very visibility. If the power of blood is driven down but not out, then the public Eucharist threatens the sublimated, secular, symbolic power of blood. As the chalice contains personal blood, not a blood object, it acutely confronts the body politics of power; its very presence interrogates which blood the state currently legitimates (declares *clean*), as well as what are its methods of enforcement.

Opening

In the homily he delivered at his inaugural Mass in 1978, John Paul II expressed a desire for the church and the wider world to open itself to the workings of God. All were exhorted to "open wide the doors for Christ," and to "open the boundaries of States, economic and political systems, the vast fields of culture, civilization and development." John Paul was setting the tone for his new papacy, invoking a spiritual and cultural freedom, and a confidence in gospel proclamation, that quashes psychic fearfulness. His words performed his own recommendation, confidently challenging any closure towards God. His mention of political systems being among those needing openness carried especial weight for Europeans living under communism.

John Paul's homily expressed his intention that his papacy be characterized by that openness he commended for church and state. Openness to God is the quintessential quality of the Virgin Mary. *Opening* used metaphorically is a basal metaphor, with strong somatic association. It is a function of many body parts, rehearsed in the myriad openings of eyes, vasal valves, and lung inflations. Its capacity for opening defines the function and purpose of the vagina. As Mary is deemed to be perpetual virgin, so perpetually sexually inactive, her vagina is associated in a sublimated imaginary with closure. The vagina, though, is an organ not only used for sexual purposes. As well as being the receptive site in sexual intercourse and providing the channel for delivery of a baby, it is also the passage through which menstrual blood leaves the body.

The vagina's histological structures mark it as remarkably extensible, able to accommodate the changes wrought by penile introitus and the more extensive strains of childbirth. Its fibromuscular layer is arranged as two layers, an inner circular layer and an outer longitudinal layer. The adventitia layer is collagen-rich and elastic, giving additional strength during childbirth and binding the vagina to surrounding structures. The vaginal walls, posterior and anterior, sit in apposition, touching each other. The vaginal walls are usually closed together.[16] So, although the vagina is commonly associated with opening, in its basal state it signs *potentiality*.

Openness and its associations with clarity, accessibility, and forthrightness is the predicate of biblical personal transformation. The Annunciation heralded the paradigmatic invitation to open self to God. Mary's act of opening herself, expressed in her *fiat*, is honored by God with the bestowal of his presence in her body. The structure of this exchange lies

---

16. O'Connell et al., "Anatomy of the Distal Vagina."

at the heart of the church's liturgy, most clearly so in the liturgy of the Eucharist.

In the liturgical assembly of the Roman Catholic rite, congregants make a penitential act during the introductory rites, immediately after the entrance of the celebrant and his greeting. This general confession at the beginning of worship is oriented toward restoring right relationship by having the community offer itself to divine scrutiny. Confession is ordered towards opening up the closure of guilt and shame, reopening the divine-creaturely channel of communication that sin had obstructed. It is ordered towards restoration of relational harmony between man and God. The original relational harmony, as expressed in the Genesis narratives, was the fruit of mutual openness. The state of trusting openness is one more frequently associated with children than adults. One of the surprising paradoxes of the gospel message is mature believers are to retrieve such a state (see Matt 18:3) which, according to the Roman Catholic Church, can be effected over time by regular, mindful participation in ecclesial liturgies, especially in the sacraments of confession and the Eucharist.

In the Anglican Church's introductory rite, the request to be opened is expressed metaphorically, identifying both concrete body parts (ears and lips) and abstract items (hearts and minds). The liturgical invocation draws its warrant from the Pauline epistles in which Paul suggests, in his "body of Christ" metaphor, that the nearest analogue for *church* is *body* (Rom 12:4–5; 1 Cor 12; Eph 4:14–16). A large part of the strength and appeal of the metaphor is its universal applicability, as every person is embodied. The liturgical itemization of body parts assumes their interconnectedness; together, they serve the good of the whole person, which is to hear, praise, receive, and contemplate God. Invoking God to open parts of the body expresses a desire to be made ready, and able, to receive grace. The expectation of the invocation is that God mediates grace through the body. Opening to God, in faith, is not only an interior, spiritual affair, but corporeal.

The liturgical invocation uses metaphor in an upwardly sliding scale. The metonyms of openness: lips, ears, hearts, and minds function with different levels of metaphoric strength. Lips that physically open, evoke both the literal and the metaphoric. Ears that do not open and close, except metaphorically, in relation to listening or not, engage *metaphor* in a stronger sense. The reference to "hearts" uses that organ as a metonym of innermost desire. The heart is therefore read as the deepest and truest indicator of the person. Talk of the mind's opening uses a submerged metaphor where an abstract thing (mind) is understood via a concrete and dynamic spatial analogy.

Body parts cannot function in isolation. The action of any one organ is held to be an action of the whole body, which is a complex organism of interrelated systems. Each member of the body acts in concert.[17] The localized attention of the invocational prayer does not aim to objectify the body, nor to reduce it to its biological mechanics. Rather, it summarizes the fulsome nature of faith which is heard, spoken, and loved. The prayer reminds the faithful to consciously and electively cooperate with God, so that the whole body is orchestrated in worship. The liturgical community is speaking as the ecclesial body functioning in Marian mode.

Open to the Father: Annunciation

In the Lucan Annunciation scene, the angelic messenger delivers a word that is both invitation and summons. The suggestion made here is that the Annunciation can be fruitfully contemplated according to the category of *opening*. The Lucan narrative implies a backstory; that Mary *heard*, on this occasion, owing to her habitual listening-out-for, or attunement to, God. This is a personal spiritual virtue of Mary's, but one anchored in her religious community that had shaped her belief. Listening is an eccentric activity, an inclination toward another, which is intrinsically social.

Muri Rubin notes that Mary's open ear was developed as a theme in the Syriac poetry of the early church, which was then more widely disseminated through the later writings of Bernard of Clairvaux.[18] Mary's ear was a convenient alternative organ, made use of by visual artists, in order to preserve Marian modesty. Transposing the conception of Christ to the open ear of Mary conveniently bypassed all obstetric sites, so distancing the event from unseemly connotations of sexual activity. While it was of the utmost theological importance that the Annunciation be shown to have effected an entirely unique form of conception that did not involve sexual relations, and the aural image answered this need with

17. A lengthy prayer for the service on the second day of Rosh Hashanah is structured around the human body which is explicitly seen as corresponding to particular aspects of revelation, so for example: "Five men are called to the law, according to the five joints in their knees" ("Service for the New Year," cited in Levin, *Body's Recollection of Being*, 194–95).

18. Rubin, *Mother of God*, 342.

its discreet decorum, it does not expunge all erotic associations. The body is still present, still open to the beloved. The Word still penetrates a body orifice, where it effects a transformation.

Continuing this reading of sublimated sexuality, we can say that Mary's *fiat* speaks her entire person. The Annunciation is the event of her radical abandonment of self, totally entrusting herself to the Other who loves her. The God who sought, and she who was found, give themselves to each other. Owing to this structure of unreserved and mutual self-giving, it is easy to understand the metaphorical attribution of the nearest human relational equivalent: Mary as bride to the divine bridegroom. This aspect is present in Joseph Cardinal Ratzinger's 1977 explication of the dogma of the *Immaculata*: "it signifies that Mary reserves no area of being, life, and will for herself as a private possession: instead, precisely in the total dispossession of self, in giving herself to God, she comes to the true possession of self."[19] As the Annunciation event reaches towards metaphors of spousal love, so the event of spousal love points towards the Annunciation. It is the fullness of Marian giving, without reserve, that renders her sexed, obstetric body a suitable metaphoric lens through which to view her.

Mary's word of assent gives form to her willing and receptive heart and mind. This willing receptivity marks the Annunciation as the paradigmatic way to live: attentively focused on the *telos* to which human life is directed. Mary openly pledges herself and it is this "trustful-risk" that "perfectly corresponds to the divine filial pattern of Jesus's life."[20] The consequence of her *yes* will become publicly visible in the literal reshaping of her pregnant body. That carnal refiguring is her body forming itself so as to visibly express what Mary already was: the habitation of God. In her maternal hosting of the god-child, Mary acts as the disciple who "willingly prepares a body for the Lord."[21] The Marian pattern of *fiat* and self-surrender enacts the Marian nature of prayer: at once spousal and maternal.

One "risk" associated with Mary's consent is the possibility that she will experience pain and suffering in direct proportion to the scale of her loving. This is made explicit early in Luke's gospel narrative: at the presentation of the infant Jesus in the temple, Simeon foretells the piercing of

19. Ratzinger, *Daughter Zion*, 70.

20. Riches, "Deconstructing the Linearity of Grace," 187.

21. Riches, "Deconstructing the Linearity of Grace," 19 [Erratum: The citation Heb 2:5–7 should read Heb 10:5–7].

Mary's heart (Luke 2:35). There is no follow-up reference to this prophecy in Luke. Christian tradition, though, draws an intertextual link with the Fourth Gospel account of Mary's presence at her son's crucifixion (John 19:25–27). The actual sword that pierces the crucified Christ recalls the "sword" foretold by Simeon, now seen as the acute empathetic suffering of Mary at the sight of her cruelly tortured son. Mary's pain affectively signifies their exceptional unity; trauma suffered by one is registered in the other's body. It alludes to another biblical symbol in the Song of Solomon, where the bride's heart is wounded with the arrow of love. Both biblical metaphors resonate with John Paul II's talk of the costliness, and beauty, of self-donation.

The heart-piercing of Mary attests to the vulnerability of openness to love. Current knowledge of heart function cautions against assuming an exclusively metaphoric reading of Mary's *piercing*. Studies of heartbeat dynamics appear to indicate that the heart can be adversely physically affected by emotional tension.[22] As an expressive figure of bodily penetration, Mary's heart piercing can be read as a transposition of those obstetric pains that she did not corporeally experience: the perforated hymen; vaginal extension at introitus; sharp uterine contractions during labor; and extensible vaginal and perineal pressure during delivery. Early Christian tradition tended to disallow the possibility of Marian pain in childbirth on theological grounds (Mary as type of the new Eve was preserved from original sin, having been immaculately conceived, and so from sin's adverse consequences, such as pain in childbirth.) The gospel attestation of Marian *piercing* nevertheless retains the linkage of love and suffering.[23]

The paradigmatic gospel image of suffering love is that of the crucified Christ. Concurrent with this image—literally in the shadow of it—is the image of Mary standing at the foot of the cross. The spousal typology is retained in the Fourth Gospel passion narrative. Paul Evdokimov points to the Eastern Church's marriage rite in which bride and groom are crowned with martyrs' crowns; a liturgical imaging of love born under

---

22. Valenza et al., "Real-Time Emotional Responses."

23. Karl Rahner nuances talk of the assumed painlessness of Jesus' birth for his mother and urges prudence concerning overly certain claims purporting to know exactly what this would have involved. While the whole person of Mary is "essentially different, through the miracle of grace," one must consider that she gave birth in an infralapsarian world; that "Mary's integrity . . . works in and through the law of suffering and pain" (Rahner, *More Recent Writings*, 160).

the sign of death. Evdokimov cites Leon Bloy's metaphor of suffering creating "spaces of the heart"; a strongly gestational allusion.[24] Mary at the cross, it could be said, is experiencing the pain of cleavage as mother and son are divested of their earthly ties.[25]

The cross-reading of Simeon's infancy prophecy with the Fourth Gospel passion narrative renders a cohesive theological poetic. Just as the Crucifixion effects salvation in and through the flesh, so, too, is it registered in Mary's body. The ingressive cross *pierces* the natural order; an event of love that truly penetrates matter. Mary's love for the God who saves, and the world that needs saving, informs her consent to participate in God's salvific plan, even though it means suffering the wound that love inflicts.

To speak of the poetics of the cross is to speak of its artistry. This is not to detract from its solemnity and gravity, but to see it in a different register. George Steiner, in *Real Presences,* asserts the moral importance of art as a way to encounter the strangeness of the other in such a way that seeks neither to domesticate nor amplify that strangeness. Artworks proceed from an artist's critical engagement with the world, purposed towards continuing that conversation with others. Art, in Steiner's understanding, is inherently social. *Otherness* is engaged with in the piece itself, and with those who respond to it. This eccentric orientation of art implies an ultimate other who does not surrender otherness and is the ground and the guarantor of all otherness. Steiner's metaphysic understands this transcendent other to nonetheless be discernible to the artistic sensibility; to sound through, or speak through, what is immediately apparent. The aesthetic experience is, says Steiner, "the making formal of epiphany."[26] This epiphanic encounter confronts us with our need to be changed, to live a better way. The "shorthand image" of this aesthetic encounter is, he says, the Annunciation.[27] It is no accident that Steiner would choose a biblical motif as his illustration of what the arts do. Each has an ingressive quality and is ordered towards changing the lives they enter. They

---

24. Evdokimov, "Sacrament of Love," 189.

25. Beverly Gaventa reads Jesus's giving of his mother to the "beloved disciple" at the Crucifixion as Jesus' divestment of all earthly attachments. Having been divested of all clothing, Jesus then divests himself of family and friends. Jesus detaches from all things earthly in order to ascend to the heavenly realm. See Gaventa, *Mary*, 91.

26. Steiner, *Real Presences*, 226.

27. Steiner, *Real Presences*, 143.

illuminate "the continuum" between the temporal and the eternal, the material and the spiritual.[28]

One type of devotional statuary, the *Vierge ouvrante*, most clearly signs Marian openness. These small figurines have hinged torsos that swing wide open to reveal Jesus inside and oftentimes, companion figures who have sought maternal refuge. The equivalent genre in Western medieval painting was the *Mater misericordiae,* where huddled figures, seeking Marian protection, crowd beneath her outspread mantle. This genre of the protective maternal, read according to the poetic of the obstetric body, would find its equivalent valence in the protective cervix that *spreads* during first-stage labor, or the extensive vaginal reach during second-stage labor. It has already been noted how the conception of Jesus has been visually cued as sound (*Word*) entering the Virgin's ear. While this makes intelligible imaginative sense, the artistic tact in handling the Mary figure is in direct contrast with the artistic handling of her son. Margaret Miles has made a study of the demise of depictions of the breast in Christian religious art, which paralleled the increasingly graphic portrayals of violence in Renaissance crucifixion paintings.[29]

The body piercing of the Virgin finds an unexpected contemporary echo in the practice of body piercing currently popular in Western secular culture. This has been variously understood as colluding in what Stephanie Paulsell calls, "our culture's relentless, evaluative gaze"[30] on the body (see also Joan Brumberg), and as a reflection on the failure of the church "to provide experiences that are deeply meaningful and so deeply marking"[31] (see also Tom Beaudoin). These decorative piercings do not aspire to the type of piercing experienced by Mary (openness to, and oneness with, the suffering God), but they do function as visible and provocative artistic endeavors where the flesh constitutes one half of the artistic materials. The role of the flesh in such artistry is sacrificial, offered up to the artistic cause, suffering its own integrity to be breached. Perhaps such an identity marker amounts to a cultural *cri de coeur*, a sign of perceived absence of sufficient meaning in the body.

---

28. Steiner, *Real Presences*, 227.

29. Miles, "God's Love, Mother's Milk," 23.

30. Paulsell, *Honoring the Body*, 63.

31. Paulsell, *Honoring the Body*, 64.

The cross is signed as the radical opener; that which punctures separate personal boundaries.[32] This opens up another way to interpret Mary's experience of piercing. As with her son, her body boundary is extended to the other in love, potentially without limit. This openness to others is the direct correlate of her openness to God, as expressed in that miniature, condensed poem-within-a-poem that was her *fiat*. Her *yes* is confirmed and honored by God's ongoing *yes* to her at the cross, where the Son expands her motherhood to the beloved disciple, also present alongside her. This beloved disciple is himself a representative and sign of all those others who faithfully follow the crucified one.

Open to the Son: Crucifixion

According to the Fourth Gospel passion narrative, Jesus is already dead when his body is pierced by a lance (John 19:34). The violent piercing would have served a practical end of either confirming, or hastening death. Within the gospel narrative, it functions as historical record while also serving theological and metaphoric purposes. Metaphorically, it serves as the cut required by Jewish law to seal sacrifices and covenants.[33] The gospel records blood and water flowing from the site of the stab wound.[34] These body fluids function metaphorically as the organizing principles around which the church will arrange her primary sacraments of baptism and Eucharist.[35] Blood and water become the identity markers of belonging to Christ's body, the church. Jesus's body, even in death, is still effectively communicating. His dead body is united to, and exceeds, the earlier tradition of temple sacrifice, which it takes up and makes new, while also proclaiming the future of the as-yet-nascent church. A more contentious metaphoric layer concerns the blood and water which are discharged at birth by laboring women. Jesus's discharge of these fluids renders him a metaphoric mother.

32. Gupta, "Which Body is a Temple?," 533–34.

33. Glick, *Marked in Your Flesh*, 19.

34. For confirmation that the spear would have been likely to have punctured the heart, and for uncoaguable blood from the heart, and water from pericardial effusion, to be the expected postmortem indications of the wound, see Retief and Cilliers, "Christ's Crucifixion as Medico-Historical Event," 307.

35. Henri de Lubac discusses Tertullian's symbolic linkage (*De Anima* XLIII) of Eve coming from the side of Adam and the church pouring from the side of the crucified Christ. See Lubac, *Motherhood of the Church*, 54.

Recognition of Jesus as mother has been a minor interpretative seam within the church and was the subject of a study by Caroline Walker Bynum.[36] Bynum investigated the imagery used in spiritual writings by twelfth-century religious, finding that Jesus's gender fluidity resonated with medieval mystics such as Julian of Norwich (AD 1342–1430), who wrote explicitly of Jesus as mother. Such a reading, sensitive to metaphor, that sees in the gospel presentation of Jesus signs that indicate his transcendence of his sex, gives positive expression to Jesus's divine nature, in which no human sex is present. It also provides ballast against an over articulation of the male.

A major potential drawback is its implications for actual women, including the real flesh-and-blood women present at the Crucifixion, such as the Holy Mother. Linn Marie Tonstad, for example, is critical of Balthasar's reading of Jesus as divine in a feminine, receptive mode, as she finds his reading overrides the actual Holy Mother, whose female body is transmuted into Christ's body, the church.[37] If Jesus on the cross is understood as being sexed male but gendered female, does this neutralize real women? Feminist theologian, Rosemary Radford Ruether, thought so. For her, interpretations of Jesus as an androgyne diminish the value of women by masking an inherently androcentric symbol system which allows for the male to represent both the divine and the creature, while restricting the female to only representing creatureliness.[38]

In arguing for women to be admitted as priests, Elaine Storkey favors a theory allowing for difference in form between the representation and what it represents. A contra position was taken in the 1976 Declaration, "*Inter Insigniores:* On the Question of Admission of Women to the Ministerial Priesthood," which argues that, lack of scriptural or historic precedent aside, women could not function as representations of Christ as they do not share his male form, and so do not have a natural resemblance to what they would signify. Storkey is critical of what she sees as a failure to maintain a distinction between a representation and a representative (for Storkey, a priest as a representative of Christ could be either male or female, while a representation of Christ would necessarily be male).[39] Storkey's distinction does not apply to the priestly original, though, as

36. Bynum, *Jesus as Mother.*
37. Tonstad, "Sexual Difference and Trinitarian Death."
38. See Ruether, *Sexism and God-Talk.*
39. Storkey, "Christology and Feminist Theology," 108.

Christ is both the representative standing *for* man and the representation *of* man. Ruether's contention that Jesus absorbs the female seems to be affirmed, not defeated. There is, though, an important Christological reason for Jesus's having been born male. Had he been born a female from a woman, his birth could have been construed as a case of (extraordinary) parthenogenesis, so casting doubt about any postulated divine involvement in the conception. This, though, would not indicate that this hypothetical Jesus were instead, purely and simply human. If this female *Jesus* were suspected of having only an earthly origin, she would, in fact, not be a person, according to Judeo-Christian understanding.[40] As the Genesis myths agree, "Adam" originates from beyond the earth, not only from it. This reminder serves to reorient Christological focus. While the means of Jesus's conception was unprecedented (the Holy Spirit impregnating a virgin), its type was not unique, as all persons originate from *above* and *below*. Jesus, from the moment of his conception, is instantiated as the new Adam precisely in the cooperation in his conception, between God and (wo)man. Jesus's male sex ensures that parthenogenesis is neither an implication, nor a possibility, of his conception, and that he is (in one of his natures) entirely human.

In her essay dealing with female imagery, Veronica Brady offers a reminder of salutary distinctions that pertain concerning the different valences of *sex* and *gender*. If *sex* refers to biological distinctions that signify difference, and so exclusion, then maleness and femaleness, following Jung, are psychological traits which each person has. Brady's deduction is that *sex* is biological, whereas *masculine* and *feminine* are imaginative constructs. This, though, significantly underarticulates the pervasiveness of sex differentiation throughout the body, and too neatly detaches biological sex from styles of thinking, relating, and engaging with the world. On the other hand, Brady's further contention that, in as far as each person "possesses possibilities which are both 'masculine' and 'feminine,' those qualities are complementary, not antagonistic nor exclusionary," is one that supports a certain desirable freedom from sex or gender stereotypes.[41] Endorsing Hélène Cixous (1937–) Brady posits *masculine* and *feminine* as two economies of interaction. The male economy is more concerned with understanding the world via rational and abstract thinking, the female economy with understanding via

---

40. Ratzinger, *Daughter Zion*, 41.

41. Brady, "Female Imagery and Imaging," 129.

attuning to the corporeal and intuitive. This broad demarcation has much in common with the ungendered categories of "daylight" and "dream" thinking proposed by Les Murray as being different but complementary modes of rationality, both of which must be present in satisfying poems. Without being rendered androgyne, the crucified Christ unites maleness and femaleness, or daylight and dream. He is a poem to be interpreted; the polyvalent symbol.

The scriptural metanarrative of salvation history illuminates this seam of Jesus's poetic figuration. Being fully human, the flesh of Jesus represents Adam of the *old* creation. Within the old order, new life springs from *old* life, each generation newly sprung from the preceding one. As one "born of woman," Jesus participates in this pattern. Jesus also participates in an exceptional way in the pattern of spiritual birth expressed in the Abrahamic succession story, where his lineage is not only through the flesh (Ishmael) but through spiritual connection (Isaac). Jesus therefore unites in his body descent via the flesh and via the spirit. This unification of the old and the new is present at the cross where the issue of blood signifies *blood descent* and the water, *spiritual descent*. The new cut marking and sealing this new sacrificial and covenantal beginning is what Ratzinger has called the "radical incision" in Christ's side.[42] What is notable is that the spiritual nature of the sacrifice does not supersede nor erase the physical nature. The cross does not effect a spiritual birth that bypasses the body; it is spiritual only by virtue of, in and through, the flesh. Read according to the concerns of Brady, et al., Jesus does not laud abstraction (*spiritualism*) over concrete knowing, in and through the body's materiality.

The gendered poetics of Jesus's crucified body is evident with his piercing by a Roman *lancia,* a phallic symbol. The reading becomes a de-potentiated, feminized Christ being literally shafted with a publicly visible opening.[43] When Jesus's body is read as maternal, the side wound functions metaphorically as a transposed vagina. As *vagina* is a direct borrowing in English from the Latin, meaning *sheath* or *scabbard*, the

---

42. Ratzinger, *Daughter Zion*, 44.

43. Christ's pierced side is the focus of a painting by Bramantino, *Risen Christ* (c. 1490, Museo Thyssen-Bornemisza, Madrid). The whole composition directs the viewer to the side wound, exposed by the dropped shroud, and indicated by the Christ-figure's left hand. The right arm hangs by Christ's side, palm upturned to face the viewer. The wounds on both hands have been minimized. The Christ-figure's eyes directly engage the viewer. All the elements of composition convey a costly openness.

epistemological linkage in this episode between the opening forged by the sword in the flesh, and the female genital, is especially acute: the weapon routinely sheathed is invaginated in Christ's side. This action inscribes Christ's body as a figure of womanly receptivity, opening up layers of metaphoric relational refiguring: Christ the son, now figured as a mother whose actual mother is figured as his daughter, the firstborn from his crucified maternal body. His actual mother, *reborn* in gospel text, is also refigured in the church imaginary as the bride of the Son.[44]

A dimension of latent eroticism is also present in a post-resurrection pericope from Matthew's gospel: Mary Magdalene and the "other Mary," on recognizing the risen Christ, "came to him, took hold of his feet, and worshiped him" (Matt 28:9 NRSV). As *feet* was a first-century euphemism for genitals, an overtone of latent eroticism seems hard to avoid.[45] In contrast, the risen Christ of John's gospel commands Mary Magdalene not to hold on to him (John 20:17), as he had not yet ascended to the Father. This prohibition is gender specific. Thomas, who had earlier insisted to his fellow disciples that he would not credit accounts of Jesus's post-death appearances unless he could feel his flesh wounds, was instructed by Jesus to "Reach out your hand and put it in my side" (John 20:27 NRSV). Jesus is seemingly continuing to respect religious restrictions on physical touch between unrelated members of the opposite sex. All the more surprising, then, is the Bernardo Strozzi painting, *The Incredulity of Saint Thomas,* held by the National Gallery, London, which renders the moment between the newly risen Christ and Thomas, in which Tina Beattie notes the painting's "implicitly sexual overtones."[46]

Christ's side wound can be read as symbolic echo, or imagistic transfer, of Adam's side opening from which God extracted a rib with which to fashion Eve (Gen 2:21–22); both male figures are shown as *birthing* females, so that analogically, *church* is to *Christ* as *female* is to *male*. The unity of male and female in each set of figures suggests "somatic homogeneity" (see *TOB* 21:6). Christ's body as birthing mother signals a

---

44. Ingrid Kitzberger notes that alongside the spiritual rebirth of Mary in John's gospel is her narrative rebirth. See Kitzberger, "Re-Birth at the Foot of the Cross," 478.

45. Rogers, *Sexuality and the Christian Body*, 244.

46. Beattie, *Woman*, 152. It deserves mention, though, that the painting is an image of an ambivalent gospel event. Although scripture does record that Thomas linked his belief in the Resurrection to be conditional upon his seeing and touching Jesus's crucifixion wounds, scripture gives no positive evidence that Thomas did touch them, once he had seen them (cf. John 20:24–9).

restitution of the homologous man which John Paul II notes precedes sex differentiation.[47] As with the Adamic side opening, Christ's opening is imperceptible by him as he, too, is "asleep." Unlike Adam's now-closed opening, Christ's open side remains open and visible in his resurrected body. Christ's final wound goes some way to answering feminist concerns about a supplementary and subordinate feminine *complementarity*, of the type raised by Elizabeth Johnson.[48] The *new Eve* of the church does spring from the side of the new Adam but through a vaginal opening startling, yet appropriate, for a birth, but riddling in its destabilizing metaphoric resonances. The phallus is no longer "the supreme power."[49] It exists alongside the maternal power of the vagina.

Sarah Alison Miller has seen the seepage of blood and water from Jesus's crucified body, which demonstrated the "permeability of Christ's corporeal boundaries,"[50] as allying him with a "monstrosity" that had come to be strongly associated with women's bodies by the twelfth century. The opened body of the dead Jesus excites both compassion (so, images of the *Pietà*) and rejection. It is at once the abjected object and the object of veneration. Within this paradox of seeming opposites is further invitation to read Jesus's crucified body as poetic text. The breaching of Jesus's body boundary by lance, and the fluids it releases, figure his body as one not oriented to self-containment. In this, too, his body metaphorically figures the female more closely than the male, situating him within the "feminine economy" of Hélène Cisoux. His body, we could say, in a real sense, cannot be nailed down. This will later be confirmed by his transformed and resurrected body which will be made available, later still, as sustenance of the church community.

47. The sexual organs of male and female are homologous during early gestational development; penis and clitoris develop from the one embryonic organ. See Schiller, "Representing Female Desire," 1162.

48. Johnson, *She Who Is*, 103.

49. Steinberg, *Sexuality of Christ in Renaissance Art*, 85. Steinberg explored a minor but intriguing seam in Christian Renaissance art. He found some two thousand images that depicted Christ's penis, either naked or referenced in hand gestures or decorative motifs. Steinberg also identified an erection motif in some crucifixion images to signal Christ's future Resurrection; life triumphing over death. Christ's penile tumescence post mortem is, argues Steinberg, a sign of Christ's volition (323–24). Steinberg also sees a maternal strain present in the topos of the side wound. He argues, though, for its being strictly metaphorical, expressive of the consolation of Christ's presence (373–77).

50. Miller, *Medieval Monstrosity*, 110.

The two piercings: the one visible, through the side, probably into the heart, of Jesus; the other invisible, through the soul of the mother, though recorded in different gospels, are linked in the metanarrative. They form one instance of a series of parallelisms connecting the lives of Mary and Jesus.[51] The generative son and the generative mother each instantiate motherhood in ways which affirm the importance of the body. The Son gives his life, that is, his entire body, for the life of the world; the mother gives her only issue. Each has given that which is most precious. It is this generative donation, in full plenitude, that links Mary and Jesus to each other, and to the "eternally generative Father."[52] Each is connected in radical openness and sacrifice for the lives of others.

Open Lips

There is no scriptural record of Mary's having spoken at the Crucifixion, and only four occasions that do attribute direct speech to her: in dialogue with the angel (Luke 1:34, 38); her Magnificat to Elizabeth (Luke 1:46–56); her interrogation of the boy Jesus when he remained at the Jerusalem temple (Luke 2:48); and at the wedding feast at Cana (John 2:3, 5). While these may seem meagre in number, they express an array of speech types which interrelate. They can be fruitfully read in the light of David Ford's hermeneutic of the moods of grammar.[53] Ford used his hermeneutic as a means of exploring the various cries of Christian Wisdom. An obvious extension of Ford's hermeneutic is to apply it to Mary who has been associated in Marian liturgies with Holy Wisdom since at least the eighth century.[54]

Ford attends to the formal usage of grammatical moods: indicative, imperative, interrogative, subjunctive, and optative. He does not, though, see these moods as always, or only, operating singly. Rather, Ford shows how the grammar of mood operates in more interesting and complex ways, such as when one mood can be inferred from, or implied by, another. A mood may be suggested without the use of formal identifiers, as for example, the interrogative invoked without the use of a question mark, or subjunctive possibilities suggested without the use of *may* or

51. See Miles, *Complex Delight*, 40.
52. Kelly, "Mary and the Creed," 20.
53. Ford, *Christian Wisdom*.
54. Boss, "Development of the Virgin's Cult," 169.

might. Applying Ford's hermeneutic to Mary's speech, we see the affirming indicative of the angelic greeting in Luke 1:28 echoed in the strong declamations of Mary's Magnificat. There is a double affirmation in this: she affirms her confidence in the imperatives of God's promises that she will bear a son who will rule "forever," and in this reciprocation, affirms the initial angelic affirmation addressed to her. She is affirming, having been affirmed. Mary's interrogative to the angel's communication of God's imperative, "you will conceive," does not express doubt that these words are from God. Her question implies a subjunctive openness, a "how may this be?" rather than the suspicious hauteur of Zechariah whose question, "how will I know that this is so?" is an implied imperative demanding of God a sign to confirm his own promise. Mary's subjunctive-interrogative is answered by the angel in a continuation of the indicative mood of affirmation with which the scene opened. Her question is respected and answered by God without giving specifics concerning the *how*. The angelic answer is delivered as a series of imperatives, but these do not effect closure. The dialogue maintains the open possibilities of the subjunctive.

Trust in God's word is maintained in the brief dialogue, not erased. Mary's *fiat* is an assent made in trusting faith because the answer she received to her wondering question was underarticulated. In Mary's *yes*, the indicative, imperative, subjunctive, and optative moods converge. The declamatory "Here am I, the servant of the Lord" speaks to the nature of her servanthood. Mary lets go of herself in order to allow the surprising possibilities of God to realize the full potential of her selfhood. She is fully, authentically, and simply present ("Here am I"), open to, and resting in, the subjunctive. Her desire is that God's subjunctive possibilities may be fulfilled in her (optative).

The crown of this intersection of moods is Mary's Magnificat, the dominant grammatical mood of which is the indicative. Mary affirms the mercy, strength, justice, and loving faithfulness of God. This, though, is enfolded within Mary's optative mood of desire for the Lord ("My soul magnifies the Lord, / and my spirit rejoices in God my Savior") and therefore for the humble, the lowly and the hungry. Mary affirms by invoking the historic faithful relationship of God with her people. As God is eternal, such relationship is also current. By her affirmation, Mary implies the obedience (imperative) that God is owed, and that she gives. This whole is nested within the implied question: what is the basis of my confidence in God? On what grounds do I optatively affirm, "Surely, from now on all / generations will call / me blessed"?

The next words Mary speaks are as "his mother" when she chides him for having caused anxiety when he went missing from his parents, staying on without them for three days at the Jerusalem temple. Although framed as a question, it contains a mild accusation, implying they were treated negligently (indicative). The interrogative is prompted by the disjunction between the parental anxiety and the boy's calm assurance "sitting among the teachers, listening to them, and asking them questions" (Luke 2:46 NRSV). His action is performative of the subjunctive mood as he is behaving in a way that "amazed" his hearers and "astonished" his parents. Jesus answers Mary's interrogative with two questions of his own that do not really seek answers yet are not rhetorical in the usual sense of not inviting an actual reply. Jesus does intend to stimulate a response, but one where the recipients interrogate themselves. Jesus returns the chiding of his mother, by asking: "Did you not know that I must be in my Father's house?" (Luke 2:49b NRSV). His question embeds an implied affirmation of His own action. Staying on in the temple was motivated by right desire: to acquire knowledge of God and to seek the Holy Presence where it may be found. It demonstrates his right priorities: honoring his heavenly Father.

The last occasion of Mary's direct speech is at the wedding feast of Cana, recorded in the Fourth Gospel (John 2:1–11 NRSV). Upon learning that the celebratory wine has run out, Mary solicits the attention of her son with a simple indicative, "They have no wine" (verse 3). Embedded within this indicative is an imperative: "Help them!" Jesus's answer in verse 4, which can read to contemporary ears as dismissive or disinterested, ("Woman, what concern is that to you and to me?"), seems to interrogate instead the desire of his mother that he take some extraordinary public action and in doing so, disclose his divine nature. Jesus's enigmatic reason for his seeming unconcern: "My hour has not yet come" (verse 4), makes sense within the embedded plea of Mary on the hosts' behalf. Her implied cry of "help them!" could be rendered as "save them!" (from social embarrassment). Jesus's reply would then mean that he had correctly understood her plea to "save them," so making it a private wordplay between them. As Jesus does then intervene, performing his first public miracle, thereby beginning the public salvific revelation of himself, this reading seems plausible. Mary's response to this conversational exchange shows no awkwardness, which also militates against interpreting Jesus's words to her as being dismissive or critical. She has confidence that, knowing of the need, he will act to meet it. Her final words in scripture are the ones she then utters to the servants: "Do whatever he tells you" (verse 5). Read figuratively, these words speak ex-textually directly to the reader. Mary has the authority to issue imperatives to the servants of the household (including those now in the church, the household of her son) in order to facilitate his saving action in the world. Her imperative antici-pates the Johannine instruction, "be doers of the word, and not merely hearers" (Jas 1:22 NRSV), linking together implied listening and acting; the performance of the two is what constitutes obedient faith. Her words articulate the foundational rule of the Christian life and are therefore fitting as the final words she imparts to the world. The import of her instruction is directly paralleled in the final words of the Father to the attendant disciples at Jesus's Transfiguration, recorded in all the synoptic gospels: "Listen to him!" (Matt 17:5; Mark 9:7; Luke 9:35 NRSV).

Spoken words are delivered through the lips of the mouth. Luce Irigaray (1930–), linguist and feminist philosopher, speaks, though, of the need to incorporate women's labial *lips* as part of a rebalancing of conceptual frameworks and language so as to include the female. Rallied by Irigaray's idea, psychoanalyst, Britt-Marie Schiller, has proposed such a labial framework for representing female desire.[55] In keeping with John Paul II, she holds that difference between male and female conditions the experience of man, so she rejects the proposals of others to frame the language of sexual development in neutral terms, as doing so would fail to offer a specifically female alternative to the dominance of the phal-lus in representing desire. Schiller allows for conceptual distinctions between sexuality, gender, and sex but insists they are "experientially intertwined." Suspending considerations of gender, and resisting a claim of a single experience of female sexual pleasure, Schiller does neverthe-less argue for a specifically female pattern based upon commonalities of body morphology. Schiller's labial framework tries to articulate the manifold erotic sensations of the woman conceptualized according to "a dynamics of fluidity and viscosity." This contrasts with, and balances, the phallic linear paradigm of sex. Searching for the language to express this means devising different metaphors, such as "vibrations in a magnetic field" or "waves breaking on the sea shore"; metaphors that express "ef-fusion and expansion" rather than a phallic restoration of equilibrium. Schiller is attempting to formulate conceptual representations that ac-commodate the full range of female sexuality. She examines, via the

55. Schiller, "Representing Female Desire."

Demeter-Persephone myth, how female sexuality and the maternal have been split, as in Irigaray's reading of myth, where sexuality is assigned to the father/male; affection and reproduction to the mother/female. The Demeter-Persephone myth seeks to redress the balance by including the character of Baubo, an old woman. To alleviate Demeter's distress, Baubo lifts her own skirt to expose her genitals, causing Demeter to laugh and her depression to lift.

The Virgin Mary, read as mythical type, seems to conform to this separation of sexual arousal and maternity; to be one of Irigaray's Symbolic "*blanks* in discourse." There is, though, a visual motif of the vulva with which both Mary and Jesus are connected: the mandorla or *vescia piscis*. This is an almond-shaped lozenge, depicted vertically, within which is an image of Jesus or Mary, as in, for example, the depiction of Our Lady of Guadalupe. The almond shape corresponds to the pudenda. Up until their official prohibition at the Council of Trent (1545–1563), wooden and stone carvings of Baubo types had been incorporated within some European Christian churches.[56] The products of deeply embedded folklore, most extant *in situ* examples are distributed in rural churches, notably in Ireland. Barbara Freitag's investigation into such *sheela-na-gig* figures led her to concur with obstetrician, Erling Rump, that they are depictions of a laboring woman. They were figures intended to aid successful parturition, their exaggeratedly enlarged pudenda, flagrantly displayed, and their vertical posture, often squatting, giving visual encouragement to supplicants. Freitag suggests their incorporation into parish church buildings would have been part of a deliberate strategy of enculturation. Even so, they were relocated high up so as to discourage touching or other types of veneration. According to Rump, their meaning within a church context is clearly the *mater ecclesia*, as the church is the mother through whom all parishioners are born. They were also spiritually protective presences from which the Devil would flee as it was through the vulva that his greatest enemy, Jesus Christ, entered the world.

Peter Fingesten, artist and academic art critic, saw a dramatic and widespread inflation of this motif written into the form of European medieval cathedrals. The floorplan of these cathedrals was shaped as an allegory of the cruciform Christ. From the twelfth century, they also incorporated an allegory of Mary. If soaring gothic arches are imagined with a pool of water in front of their base, the ground acting as a plane of

56. Freitag, *Sheela-Na-Gigs*, 115.

reflection, then the arched doors and surrounds would form a complete lozenge shape. The faithful enter through these "symbols of her virginal organ, [which] lead into the interior which resembles a dissected female body."[57] Anglican bishop, Martin Warner, has, in parallel vein, suggested that Mary is so fully invested in the expansion of her radical maternal relation, now extending to all the faithful, that she can be seen as "the very walls of our church building."[58]

The highly stylized church paintings of Jesus or Mary enclosed within a mandorla are linked to their roles, and the role of the church, as fertile, fecund, and generative. It is a visual-poetic rendering of the sacred mother.

Expanding

Virgin Mother: The Paradox of Converged Boundaries

Attending now to uterine expansion in pregnancy, which stretches to accommodate growing fetal life, the metaphoric resonances of that organ and its action are brought especially to mind. To *attend* is, as the etymology of that word expresses, to stretch towards something; we could say, it is to put ourselves out for the other, as is literally the case, in pregnancy. The pregnant woman is both herself and more than herself, restructuring the concept of singleness and deepening the concept of unity. This paradoxical nature of pregnancy helps illuminate the paradoxical relationship that Christians see as pertaining between the presence and absence, or withheld presence, of God-in-the-world. The earliest stages of pregnancy are usually indiscernible to third parties. When the fetus has developed sufficiently so as to alter maternal body shape, it has made its preliminary entrance into the world. Now occupying the liminal ground between actualized presence and withheld presence, it becomes a visual, anthropological representation of the coexistence of transcendence and immanence. The gestating fetus which cannot be ordinarily seen, touched or imagined, signs that which is beyond human knowing. However owing to its maternal mediation, the fetal presence is indirectly seen in the mother's changed shape and indirectly felt through her body. It is slightly and imperfectly knowable.

57. Fingesten, "Gothic Cathedral," 18.
58. Warner, *Say Yes to God*, 6.

There is an analogy in the signage of a pregnant woman with the Eucharist, as it is understood in Roman Catholic doctrine. The eyes of those present see the sign of the consecrated host as immanent matter. The Holy Presence within the sign is concealed. Someone, therefore, who is unfamiliar with, or resistant to, eucharistic theology and practice may say of it: there is nothing there except a wafer of bread. Christian orthodoxy, strongly expressed in Roman Catholic doctrine, sees a perfect cohesion of the sign and the signed. The priestly act of consecration is understood to really and effectively realize this cohesion. The consecrated host, sign of God's presence, actually, and truly, becomes Christ Present. It is the apogee of the sacramental sign. Veiled by the opaque sign of bread, it is *seen* rightly only with the eyes of faith.

Something of this paradox is sensed during pregnancy. The non-pregnant womb is transformed upon conception into a place of presence; the developing someone is veiled within the flesh of its mother. The cry of Eve upon giving birth to her first-born: "I have produced a man with the help of the Lord" (Gen 4:1 NRSV), expresses her recognition that we are more than our biology; that immanence and transcendence coexist. It also indicates an acknowledgement that in the natural order, whether or not procreation occurs is something philosophically extrinsic to sexual intercourse.[59]

Eve's cry is uniquely literalized in Christ's conception, gestation, and birth. Mary's signification, *virgin mother*, expresses paradox so acute the boundary of each term contests its neighbor's, threatening the viability of their union in an extreme example of the nonequilibrium of paradox. The affective resonance of the term differs according to one's sex. For a man, *virgin* may be one to whom he could properly direct sexual desire (the concupiscent version being *virgin* as the boundary he wants to trespass). *Mother* thwarts male desire as it resonates with his memory of his own mother, his ultimate sexual taboo. The term *virgin mother* signals the inherent tension in the linguistic linkage of unrealized sexual potentiality and consummated maternity. Part of this tension Luce Irigaray would attribute to the history of sociosexual politics. Societies, she claims, are premised upon the exchange of women, and that mothers as "instruments" must be "private property, excluded from exchange."[60] This system leaves sexually inexperienced women vulnerable to commoditization: "*The*

---

59. Lee and George, *Body-Self Dualism*, 204.
60. Irigaray, *This Sex Which Is Not One*, 185.

virginal woman, on the other hand, is pure exchange value. She is nothing but the possibility, the place, the sign of relations among men."[61] Mothers, that is, are a nonexchangeable currency while virgins are fungible. While in some contemporary cultures this may still hold true, the burgeoning reproductive industry has largely upended Irigaray's analysis. For a significant minority of women and children, the unified integrity of motherhood has been rent. It is increasingly necessary to qualify motherhood as biological, gestational, social, or legal. Women's childbearing capacity, or more reductively, women as *providers* of biological material necessary for the production of an embryo, are increasingly the new fungible commodity.[62] While for a woman, the resonances of *virgin* are freighted with an edgy sense of her vulnerability, especially in as far as she is aware of virginity's exchange value, perhaps the term *mother* is today becoming even more unsettling.

The maternal virginity of Mary has, not unreasonably, unsettled even some of those who accept it as a matter of faith. The linkage of *virginity* in its three modes: the conception (*virginitas ante partum*), the birth (*virginitas in partu*), and the ongoing motherhood (*virginitas postpartum*) impacts on *motherhood*. In the birth narratives of Matthew and Luke, the writers are in agreement concerning the virginal conception. Each constructs his story from different sources so as to make clear the exceptional conditions of Jesus's conception without a human father.[63] Matthew's genealogy of Jesus (Matt 1:1–16) lists the lineage of thirty-nine fathers who begat sons, using the active voice. The final verse, though, carefully and deliberately records a variant: "Joseph the husband of Mary, of whom Jesus was born" (Matt 1:16 NRSV) which uniquely uses the passive voice of Jesus's conception.[64] This mark of discontinuity is affirmed two lines later: "When his mother Mary had been engaged to Joseph, but before they lived together, she was found to be with child from the Holy Spirit" (Matt 1:18b NRSV).[65] It is iterated a third time by the angel

---

61. Irigaray, *This Sex Which Is Not One*, 185–86.

62. For analysis of the legal, medical, and ethical issues surrounding the commercialization of body tissues, see Dickenson, *Property in the Body*.

63. O'Carroll, *Theotokos*, 357.

64. Lagrand, "How Was the Virgin Mary 'Like a Man'?," 7–8.

65. The explicit mention of Mary in Jesus's genealogy has precedent in Hebrew scriptures. Genealogies are given when introducing Davidic kings and the royal Queen Mother is always named. The naming of Mary conforms to this pattern. See Pitre, *Jewish Roots of Mary*, 82.

who appears to Joseph in a dream (Matt 1:20). In the Lucan narrative of the Annunciation, Mary is three times within nine verses referred to as *virgin* (Luke 1:26–34). The angelic announcement proclaims, "And now, you will conceive in your womb and bear a son" (Luke 1:31 NRSV) rather than the usual formulation of "giving a son" to the husband. There has been uncontested acceptance of Mary's virginity at the time of Jesus's conception since the earliest days of the church, hence there has been no direct intervention by the magisterium, concerning this.

The *virginitas in partu* has been less unanimously received, although neither has it been widely denied.[66] The years post–Vatican II saw much questioning of theological positions once deemed untouchable. The notion of Mary's perpetual virginity was one such dogma that was scrutinized. Some Roman Catholic theologians sought to press the dogma, so as to answer modern skepticism of it. Karl Rahner contributed to the debate in volume four of his *Theological Investigations*. Rahner is delicate and nuanced in what he writes. He upholds Mary's "bodily integrity," that she is "*semper virgo*," as a matter of faith but calls for "a certain reserve" as to the content of that designate.[67] Rahner points out that the exact meaning is not clear from Patristic sources.[68] Some of the early church Fathers understood it to mean preservation of the hymen during birth; some as pain-free delivery; one, St Ephraim, as the hymen restored after parturition. One of the difficulties of claiming Mary's body was unaffected ("incorrupt") by the birth is that this could lead to Docetism; that is, claiming a birth that somehow bypassed the vagina and was not really of the body, hence Pope Martin the First who, at the Lateran Synod of AD 649, declared, in Rahner's summary, that "Christ did not pass through Mary as through a fistula."[69] The affirmation that can be made, in keeping with Church doctrine, says Rahner, is that Jesus's birth from Mary was "unique, miraculous and virginal," but that "this proposition, which is directly intelligible, does not offer us the possibility of deducing assertions about the concrete details of the process, which would be *certain* and

66. O'Carroll, *Theotokos*, 361.

67. Rahner, *More Recent Writings*, 137.

68. Rahner, *More Recent Writings*, 138n15. Rahner also cites Clement of Alexandria, who wrote in the late second century that only "some" held to Mary's *virginitas in partu*. This minority Rahner sees represented in the mid-second-century apocryphal infancy narratives. These nativity accounts, he notes, have "an unmistakably docetic tinge" (Rahner, *More Recent Writings*, 148–49).

69. Rahner, *More Recent Writings*, 139–40.

universally binding."[70] Rahner is carefully attentive to the specific state-ments of the early Fathers, adheres to binding dogma, yet respects the limits of knowledge. He sits within the tension of the known (or know-able) and the unknown (or unknowable), ceding ground to neither but inclining to the latter.

One generation later, in his contribution to the Anglican-Roman Catholic International Commission (ARCIC) working papers on Mary, Jean-Marie Tillard sketches a position that tries to distinguish between two broad types of gospel writing, each of which is truth-bearing, but in distinctive ways. They are, he says, "two complementary ways of transmitting the same revealed truth": the "*descriptive*, based on his-torical evidence" and the "*interpretative*, trying to make clear the inner signification."[71] Tillard illustrates this by referring to the nativity details in the Matthean and Lucan gospels such as the choirs of angels, the bril-liant star in the sky, and the pilgrims appearing, and calls them "beautiful poetical or symbolic images," further elucidating: "Such language does not 'describe.' Strictly speaking, it 'reveals.'"[72]

This assertion of Tillard's is contentious for two reasons. Firstly, it begs the question of who determines what is descriptive and what inter-pretative, and what criteria is used to make that determination. The cri-teria he implies for the category distinction he sets up is whether or not the description is consonant with a scientific worldview. If it is not, then it is relegated to the category of interpretation which in Tillard's scheme amounts to an attractive fiction; a weak kind of dispensable *poetry*. Til-lard's category distinction sees interpretation as an interpolation of sub-jective opinion upon objective fact. Secondly, Tillard begs the question of why descriptive language cannot also be revelatory or *poetical*. In Tillard's scheme, physical reality carries a restriction that limits it to being only *of the earth*, something that only ever conforms to known rules of expres-sion. Interpretation for Tillard is a supplementary act of the mind whose interiority is essentially detached from what is observable exteriorly. His allowance that revelation is discerned under the guidance of the Holy Spirit, who aids persons in perceiving the transcendent dimension, does not help overcome this interior-exterior divide, nor that between *descrip-tion* and *revelation*. Although Tillard cautions against "the temptation to

70. Rahner, *More Recent Writings*, 162.

71. Tillard, "Marian Issues," 5–6.

72. Tillard, "Marian Issues," 6.

reduce everything to the descriptive, the chronological, the obvious, the empirical," his position does not present complementary ways of knowing so much as mutually exclusive ones.[73] His presentation of poetic *truth* sounds more like poetic fiction, so for example, in his saying of Mary's assumption, it is "a poetical vision which is not to be understoodliterally."[74]

By contrast, in his 1995–1997 series of General Audiences on the Virgin Mary, John Paul II tended strongly towards affirming the literal and descriptive. In his General Audience of July 10, 1996, he said of the *virginitas ante partum* that Luke's account is not just the "development of a Jewish theme" nor "the derivation of a pagan mythological legend." Contra Tillard, for whom poetic language expresses the inner signification of events and in that sense, can disclose truth, John Paul implies the unreliability of such interpretation. When applied to gospel texts, it can inhibit a correct reading of a biblical event. The pope explicitly states that "the structure of the Lucan text (Luke 1:26–38; 2:29, 51) resists any reductive interpretation." *Reductive* here means reading as a weak symbol, metaphor or other literary device, what was intended to be read as objective realism. John Paul further says: "several recent interpretations which understand the virginal conception not in a physical or biological sense, but only as symbolic or metaphorical" are to be rejected, as is calling the event a theologoumenon.

As John Paul II was himself an accomplished poet, it would be highly unlikely that he was positing a literal, factual reading at the expense of a metaphoric one. In *Mulieris Dignitatem*, some of the pope's words echoed more closely those of Tillard concerning the relation between poetic language and disclosure of truth. The Genesis creation stories, he says, were written "in language that is poetic and symbolic, yet profoundly true" (*MD* 7). These, though, are ancient mythological texts. The much more recent gospel texts are written as testimony of historical events and persons from writers already convinced of their extraordinary import. As the Lucan gospel contains information dependent upon firsthand disclosure, notably the annunciation scene, it may have been based on direct testimony by Mary.[75] While allowing for the differences between different

---

73. Tillard, "Marian Issues," 6.

74. Tillard, "Marian Issues," 10.

75. The Lucan gospel opens with a declaration of authorial intent: "I too decided, after investigating everything carefully from the very first, to write an orderly account for you, most excellent Theophilus, so that you may know the truth concerning the things about which you have been instructed" (Luke 1:3–4 NRSV). Luke's words

biblical texts, John Paul strongly affirms the plain sense of the gospels, as stated in his July 10, 1996, General Audience: the gospels "contain the explicit affirmation of a virginal conception of the biological order, by the Holy Spirit, and this truth has been endorsed by the Church from the earliest formulations of faith (cf. *CCC 496*)." That the Lucan account presents a recapitulation of the much earlier Old Testament material concerning the ark of the covenant is not, for John Paul, to suggest that it is a literary fiction, consciously constructed as a parallel typology.[76] It is both a literary presentation of events that happened, and an arrangement of those events which provokes recognition in those familiar with the earlier Scriptures.

John Paul's intention concerning the virginal conception seems to be to retain the co-existence of the plain meaning, and the poetic, without seeing the latter as negating the former, nor of its discounting the historicity of the event. John Paul is reiterating the gospel tradition, which had not been subject to much challenge until after Vatican II. He is disallowing a distance between the words *virgin* and *mother*. Each term is to be accorded its straightforward meaning, and together, through contemplation, the composite term can unfold further layers of meaning. He is concerned to safeguard the reliability of words and their connection with primary meaning. The gap implied with Tillard's rendering of "descriptive" and "interpretative" language, notwithstanding his talk of their complementarity, supports their distinction but not their unity.

John Paul II, despite initial appearances, supports a unitive approach to gospel language. While seeming to rein in poetic readings, John Paul's insistence on literality paradoxically opens up Rahnerian "space" for "what is uncertain and unanswered."[77] This unitive, or spousal approach, is present in the designate *virgin mother* which John Paul explicitly references in *Mulieris Dignitatem*, saying virginity and motherhood "united in her [Mary] in an exceptional manner, in such a way that one did not exclude the other but wonderfully complemented it" (*MD* 17). In the same document he writes of the peaceful coexistence of opposites within consecrated virginity: "virginity is not restricted to a mere 'no,' but contains a profound 'yes' in the spousal order: the gift of self-love in a total and undivided manner" (*MD* 20).

---

indicate his interest in an historical hermeneutic and, as his ante-natal narrative indicates, an interest in contextual biography.

76. See the editor's introduction in Boss, *Mary*, 3.

77. Rahner, *Faith and Ministry*, 228.

Mary's paradoxical body ushers in the ultimate paradox of the god-man. Paradox is a category favored by Henri de Lubac in his ecclesiology as being particularly supportive of the expression of mystery. Mary's unique motherhood also expresses her continuity and discontinuity with the religious past of her people. In *Daughter Zion,* Ratzinger writes of Mary's improbable maternity in the context of the "unblessed-blessed mothers" of Israel, among whom: Sarah, Rachel, Hannah, Esther, and Judith. Infertile, or otherwise powerless, women become the persons in whom God manifests his power. Mary's motherhood works within the logic of this religious inheritance: she is the lowly one for whom "the Mighty One" does great things. Ratzinger sees a deeper dimension to Mary's motherhood, which sets her apart from her womanly forebears. As *Theotokos,* Mary, he says, "is more than the organ of a fortuitous corporeal event. To bear the 'Son' includes the surrender of oneself into barrenness . . . barrenness is the condition of fruitfulness."[78] The "barrenness" is Mary's emptying of herself into the will of the Father, signed biologically by her virginity.

John Paul II writes from the same perspective when he says of virginity and motherhood that they are "two dimensions of the female vocation" which complement each other and are united in Mary (*MD* 17). He means by this the sacrificial giving of the whole self to God, including one's sexual and reproductive potentialities. This utter *yes* to God, even freely taking on barrenness, is the means by which God confers blessings of fruitfulness; in Mary's case, concrete fruitfulness springs from the ground of her virginal barrenness. She is the anticipatory sign of voluntary virginity for the sake of the kingdom of God (see Matt 19:12). While this was not, perhaps, an entirely new possibility for God's people, it is radically expanded within the new covenantal relationship.[79] It becomes a mode of participating in the freely-laid-down life of the Son: the virgin or "eunuch" freely lays down passing on her/his family lineage. Freely given sacrifice, as modelled by her son, inverts notions of blessed and unblessed, and becomes a new way to live for the furtherance of God's rule.

---

78. Ratzinger, *Daughter Zion*, 52. Ratzinger sees the unity between Jewish and Christian scriptures as essential in fostering understanding of Marian dogmas. These cannot be deduced from the New Testament alone. When scriptural unity is lost, "healthy Mariology is lost," veering either towards "rebellion" or "dangerous romanticism" (32).

79. Michael O'Carroll notes that although the "general rule" for a first-century Jewish woman may have been to equate blessedness with offspring, whether "voluntary childlessness" was unheard of is "not certain" (*Theotokos*, 364).

Mary's virginity overturned the Old Testament typology of the *cursed* infertile woman. Instead, sexual renunciation, signed as virginity, becomes wedded to fruitfulness. In electing consecrated virginity, women are affirmed as worthwhile, independent of their potential to bear children. In their different mode of giving to others, they realize a different kind of fruitfulness. Such virginity is an expression of the so-called radicalism of the gospel; of leaving all to follow Christ. It is therefore a state not only of self-denial but of self-giving, and the concomitant self-reception this brings.[80] *Virginity* as representative of the non-child-bearing woman also accords with the fertility pattern of women whose natural biological reproductive phase is about thirty years in length, or under half her life expectancy. Most women can expect to live decades without the possibility of pregnancy, so need symbolic access that affirms this pattern.

The gift of the self can be understood via the analogy of the gestational uterus. The uterus realizes itself in its dynamic pattern of supportive self-donation, stretching and enlarging to accommodate the maturing fetus. The uterine enlargement is not a passive displacement. At term, the uterus will have increased ten-fold in weight with a ten-fold increase, between week ten and delivery, of uterine blood volume.[81] The uterine boundary is secure but also plastic, engaged in a *speech pattern*, a chemical dialogue. Within this speech pattern, it performs a series of alterations and adjustments cyclically, intra-cyclically, and throughout a pregnancy's term. In response to hormonal signals, the endometrium thickens so as to fashion itself as a receptive site of a conceptus. Endometrial receptivity is realized by different chemical markers which variously ensure it continues its *rolling* movement prior to implantation, repels it from those areas with a poor chance of implantation, attracts it to a more suitable site, and ensures adhesion to the endometrium. Its properties are not arbitrary but exist so as to foster life. The uterine boundary is dynamic, responsive, and alterable, yet the uterus retains its integrity as a distinct and distinctive organ.

80. "Being a person means striving towards self-realization . . . which can only be achieved 'through a sincere gift of the self'" (*MD* 7).

81. Collins et al., *Oxford Handbook of Obstetrics and Gynaecology*, 30.

Boundary Transformation:
The Crucified Christ As Birthing Mother

The expansive uterine boundary is given painterly allegorical expression in the West as the *Mater misericordiae*, in the East as the *Pokrov*. Mary stands with her mantle outstretched in a wide, inclusive embrace while numerous adult children huddle within its protective reach. Her mantle functions as a uterine motif, competent to offer refuge to all people. Mary imaged as maternal protectress is modeled upon Christ, with arms outstretched on the cross. Reversing the direction of the analogy, Christ's crucified form, interpreted as embrace, figures him as welcoming all who would approach. Mary, in a figuratively less complex way, iterates this welcome, cooperating with Christ to offer protection to any who seek it.

Mary and her son are bound together in the shared imagery of defensive, protective maternity, each laboring to bring forth children of God. Mary, Jesus's physical and spiritual mother, works to bring him brothers and sisters in the faith. Christ's crucified body, stretched upwards, downwards, and sideways, enacts uterine gestational, or parturient vaginal, stretching. This figuration of Christ as natal deliverer stands within a history of biblical birthing motifs associated with God's salvation, such as the parting of the *birth canal*[82] of the sea, and the bloody lintels of the doorways at Passover.

Interpreting Jesus's death on the cross as enacting metaphoric birth introduces a problem of the male Jesus seemingly appropriating the maternal feminine. In Nancy Jay's oft-quoted words, the cross could seem an instantiation *par excellence* of "birth done better."[83] I have suggested above that this is not the case: that Jesus as male is figured as one of strongly articulated feminine traits of nurturance, openness, and boundary porosity. A different but complementary perspective comes from the field of anthropology. Anthropological studies have documented an almost universal transcultural practice of *couvade*; that is, fathers' culturally prescribed behaviors during and after birth which may entail acting out labor pains.[84] Daniel Boyarin proposes, contra Freud et al., that

---

82. Margalit, "Priestly Men and Invisible Women," 311. The gospel's narrative connection with the bloody lintels is quite explicit as Jesus's Crucifixion took place on the day of Preparation for the Passover.

83. Jay, *Throughout Your Generations Forever*, xxiv.

84. Lundell, "Couvade in Sweden."

male envy of the female body may be at play.[85] Inverting the classical Freudian notion of penis envy (that is, a female purportedly perceiving her own genitals as a lack, so envying the male who has the organ she desires), Boyarin sees this "phallus-myth" as a constructed "mythic opposite" (itself a kind of *couvade*), which obscures the male's real desire: to be female. The counter-part of this myth is castration anxiety or being rendered *female*. Boyarin, though, counter-intuitively interprets even the counter-myth as masking "the fear of *not* being female."[86]

As ingenious as Boyarin's interpretation is, it does not satisfy. The castrated male is still chromosomally male. He is not rendered *female* so much as *neither-male-nor-female*. As Jesus in the gospels shows no fear of, or aversion towards, women, a case could be mounted that the crucified Christ takes upon himself the deep castration phobia by virtue of his body enacting sexual indeterminacy, in the sense explained above. If Jesus is figured metaphorically as female, then in a chiastic refiguring, Mary becomes male. Read according to the *couvade* motif, Mary at the foot of the cross occupies the symbolic place of the father, or other male support. One of the reasons Torborg Lundell cites for a male presence at a birth was to share, if only secondarily and empathetically, the wife's pain and anxiety, and to hopefully mitigate it by his presence. The linkage of the Simeon prophecy (Luke 2:35) with Mary's presence at the Johannine crucifixion strengthens this reading of Marian *couvade*. She, as metaphoric male, functions as the faithful and loving spouse, who shares so fully in the birth pain that she experiences it in herself.

Mary's spousal relation with her son does not negate her maternal relation, as attested to by the crucified Christ declaring her mother of the disciple who was present at her side. This disciple was present not only in his personal capacity, but as representative of the nascent church. Notably, Jesus calls Mary "woman" as he had at Cana. This indicates, as observed by John Paul II in *Redemptoris Mater*, that Jesus addresses Mary in a triple modality as individual, as representative, and as type. Jesus's words are declaring, so establishing, a bond between the believing community and his mother. The church, as Christ's mystical body, will henceforth share in their maternal-filial unity.[87] Christ's filial act from the cross makes temporal provision for his mother while also affirming her

85. Boyarin, "Couvade."

86. Boyarin, "Couvade," 15.

87. Howell, "Mary's Bodily Participation," 210.

as the archetypal good mother. Her maternal ministry is exponentially expanded. Christ's declaration means that Mary cannot be fully understood, nor fully honored, if she is only considered from the temporal dimension as one individual mother of one individual son. Mary's motherhood is not limited in that way; it has transcended and exceeded temporality. If, as Christians believe, she is the mother of God, then she is the mother of the living, as those who live, live in and through God's grace. Mary's motherhood of Christ is not rendered redundant, irrelevant, or discontinuous upon his death. As will later be made clear, at the Resurrection, the body she gestated, lives on. The connection between her son and his followers will be of the closest possible intimacy, exceeding even that of gestation. Not only do his followers live through God's grace; they live in union with the Second Person of the Trinity. One of the metaphors by which they shall come to be known is the *body of Christ*. Mary is the mother not just of one person but of the one corporate person, Christ. The first commandment in the Decalogue which follows those that deal directly with how to relate to God, is: "honor your father and mother." In continuity with this directive, the Christ-ordained implication for Mary's many spiritual children is: honor her.

It is by virtue of having been the good mother that Mary becomes the "helper meet," or ideal spouse, of Jesus, aiding him in the ongoing work of salvation, and helping to bring persons into the body of her son. This Christic ecclesial body is figured imaginatively as the bride of Christ, a different iteration of the revealed self-completeness of Israel's God ("I Am Who I Am"). The uncomfortable metaphoric shift that figures Mary the mother as spouse of her son has found disconcerting expression in medieval paintings of Mary and Christ as lovers. Motherhood can, though, be construed analogously as a spousal relationship between mother and child, as it echoes the intention ("I take you"), the promise ("to be mine"), and the permanence ("till death do us part") of the wedding vows. Motherhood, not only marriage, can be construed as a sign of the mystery of God's self-gift as spousal love.

A reading of the crucified Christ as a realization of the impossible—male birth—reprises at his death the impossible boundary-crossing that took place at the Incarnation in the Virgin. Mary's presence as birth assistant or doula recalls her self-identification as the "handmaid" of The Lord. It is not motherhood that is usurped by Christ's birthing body but the culturally assumed dominance of the phallus. In Christ's body, by contrast, the power is in the wounds, open and bleeding. His body upon death has become an open invitation to enter inside it; the two-in-one of pregnancy is now the two-in-one of Christ and believer. This body statement, or somatic metaphor, claims that the nature of that unity far exceeds the merely moral. The union is ontological.[88] Christ's body has become a dwelling place, and in a metaphoric mirroring, expressive of the mutuality of relationship, the believer is to become a dwelling place for Christ, as was Mary. Believers, that is, are to imitate Mary, modelling themselves on her. This is metaphor expressed concretely. Consistent with the human experience of embodiment, the human body is not "an object placed before us" but the "environment in which we dwell."[89] The Johannine crucified Christ can be read as expressing the structure of metaphor in the connection between the related terms (here, of *male* and *female*) and of the distinction between them; of Jesus being male according to his humanity, and neither-male-nor-female according to his divinity.[90]

Furthermore, Jesus's death unifies the two modes by which social groups establish belonging: via familial, blood relations, and via the strategy of establishing male patterns of descent according to ritual prescriptions. In Jesus's death, the two lineations of descent, maternal and paternal, are unified. The spear wound is a composite sign of the blood of birth (female) and of battle (male). Jesus's death does not operate to the exclusion of women and mothers. It reconciles in his person the social and ritual competition between the modes of descent and identity formation. The bounds of the metaphoric predication of Jesus as birthing mother are that Jesus is male; that followers are invited to dwell in his death; and that the site of gestation is his *uterine* heart. The metaphoric meaning has not erased Jesus's male body, but its illocutionary message is that Jesus's maleness is not *ad idem* with the phallus. Salvation is not simply a case of *mankind saved by a man*, but of *mankind saved by God who was born as a man of a woman*. It is not Jesus's maleness that saves. Salvation comes from God via mankind in his fullness, male-and-female.

A straightforward interpretation of the crucified Christ as the one who bridges in his body male-female distinction, restoring the homologous man of creation, is problematic if viewed as a male body which has

---

88. Naumann, "Kenterich and the Image of Mary," 237.

89. Granados, "Body, Family, Order of Love," 202.

90. This, though, is not the final word on the matter. As Graham Ward has insightfully observed, the body of Christ was transposed to the broken bread by Christ himself, and "Jesus' body as bread is no longer Christ as simply and biologically male" (Ward, "Displaced Body," 103).

absorbed the female. While his opened body invites entry and signs the possibility of birth, Son gestating mother-church, it need not be rejected as male appropriation and *improvement* of birth, as per Nancy Jay's critique. Rather, it follows the metaphoric precedent of Genesis where the male, Adam, is opened to enable the *birth* of another. As noted by John Paul II, it is upon discovering an adequate relation "to" a person, that one is then able to open up more fully in a "communion of persons" (*TOB* 9:2). Jesus on the cross reprises this opening, a reading that retains, rather than abolishes, male-female identities. The cross is the place where the two become one (cf. Gen 2:24; *TOB* 10). Jesus is the person in whom this happens, the complete image of man.

Strengthening, Effacing, Dilating

The lower part of the uterus, the cervix, functions variously to aid conception, support the growing fetus, and aid the delivery of the baby at term. It undergoes extensive changes during gestation and parturition. The nonpregnant cervix is predominantly made up of collagen proteins which are rigid and non-extensible. These collagen bundles are densely and irregularly packed. During pregnancy, the cervix undergoes extensive remodeling, becoming palpably softer owing to increased water concentration. It increases in mass and tensile strength through the reorganization of collagen. The realigned collagen fibers are remodeled into a structurally stronger pattern that allows the cervix to support the fetus *in utero*. The second structural change reverses this procedure, the collagen degrading and dispersing prior to cervical effacement and dilation at the onset of labor.[91]

This pattern of cervical remodeling offers possibilities for a metaphoric reading. One of the criticisms of some feminists concerning the construal of Mary within the church is the overdetermination of what could be called her *effacement*. The associations of effacement are of modesty, and withdrawal from sight, scaling down to insignificance and erasure. Such concepts have come to be particularly associated with the Virgin Mary. Tina Beattie criticizes Augustine's (and consequently, the church's) construal of Mary's humility before Joseph as absorbing her into prevailing social codes: "domesticated and incorporated into the law of the father through an emphasis on Mary's modesty, humility

---

91. Reece and Hobbins, *Fetus and Mother*, 639–40.

and silence."[92] These last three designators are strongly associated with effacement.

John Paul II, in *Redemptoris Mater*, seems to understand Mary's consent at the Annunciation in such terms. In paragraph thirteen, he praises the attributes nominated in Vatican II's document, *Dei Verbum*: "submission of intellect and will" (*DV* 5) and "the obedience of faith" (*DV* 5). When these virtues are directed towards the biblical God, they are fitting and proper. They are also vulnerable, though, to being disproportionately expected of women in the Roman Catholic church structure, and of anyone, whether female or male, who does not occupy a position of ecclesial authority in other church structures. While submission and obedience can be improperly leveraged for political ends, there is also a contemporary resistance to those qualities, as such. The qualitative changes of the cervix during gestation and labor—softening, thinning, effacing—when read metaphorically, can help lessen such resistance, and some of the concerns which underlie it. So, for example, the structural changes of the cervix prior to effacement put a different gloss upon *softening* which is not associated with lack (of resolve, courage, et cetera), but with strengthening. The partnership of softening and strengthening has strong biblical resonances. *Hardness of heart,* meaning obdurate refusal of critical self-examination, or ingratitude to God, is a constant theme. The opposite, *the heart of flesh*, is the soft heart that is the heart strengthened through having admitted God.

Sarah Coakley advocates for the practice of contemplative, silent prayer as it "inculcates mental patterns of 'unmastery'" by fostering patient waiting upon God and relinquishing self-dominion.[93] This argument forms part of Coakley's defense of systematic theology as a discipline, against criticisms that it represses areas of knowledge that have been traditionally associated with the feminine. Purported theological knowledge of God—knowledge which is unlike any other—is well imagined, for Coakley, as a transparency of the subject before God's knowing; Christian contemplation is a "bodily practice of dispossession, humility and effacement."[94] Coakley re-centers effacement, seen as the ground of attentiveness to the other, as a desirable ascetic practice.

---

92. Beattie, *God's Mother, Eve's Advocate*, 177.

93. Coakley, "Future for Gender and Theology?," 53.

94. Coakley, "Future for Gender and Theology?," 55.

Within the gospel context, Marian effacement operates positively. While Mary appears on few occasions, each is at a crucial narrative juncture that covers the whole span of Christ's life: conception (Annunciation); the inaugural mission event (Visitation); Nativity; dedication to God in the temple; the precocious start to his teaching ministry in the Jerusalem temple; the inauguration of his public ministry (Cana); the occasion when Jesus teaches about how the *family* of God is constituted; the Crucifixion; and Pentecost. Luke's gospel is the one most interested in the earthly genesis of Jesus and the only one to record the Annunciation, Visitation, and Presentation, key episodes of Jesus's earliest life reliant on, or notable for, Mary's presence. The gospel inclusion of a pericope (Matt 12: 46–50; Luke 8: 19–21) where Mary seems entirely overlooked (effaced), is highly significant. Told that his mother and "brothers" are waiting outside for him, Jesus responds by asking, "Who is my mother, and who are my brothers?" (Matt 12:48 NRSV) in seeming reproof, the adult Jesus apparently trying to redress the maternal overdetermination of his lineage. His answer to his own question: "For whoever does the will of my Father in heaven is my brother and sister and mother" (Matt 12:50 NRSV) undoes that initial assumption. Mary is preeminently the one who heard and did the word of God, hence the words of Pope Benedict XVI: "It is Mary's obedience that opens the door to God."[95] Mary and his brothers have not been superseded but recast within a hugely expanded familial network. Jesus reveals that the human biological family is a metaphoric analogy for the intimate type of relational unity each person can experience with God. It speaks of an ontological bond unable to be unmade. This enduring strength of bond can be consciously invoked by any and all of God's *children*. Human blood-bonds provide a strong analogy of the bonds between those who internalize and live the Word of God. Applying this logic to Jesus's reaction to the interruption of Mary and his brothers, Jesus is not repudiating his sonship of Mary but properly contextualizing it within her first having lived as "Daughter Zion." His response effaces their biological connection only in order to dilate their spiritual one. That such effacement does not amount to erasure is confirmed by Mary's presence at the cross in John's gospel where she is given as mother to the whole community of believers—which could potentially amount to the whole world.

95. Benedict XVI, *Infancy Narratives*, 56.

Cervical *thinning* serves a specific good and is necessary prior to dilation. The softened cervix, preparatory to the thinning of effacement, involves remodeling and physiologic cell death. While caution may well be in order so as to not press the metaphor too keenly in its applicability to Mary, and to women as a group, this notion of voluntary (and partial) deconstruction, in order to facilitate bringing forth another life, correlates with Jesus's strongly worded injunction that one must lose one's life in order to gain it (Matt 16:25) where *loss* refers to personal self-determination which is voluntarily ceded to God. Seeing the maternal cervix as such a correlate is benign because it signifies gain, rather than permanent loss or damage. The deconstructed cervix institutes a process of repair, possibly beginning even during dilation, so that a future pregnancy cycle will become possible. Cervical effacement expresses a repeatable pattern of active and self-giving support for another.

In the action of dilation, the cervix is metaphorically linked with the other organs of dilation: the eyes. Unlike the swift and unconsciously performed optical dilations, cervical dilation is slow, painful, and intrudes upon consciousness. The constant modifications of the pupils operate unnoticed, increasing or decreasing the entry of light so that sight can continue. Vision has historically been considered preeminent of the senses. In his article exploring the nature of Christ's Transfiguration, José Granados attaches particular importance to divine glory having been manifest in Christ's human body, as this enabled it to be witnessed (*seen*) by others.[96] Sight is an operation of the eyes but is a function made possible by the whole living organism. Philosophically, human sight has been linked to human mobility; that we see because we move. Vision therefore is a synthesis of two functions: seeing and moving.[97] Sight enables the input of constantly adjusted data concerning depth of field so that a person can successfully navigate through space. This linkage between sight and movement provides the origin of an embedded, implied gospel wordplay: insight comes through admitting more L/light which is always moving, so stimulating disciples to move and follow.

The experience of seeing prompts a metaphoric strand in the gospels relating it to spiritual insight. This insight, or dilation, moves a believer on, in the pilgrimage of faith. Mary, in Luke's gospel, is associated with this type of spiritual dilation. Luke links Mary's insight with her tendency

96. Granados, "Embodied Light, Incarnate Image."
97. Granados, "Embodied Light, Incarnate Image," 22.

to contemplative reflection—an "ingathering" of her experiences.[98] Mary ponders the angelic greeting (Luke 1:29); the account of the shepherds (Luke 2:19); and finding the child Jesus in the temple (Luke 2:51). Art historian and critic, John Drury, has seen this confluence in Mary of sight, fruitful contemplation, and knowledge represented in The National Gallery's painting of the Annunciation by Fra Filippo Lippi. The painting depicts a stream of heavenly light beamed into the lozenge shape, or *eye*, made by the parted tunic over her stomach.[99] Associations of vision, heightened inner sight, dilation, and fecundity coalesce. Mary is the seer whose vision has been dilated by the Light of God. Her spiritual insight exceeds that of the later disciples of her adult son, whom he often castigated for blindness.

Mary's deep sightedness, though, does not equate with perfect understanding. Mary in Luke's account is not given data that would satisfy her understanding. She consents on the basis of dark faith that will gradually be enlightened throughout her own life pilgrimage. In one of his published sermons, Rowan Williams expounds upon an image of Dionysius—God as a "ray of darkness."[100] God's divine light dazzles the eyes, pure radiance that blinds. This is light so searing that it can obliterate hitherto firmly held certainties. This may cause such a fundamental rethink that one is compelled, in Williams's words, to "find a new way of knowing myself, identifying myself, uttering myself, talking of myself, imaging myself."[101] Luke's Mary is prepared to welcome this incomprehensible Light. Her trusting incomprehension is narratively balanced with her expressive Magnificat. Neither silenced nor blinded by her encounter with God, her Magnificat praises God with expectant trust that he will institute his justice in a disordered world. Her dilated understanding knows that all things will be made new but not the means by which this shall be effected.

Cervical and optical dilations are related in their contrasts and inverse mechanisms, as well as in their rude mechanical similarity. Optical dilation allows more light to enter the body; cervical dilation allows more life (light) to enter the world. One of the recurring biblical figures for God is light. If God is understood as light, then human life, God's

98. Granados, "Embodied Light, Incarnate Image," 25.

99. Drury, *Painting the Word*, 48–54.

100. Williams, *Ray of Darkness*.

101. Williams, *Ray of Darkness*, 100.

image, is also imbued with light. In a surprising metaphoric twist, the Lucan Jesus draws a parallel between a lamp on a stand and, "Your eye [which] is the lamp of your body" (Luke 11:34 NRSV); that is, the eye is presented in strikingly inverse manner as emitter, rather than receiver, of light. The Nicene Creed expresses the intra-Trinitarian mission of the Son from the Father as "Light from Light." Every human birth can be read as a recapitulation within the natural order of the divine mission, "light from light."

Even prior to conception, the cervix acts as enabler. Cervical mucus facilitates possible conception. It alters in viscosity throughout the menstrual cycle, increasing in volume and fluidity at the time of peak fertility. The maximal mucosal elasticity at this phase, together with the increased mucosal hydration, facilitates sperm penetration into the uterus. Filtering out suboptimal sperm, the cervical mucus guides healthy sperm along structural troughs or runnels that run the length of the cervix. When sperm does come into contact with an ovum, it does not aggressively force itself inside with the troubling associations of that conceptual frame. Rather, the binding sites of the sperm and the surface receptors of the ovum cooperate.[102] Eschewing an aggressive hierarchy, this model recasts female receptivity as an active, cooperative partnership. The mucosal plug that fills the cervical *os* after conception prevents pathogens from entering the uterus, keeping the uterine environment aseptic.

As seen in the example above, altering the language used of conception alters how it is thought about. The language used to describe biological functions can do more than disinterestedly denote. It can expose and build conceptual frameworks by which we understand ourselves. Word choices descriptive of biological processes may convey secondary meanings of a political nature. Mary Shivanandan analyzed the findings of feminist ethnographer, Emily Martin.[103] Martin had investigated the language choices of the main medical textbooks used at Johns Hopkins University during the few years prior to her study. Her aim was to determine what messages they conveyed about the male and female reproductive systems. Shivanandan commends Martin's critique of the texts' language, finding that they favored male tissue and actions over the female, so for example, the transformation of spermatid into sperm is "remarkable," the "sheer magnitude" of sperm production a "feat." This

102. Ory and Barrionuevo, "Differential Diagnosis of Female Infertility," 1016.

103. Shivanandan, "Body Narratives."

valorization contrasts with the words chosen to describe menstrual shedding: "losing," "dying," "denuding," "debris." Martin finds the ascription of cultural sex stereotypes regarding masculine and feminine, so the imputed passivity of the ovum moving along the fallopian tube where it "is transported," "is swept," "drifts." The sperm on contact with the ovum is "penetrating," "burrowing," so as to "activate" conception. Such stereotypically gendered language usage undermines claims of its neutrality. The language choices do more than transfer information. They embed a particular worldview that is competitive, dualistic, and hierarchical; male is pitted against female. Conception framed in a language of invasion, conquest, and hostility is highly problematic. Shivanandan contrasts this aggressive textbook vocabulary with that used in fifteen natural family planning manuals. These, in contrast to the textbooks, used language of uniting, meeting, and cooperating. This alternative vocabulary declines viewing either the sexual act, or conception, as inherently competitive or hostile. Furthermore, this politically more appealing language seems to more accurately reflect the biology. Shivanandan found the gentler language of mutuality correlated with biological research, current at the time of her writing, in which conception was being revealed as an act of cellular cooperation.

The softened, effaced, and dilated cervix forms a portal through which the fetus descends into the world. This association of the open doorway that allows passage into an alien environment, never before experienced, but for which one was always intended, correlates with the Christian understanding of personal life extending beyond physical death, hopefully into union with The Divine. Jesus's death communicates this notion of death as a doorway into something beyond, through the cluster of gospel images surrounding his death: solar occlusion, earthquake, and the tearing of the temple curtain. This metaphoric cluster registers the poetic domain the reader has entered.[104] The dramatic solar occlusion, temporarily plunging the visible world into darkness, expresses in the celestial order the extinguishing of The One who had lived as light on the earth. As it is an occurrence in the natural order, which is beyond human manipulation, and as it is concurrent with the death of

---

104. *Metaphoric* and *poetic* are not intended to mean contrary to what actually or physically took place. They are used to indicate that the images interact among themselves and with the actual event of Jesus's death. Both of themselves and in their relationships, the metaphors communicate meanings which elucidate, echo, and illuminate dimensions of the meaning of Jesus's death on the cross.

Jesus, it is understood to be spoken by God—a dramatic visual metaphor for the benefit of those who see it, record it, and will read of it.

The inexplicable solar occlusion (not a predictable solar eclipse) is multivalent. It is a sign of destitution (life-giving light/Light withheld); a sign of judgment (an earthquake ominously accompanied the eclipse), and a sign of hope (God has opened a portal to the heavenly realm). The earthquake expands the affective range of the signs and serves as meta-phoric balance to the suddenly blacked-out sun. An earthquake is heard and felt with the whole body. While no mention is made of fractures and fissures opening in the earth as a result of the quake, they frequently accompany violent tectonic activity. The heavenly portal now signed, through which people may, pending their assent, *ascend*, is balanced by a suggestion of a possible *descent* into the depths of a shaken, riven earth.

The Lukan and Matthean gospels also record the rending in two of the temple curtains at the Crucifixion (Luke 23:45; Matt 27:51).[105] These curtains are commonly agreed to have been those that screened off the Holy of Holies in the Jerusalem temple. They formed a highly symbolic opaque veil that represented all created matter.[106] In passing through them once a year at *Yom Kippur*, the High Priest was passing beyond earth, through the visible heaven into the celestial realm, impenetrable and indiscernible to human eyes, where God dwelt. Applying the cervical motif to them, they protect (God's people from God's intolerably holy presence) and enable (expiation of sins, annually, through the temple cult). Academic biblical scholar, Margaret Barker, says that these portals "represented the division between the material world and the spiritual."[107] Those who pass from the heavenly side through the curtain become vis-ible by taking on flesh; the High Priest who passes through from the opposite direction changes his vestments to angelic white linen. Barker draws attention to their great size and extreme weight: "two hundred square meters of wool and linen fabric."[108] Both gospels mention they were "torn in two," with the Matthean emphasizing the extent of the rent: "from top to bottom." Both gospels intend this to be read as a divine

---

105. Luke's gospel situates the tearing of the temple curtain just prior to Jesus's death. Its tearing releases a prayer from Jesus commending his spirit to the Father. Dennis Sylva proposes this as the place of Presence being opened to allow communion between Jesus and the Father. See Sylva, "Temple Curtain."

106. Barker, "Veil."

107. Barker, "Veil," 118.

108. Barker, "Veil," 106–7.

action which ruined their functionality as a cultic boundary.[109] One way to interpret this is that God's dwelling place is no longer concealed nor exclusionary; access is opened to that which had been denied.[110] Another reading would be that God's holy presence no longer dwells there, the rent curtains a mourning rite of the Father for the dead Son.[111]

Mary's presence at the Crucifixion adds yet another dimension. Mary's womb gestating Christ can be read as a figure, or personal embodiment, of the Holy of Holies. The holiest inner sanctum of the temple was the *raison d'être* and pinnacle of the temple precinct's architectural divisions, which marked off progressively stringent, and exclusionary, cultic separations. Mary's uterus separates the holiest child within her own holy body from the profane world. Developing inside Mary's womb in fully human fashion, the gestating Jesus is enclosed within the uterine membrane, pierced upon his birth. Birth and death are linked in the poetic accretion of piercings: uterine membrane, Jesus's body, his mother's heart, the temple curtain. These constitute a progressive unveiling of Jesus's identity, culminating in the revelatory moment of his death. The natal and terminal shared metaphor contracts the perceived distance (and difference) between them.

The extraordinary rending of the temple curtain is decoded in the book of Hebrews. The sign is interpreted as concretely signaling the meaning of Jesus's death. Jesus's salvific mission was to close the distance between the divine and the creaturely. Having already passed through the veil in order to enter creation, as the Christmas carol says, "veiled in flesh" (see also Heb 10:20), Jesus is able to make the return passage to the celestial realm. The pattern, materials, and colors of the temple veil were repeated in the ordinary vestment of the high priest (as distinct from the linen vestment worn only once per year), so forging, as Barker notes, an "intimate connection between the two."[112] The torn curtain at Jesus's death is therefore a sign of his tearing out from his fleshly veil, an actualization of the ritual performed annually by the high priest. The paradoxical sign,

109. Gurtner, *Torn Veil*, 199.

110. These images of earthquake and occluded sun recur in the prophetic apocalyptic text of Revelation: "The sun became black as sack" (Rev 6:12 NRSV), and in place of the riven temple curtain, the sky itself vanishes "like a scroll rolling itself up" (Rev 6:14 NRSV).

111. Tearing clothes upon hearing of the death of a loved one is an ancient Jewish mourning rite (see Gen 37:34; 2 Sam 13:19; Job 1:20).

112. Barker, *Gate*, 124.

and means by which this was effected, is Jesus's torn flesh, re-signed in the torn curtain (cf. Heb 6:19; 10:19–20); *rift* is mended by *rift* signed as *rift* in a dense metaphoric circle that fuses the boundaries between literal and figurative, concrete and metaphoric. The connection discerned by the writer of the Hebrews between Jesus's flesh and its signage in the temple furnishing made by human hands, follows the pattern of signage in Christ's eucharistic body. The eucharistic flesh—his differently-veiled body—is signed by the torn bread made by human labor.[113]

The temple curtain as representative of heaven marks the outermost boundary of the created, visible world. Beyond this veil is the realm of the unknown and inadmissible (except, exceptionally, once a year by the High Priest alone). It can therefore also be seen as an analogous metaphor of Mary's virginal motherhood: the boundary between the known (*virgin*; *mother*) and the impenetrable (*virgin-mother*). Mary's flesh uniquely distinguishes her and sets her apart, in a way analogous to Jewish male circumcision. It is not the removal of flesh, though, but its retention, which distinguishes Mary; her intact hymen signs her body as set apart in its unaltered integrity. Mary has long been imaginatively connected with the woman in the Song of Songs: "A garden locked is my sister, my bride, / a garden locked, a fountain sealed" (Song 4:12 NRSV). Mary as the inaccessible garden is the one reserved exclusively for God, the One in whom she delights. The image cluster of locked gate, enclosure, and being sealed up, has quite overt associations with virginity but is equally suggestive of pregnancy. Mary's hymen as the carnal correlate of the temple curtain shares its function of simultaneously veiling, and indicating, the divine mystery. What would have been the usually -expected rupture of the hymen is transposed to the torn curtain. Torn curtain and intact maternal hymen share the distinctive and crucial characteristic of existing in such a way as to preclude any humanly accountable cause. The divine actor abstains from enacting any violence upon his creature. The crucified holy one erupts through God's own hymen-curtain, signaling the consummation of God's love for man. The cost of God's venture is exacted from the incarnated divinity and registered in his breached body boundary. Mary's creaturely body, by contrast, remains intact. (Although Mary feels a sword pierce her own heart, this is an acute empathetic piercing that does not cut her flesh.)

---

113. This connection is not clearly apparent in current Roman Catholic liturgical practice where the eucharistic bread is not recognizable as such. Overly refined into a crisp wafer, it is neatly snapped rather than torn.

The church has traditionally taught the perpetuity of Mary's virginity. The birthing of Jesus in such a way that his mother remains virginally intact anticipates and mirrors the passing of the deposed, adult Jesus from the sealed sepulcher. Each passing-through is rendered indiscernible to eyes searching for physical evidence. The evidence, instead, is that which confounds the natural law of cause and effect. Each exceptional sign—maternal, intact hymen; sealed, evacuated tomb; torn temple curtain—confounds and confronts with its inexplicability. They exceed and transcend the bounds of human rationality. These physical anomalies challenge those who either see them, hear of them, or read of them. They are left with a choice of either disregarding their own eyes (or the testimony of contemporary eyewitnesses) or accepting that the *words* reliably mean what they say. To commit to the reliability of the text is to commit to *seeing* differently. Such seeing opens mind and heart and transforms one's perception of the real. This type of seeing becomes, as with Fra Filippo Lippi's Virgin, an act of the whole body. Such sight ignites the seer's understanding into an inflationary awareness of the possibilities of the world in which God acts and is present, "For nothing will be impossible with God" (Luke 1:37 NRSV).

The gate is a recurrent biblical motif of safety, protection, and boundary. The closed protective gate through which only the righteous can enter (cf. Ps 118:20) is reiterated and elaborated in several places in the New Testament (Matt 7:13; Luke 13:24; Heb 13:12). The characteristics of the motif are narrowness (few will be able to pass through) and finality (many will clamor unsuccessfully for admittance once the gate has been shut). Jesus in the Fourth Gospel refers to himself as the gate: "I am the gate. Whoever enters by me will be saved" (John 10:9 NRSV; set within the larger passage, John 10:1–10). Jesus here figures himself as the maternal gate (*cervix*) through whom all who would be born to eternal life, must pass—a message of personal exclusivity iterated later in the same gospel: " 'No one comes to the Father except through me' " (John 14:6 NRSV). In the sixth-century devotional Akathist Hymn of the Eastern Orthodox rite, two of the vocatives used of Mary are "door of solemn mystery" (*Ikos* 8) and "gate of salvation" (*Ikos* 10). This prompts the question of how it is that Jesus and Mary can each be identified as the gate of salvation.

One answer is that the flesh of Christ was formed from the flesh of his mother. Mary's maternal body was the gateway through which salvation was born. Mary is therefore the immanent gate, according to the flesh; Jesus the transcendent gate, according to the spirit. This construal alone, though, runs the risk of reducing Mary's person to her flesh, which scripture is careful to avoid doing, and of reducing Jesus to spirit. More helpful is to draw upon the work of Trevor Hart.[114] Hart proposes a strong theological underpinning for creative works of the human imagination. He argues that it is possible to safeguard the absolute, unaided initial creation whereby, in a free act of donation, God chooses to generate something other than himself, while also allowing for the ongoing unfolding of the created order. This unfolding completes God's original creative act. Such human collaboration is also willed by God.[115] This provides the basis by which it is possible to understand Mary and Jesus by the same motif. Jesus figured as birthing mother does not erase his earthly mother. Rather, the motif they share speaks of the reliable resemblance between mother and son, and the relationship between them, as *portals* within their respective orders. Mary as created, cosmic representative, and as specific creature, was essential for the realization of God as an embodied human, an internal participant, within his own creation.

Separating

Childbirth remains the ubiquitous and defining trans-temporal event. Even within the protective ambit of Western medical care, childbirth still exposes the mother to the primal constants of crisis: danger, desire for deliverance, and reliance on the aid of others. She is taking part in an acute way in what Edwin Muir would call the "ancestral pattern," including experiencing at least some of the primary emotional universals: hope, fear, and love. During labor, the mother psychically withdraws from the world; her bodily experience progressively absorbs all her concentration, interest, and energies. A note of dissonance is introduced by the ambivalent status of the vagina. Once the site of receptive *jouissance*, it is now the site of expulsive trauma. While vaginal plasticity is equally able to manage ingress and egress, the disparate maternal experience of birth intrudes into, and shapes the contours of, the wider sexual relationship.

Childbirth is an ambiguous event in terms of personal agency. The mother's body expends energy, but such labor is not always, nor ever only, the effect of deliberate will or effort. The particular mother is the

114. Hart, *Between Image and Word.*
115. Hart, *Between Image and Word,* 124.

one actively giving birth, but birth is also biologically determined and regulated, as are all bodily functions. The birthing process proceeds according to a cascade of chemical cellular signals which are activated irrespective of the mother's will. The status of the laboring mother is therefore ambivalent in philosophic terms, as birth is not unambiguously an act of the acting person. An alternative manner of presenting it is as an act of submission to one's body. A large measure of its poetic force as typology seems to lie in the radical disempowerment of will and ego that it entails, its evocative power lying in maternal dispossession of agency and concomitant reliance on the good will and aid of others.[116] To labor is to be led by the body into a risky and profound new order of knowing.

The difficulty and pain of human birth redounds to the heart of "spousal communion." The causal relationship between sexual union and laboring birth seems ordered towards sharpening consciousness of the meaning, and potential cost, of the sexual act. Coitus, designed from "the beginning" to be organically linked to the fullness of the couple's relationship, is intended to be more than an expression of animal sexual drive. The human sexual urge is not only biological but has an existential dimension.[117] It is ordered towards the continuance of the species but also towards the unique expression of the love between husband and wife. Its moral dimension arises from the conscious decision made as to whether to act upon the sexual urge. The sexual act's potential long-term outcome—the birth, nurturance, and education of a child—demands rational thinking. Human sexual union is intended to be an act of will exercised by both participants in love, where both willingly share in the consequences.

Interest in birth as biological event, and as a personal experience, has burgeoned in the latter twentieth century. One of the influential essays from this period is Julia Kristeva's "Stabat Mater." A reading of Kristeva's essay follows, looking at how it construes the gestational and *postpartum* bodies, and how this speaks to John Paul's theological anthropology.

116. This note of embedded carnal humility acts as reproof against the advice of the panel commissioned by Pope Paul VI to advise about the possible moral permissibility of allowing the use of artificial contraception. The majority report strongly recommended it be allowed on the Baconian ground that technical mastery (that is, imposed human will) of nature was a good. See Waldstein, "Introduction," 100.

117. This is dealt with at some length in Wojtyła, *Love and Responsibility*, 51–54, 62–63.

Julia Kristeva, "Stabat Mater"

The post–Vatican II decade saw a reduction in the Roman Catholic Church's recourse to Mary as an expressive symbol. This demise of the Marian devotional cult left a representative void concerning motherhood. Stimulated by Marina Warner's *Alone of All Her Sex*, Kristeva intended to help fill the void by offering an analysis of motherhood. Her own pregnancy at the time of writing added an unanticipated subjective dimension to her resultant essay, "Stabat Mater." As her essay's title, an incipit of a thirteenth-century hymn, implies, her interest is both historic—how the Virgin's sufferings at the Crucifixion helped shape the church's discourse on motherhood—and contemporary.

Kristeva's abstract mental analysis is counterpointed and tempered by her experience of pregnancy. The resultant text imaginatively registers these two strands in typological fragmentation. The left-hand column of type gives her impressions of being pregnant, occasionally interrupting the more academic text which has to flow around it in typological accommodation. Several pages of two distinct columns of print parallel the experiences of mental analysis and physical experience (*SM* 166–69; 17–25; 175–183). The poetic prose of her pregnancy text amounts to a condensed, non-systematized phenomenology.[118] Broad ranging, her text reflects upon her pregnant self-consciousness; pregnancy as a physical and emotional state; her changed perception of her own body; awareness of her changed position in the social body of women; and her refigured self within the linguistic domain. Her dual texts enact displacement and condensation, two of the actions Kristeva, following Freud, postulates for the prelinguistic, "so-called *primary processes*."[119]

For Kristeva, pregnancy represents a crisis of language. This is made plain at the outset; knowledge of her pregnancy intrudes into the text— "FLASH" (*SM* 162)—with uppercase urgency. Typological orthodoxy is abandoned; conventions of formal presentation, overridden. The spatial irruption forces the reader to decide how to navigate the remaining text: to continue to the section end of the academic text, or to follow the newly

---

118. Kristeva's use of poetic text is a strategy consistent with her theory of the emergent self within the sign-system of the symbolic. She augmented Freudian psychoanalytic theory with the Platonic term, *chora*, which she uses to denote the regulatory process that orders the drives; a process that is a necessary precursor to language acquisition. Kristeva, *Revolution in Poetic Language*, 25–29.

119. Kristeva, *Revolution in Poetic Language*, 25.

inserted left-hand text, or to attempt to read piecemeal, from one text to the other. Pregnancy has brought Kristeva to the edge of linguistic possibility: "language necessarily skims over from afar, allusively. Words that are always too distant, too abstract" (SM 162). For Kristeva, the gap between language and somatic experience threatens, with pregnancy, to become an abyss—the qualitative difference between observation and participation. Pregnancy has thrust her into the gap between the meaning that resides in language signs, and the reality which transcends those signs.[120]

In the experiential storm of pregnancy, Kristeva reaches for the poetic, the function of which is, she says, "to introduce through the symbolic that which works on, moves through, and threatens it [that is, 'the sociosymbolic order']."[121] She therefore uses reconstituted or radically reduced syntax in the left-hand text.[122] By minimizing syntax, the structure that aids intelligibility, she is evoking the roots or "mystery" of language in the musical and rhythmic.[123] Grappling with the limits of communicability is at the root of her experience. Her new knowledge confounds language; the conceptus is quite literally, "unnameable." This apophaticism colors her reflections upon the Virgin whose son, although male, confounded the symbolic. Mary's was the supremely "unnameable" pregnancy; the "Word" she carried was not only electively silenced in her womb but eluded the grasp of words throughout his life.[124]

To be born, though, is to be born into language; each person must "take a chance with meaning under a veil of words" (SM 162). Kristeva frames language as a gamble that may or may not express real meaning. Persons are obliged to speak but speaking embroils the speaker in compromise where words obscure ("veil") even as they attempt to communicate. Language so framed loses its authority and its confidence. It is a none-too-reliable tool. This reductive view of language as "a kind of

---

120. Hart, *Trespass of the Sign*, 115.

121. Kristeva, *Revolution in Poetic Language*, 81.

122. The left-hand column of text becomes less poetic the further removed Kristeva's narrative becomes from the events of pregnancy and birth. The passage of time changes the passage of text which transitions to prose by essay's end, with regularized sentence structure and analysis (180–83).

123. Kristeva was attentive to Mallarmé's connection of the foundational musicality of text with woman. See Kristeva, *Revolution in Poetic Language*, 29.

124. Jesus directly questions his disciples, "But who do you say that I am?" (Mark 8:29 NRSV; cf. Matt 16:15; Luke 9:20).

failure" is one repudiated by Rowan Williams in his book, *The Edge of Words*. Williams makes the case for a more dynamic understanding of the relationship between words and what they represent. In support of this thesis, Williams cites as evidence that words operate in an evolving universe, not a fixed one, and words themselves are part of this dynamism, present within a temporal flow. Words do not effect closure but remain open as the world is "negotiated" anew with each refinement and extension of speech. Rather than seen as a failure, language is seen to be endlessly generative, "prolonging or extending in another mode the life of the environment we inhabit."[125] Williams is proposing what may be called a more feminized view of language and its workings which respond to, and participate in, a motile world. His alternative framing speaks to Kristeva's concerns about the incommensurability of language and fluctuating experience. Williams's view is attractive for its image of accommodating mutuality between words and world.

Kristeva understands language negotiations differently, according to the terms by which she sees it operating. As language belongs, within her scheme, to the male domain of the symbolic, it is part of a world that involves "contests and negotiations over power or . . . play and improvisation."[126] She joins in this game, integrating a type of formalized improvisation in her essay through a series of word associations (Virgin Mary > maternity > language) that culminate in an extended and embedded wordplay upon the incarnated Word -made -flesh. Kristeva omits the verb in her uppercased "WORD FLESH," each term kept discrete. No longer unified with a connective, *word* and *flesh* are kept apart, with the space between the words dividing them.

Kristeva construes *living* and *writing* as oscillating between the two domains of culture ("WORD") and experience ("FLESH"). This oscillation generates the paradox of "deprivation and benefit" (*SM* 168), the binary Kristeva sees as characterizing maternity. In the Christian imaginary, Kristeva sees such "deprivation" in the reduction of Mary's visible maternal body to ear, tears, and breast (*SM* 172–73). Milk and tears are "the metaphors of non-speech, of a 'semiotics' that linguistic communication does not account for" (*SM* 174); here is flesh without word. It is lactation, though, that releases Kristeva's first address to her child: "My son" (*SM* 171); milk flow stimulates word flow. Her simple relational

125. Williams, *Edge of Words*, 109.
126. Williams, *Edge of Words*, 157.

words augment the intimacy her body has already experienced, implying the interdependence of the prelinguistic and the symbolic. The use of the possessive personal pronoun is a hallmark of the language of love and its use communicates a sense of the "spousal meaning" of the body where a subject knows itself through belonging to another. Even after the separation of their shared gestational embodiment, their belonging together is retained and expressed analogically as ownership (cf. *TOB* 33:3). Kristeva shares ground with John Paul II in her experience of the interconnectedness between knowledge, language, and the body.

Both she and the pope intend, in their reflections, to draw upon the fullness of human experience. Kristeva reports objective changes to her body—her new self-knowledge—in highly subjective language. This convergence of the objective and subjective contributes to anthropology by incorporating reflection from within the natal process and event. Where her approach crucially differs from John Paul's is in making no theological connections with her experience. Whereas John Paul saw the meaning of the person in the personal experience of being loved and of loving, Kristeva offers no sense of her relationship with her child's father and treats her motherhood in highly ambivalent fashion. Her ambivalence about motherhood and attendant sense of loss, could speak theologically in its being a type of poverty, for example, in its expenditure of time and energy. Kristeva's personal experience of motherhood alters her own perspective of herself. She seeks to understand motherhood within a postmodern feminist paradigm, focusing on the differences and distance between women and men. Mothers, in Kristeva's analysis, are distant, even excluded from, the paternal symbolic. Motherhood is perceived by Kristeva as somatic suffering. Her poetic text luxuriates in physical descriptions of birth, her child, and her emotional responses to motherhood. She maps the intrusive effects on her body: the baby's cry is "tearing" (*SM* 166), entering into "my skull, the hair" (*SM* 167). The child seems "an inaccessible other" (*SM* 178) and "irreparably alien" (*SM* 179), perceptions that sit in tension with her earlier sense of their belonging. Her chronic perception: "My body is no longer mine" (*SM* 167) ruefully expresses her sense of maternal subjugation. Her maternal body is the ambivalent locus of alienation and communion; ironically, the strength of the gestational bond is that which triggers her sense of somatic alienation. Her *postpartum* body continues to shape itself to the needs of the child in lactation, thereby continuing to undo any sense of an autonomous, contained self.

This overwhelming sense of connectedness does not, for Kristeva, foster a sense of fulfilment. Birth is expressed as a manifestation of the

Freudian death drive, in images of darkness and of proliferating, night-marish displacements of her own body parts. The visibility of written text belies the invisibility of pain which words struggle to adequately articulate. Kristeva's strategy is to use unusual metaphors of spatial ab-stractions: "volumes, expanses, spaces, lines, points" (SM 168) to give a sense of pain's presence, which may be amorphous and diffuse ("volume"; "expanses"), or distractingly precise ("points"). Her metaphors suggest the challenge pain poses to linguistic expression, nudging, as it does, on the frontier of unintelligibility.

More troublingly ambivalent are her dark terms of indeterminate referent: "a living dead"; "monstrous graft"; "My removed marrow." Each phrase could as well refer to her newborn as to the placenta. What the terms do make clear is Kristeva's exaggerated sense of bodily disenfran-chisement. The separation of birth is experienced as a severance, or split, within her own person which is only weakly overcome through respond-ing to her child's laughter (SM 179). Her identity is fissured by a sense of her new and alien maternal corporeality, and her ongoing connection with the "irreparably alien" child. Birth not only separates mother and child, but detaches Kristeva from her sense of self, the birth-event refig-uring her as a new subject (*mother*) within a re-worked body.

Kristeva's psychoanalytic conceptual frame sees *male* and *female* as competitive opposites. The maternal body and what it indicates: the pre-verbal; the "division of language" (SM 178); corporeality, is pitted against the masculine order of the symbolic: law; the analytic. She expressly links the cult of the Virgin Mary with Christianity's strong articulation of the Word, notably in the Johannine prologue, suggesting the Virgin's cult is "compensation" (SM 176) for something difficult to believe in; the physi-cal experience of mothers and mothering providing concrete ballast for the abstraction and conceptual fragility of fatherhood.

Kristeva's bipartite scheme contrasts with the conceptual frame of John Paul's *Theology of the Body* which integrates nature and language. Underpinning John Paul's primary metaphor, "language of the body," is a commitment to the intelligibility of physicality where the body itself, inserted into a receptive world, is part of a meta-system of intelligible, organic patterns. Male-and-female is one of these fundamental patterns. The two sexes incline towards each other, in simultaneous recognition of their homogeneity, and acknowledgement of their complementary differ-ence. By contrast, the father of Kristeva's child is notably absent as *father* exists within the symbolic. John Paul II acknowledges the differences between fatherhood and motherhood, noting in *Mulieris Dignitatem* that a man's parenthood does not have the direct bodily mediation a mother's does. While the father is an observer "outside" pregnancy and birth, this distinction, contra Kristeva, is held within the committed spousal relation which allows the father to "learn his own 'fatherhood' from the mother" (*MD* 18:6).

Becoming a mother activates Kristeva's memory of having been mothered by "a shadow that darkens, soaks me up" (*SM* 180), even in the act of recollection—"Mamma: anamnesis" (*SM* 166). Mothers are viewed as social predicates participating in structures of socio-sexual-linguistic power. Maternal self-sacrifice, interpreted psychoanalytically, anonymizes the mother in order to pass on the "social norm" (*SM* 183). Motherhood on this account is a masochistic collusion with the male, rather than, as in John Paul II's account, a fulfilment of one of the "dimensions of the female vocation" (*MD* 17). Fulfilment is a holistic measure but for Kristeva, such integrated flourishing is inconceivable for a woman whose body is "a place of permanent scission" between upper (head and heart) and lower (legs, signifying mobility and action) by means of the pelvis (reproductive center).[127] Non-integration extends to the female social body, marked by disunity and a judgmental social code, preoccupied with imposing regulatory admonitions; furtherance of group conformity supersedes interpersonal communion. To be singular, or to aspire to singularity, is to invite the opprobrium of other women (*SM* 181–82) as singularity jeopardizes group cohesion.

Kristeva's psychoanalytic focus interprets persons as objects of culture (cf. *TOB* 60:3), her experience of gestation and birth insufficient to redress the balance of cultural (*male*) dominance.[128] As God is not admissible within a psychoanalytic frame, the human is overly determined and there is no grounding of human relationships within the category of *gift*. Human relations are seen in terms of self-enhancement, self-protection and competition, even between mother and child; the group is formed and maintained at the cost of the individual. Kristeva's interpretative frame gives a disturbing overlay to her contemplation of her sleeping son: "neither being nor unborn, neither present nor absent, but real, real inaccessible innocence" (*SM* 172–73).[129] The apophatic contours of her

127. Kristeva, *Revolution in Poetic Language*, 27.

128. See the sometime dominance of the right-hand text, which effectively silences the text dealing with the body (e.g., *SM* 162–66, 169–71, 183–84).

129. Her infant son is not yet, on Freudian terms, a subject, as he is at too early a

response to her son give way to a progressive knowledge of him but she gains fuller "epistemic access"[130] to him only once he is ill; illness is both separator and connector, as it is the *de facto* condition of humanity (*SM* 173). Having expressed her ambivalence about group identity, Kristeva, ironically, only engages more fully with her son once he has exhibited the wounded signs of belonging to the human family.

Kristeva's psychoanalytic approach does not have the internal resources to make satisfying meaning of maternal suffering. Margaret Bruzelius has observed that Kristeva failed, in "Stabat Mater," to reach her intended *telos*.[131] While Kristeva had wanted to move outside a traditional moral frame ("herethics"), and to prioritize maternal somatic experience, she ends, says Bruzelius, at the old destination, where mothers "purchase speech at the price of suffering." Bruzelius attributes this directly to the inspiration Kristeva found in the *Mater Dolorosa* figure. This figure, for Bruzelius, identifies so intensely with the death of her son, that her own identity is erased. (John Paul II would see a misunderstanding of Marian self-identification in Bruzelius's assessment. Mary's suffering was attributable to the unity in love of mother and son. In that suffering unity, Mary has not lost, but rather found, her truest identity.) Contra Bruzelius, suffering within a classical Christian worldview can become a way to draw near to the heart of God, a theme developed by Paul in the second epistle to the Corinthians, and the subject of a study by A. E. Harvey.[132] Harvey sees Paul's letter as reversing the usual negative evaluation of suffering. This reevaluation followed Paul's recognition that his own suffering had brought him closer to the suffering Christ. Proximity to the suffering Christ can transform the fellow sufferer. In direct proportion to the extent to which one's suffering is conjoined with Christ's, it can be transformed into a meaningful positive, aiding Christ in the ongoing work of salvation. The transformative experience of birth can be understood in Harvey's terms as suffering for the sake of another that aligns the sufferer with Christ's laboring passion. This conformity to Christ constitutes one part of the ongoing project of salvation: restoration of the divine image.

---

developmental stage. See Kristeva, *Revolution in Poetic Language*, 25. Kristeva's use of "real" contrasts with "symbolic" (26).

130. Hart, *Trespass of the Sign*, 93.

131. Bruzelius, "Mother's Pain, Mother's Voice."

132. Harvey, *Renewal through Suffering*.

Overview of Kristevan Perceptions

The typology of Kristeva's essay performs a textual destabilization—a literary representation of the destabilizing experience of gestation and birth. As already noted, though, the analytic text dominates the emotional, subjective text, in some places effectively silencing it. This analytic textual dominance ironically promotes the male domain, confirming what Kristeva understood to be entrenched male cultural determinism. Her stated intention—to redress the female-maternal representational void in the church—shows the strain of the attempt in the overtaking of her poetic prose by the male language domain. This tension illustrates the problem of whether it is possible for *knowledge* to cross the sex divide, especially when each sex is seen to operate within different linguistic domains (cf. James McAuley's "Pietà"). This crisis of knowledge is exacerbated by her child with whom she feels overwhelmingly conjoined. Her troubling sense of overconnection with her infant will be eased, though, through the child's entry into the male language domain, as learning to speak accelerates mother-child separation.[133] It is therefore the male domain that facilitates and helps realize a restored (and, at least in Kristeva's case, desired) maternal sense of individuated identity; a cooperative pattern of male-female inter-relation lends support to just the sort of paradigm that is explicated in John Paul's *Theology of the Body.*

Kristeva's difficulties around *knowledge* can be compared with the Genesis 4:1 account of knowledge acquisition. Adam comes to know himself as differentiated from the animals, sensing himself to be a personal subject (*TOB* 21:1). John Paul comments (*TOB* 21:2) on the active-passive distinction within the text (man who knows; woman who is known). John Paul does not see this as entrenching male hierarchy and female subordination, rather as indicating the hiddenness ("mystery") of femininity which waits until it is manifest and revealed through motherhood (*TOB* 21:2). John Paul explicitly claims the mutuality of male and female knowledge owing to the nature of their spousal relationship (*TOB* 21:3). While there is no hint of such knowing through begetting in "Stabat Mater," Kristeva's text orients itself towards the possibility of such mutual knowledge in that she, as woman and as mother, gives analytic attention (*male*) to gestation and early motherhood (*female*), so tentatively beginning to bridge the otherwise estranged two.

---

133. Stadlen, *What Mothers Do*, 181.

Separation is one of the implied, recurrent concerns of "Stabat Mater." For Kristeva, the predicament of motherhood is how to retain an interior sense of, and an actual experience of, her subjectivity through her mothering. Kristeva's attitudes to her changed status, newly recontoured life, and to her child, express her maladjustment to her transitional lifestage. Her reportage is valuable for the contribution it makes to a fuller imaginary of motherhood, part of a wider secular discussion with theological relevance (akin to Sarah Coakley's stated intention to "grope towards a more equitable representation of male and female creatureliness").[134] Kristeva's preparedness to face, and name, her ambivalent, even negative, perceptions of motherhood provide an alternative perspective from that of John Paul II's *Mulieris Dignitatem*, for example, which seems to assume that mothers adjust seamlessly to motherhood, even while acknowledging that it is the woman "who *pays* directly for this shared generation" (*MD* 18). Gestation and early motherhood are personally significant for Kristeva in their felt force although she does not give a sense of how this force may be otherwise, and more widely, significant.

Janet Soskice sees in the Christian doctrine of the Trinity a defense against a style of egotistical thinking that does not admit true otherness. These so-called "philosophies of the One," have been criticized, she notes, by Simone de Beauvoir and Luce Irigaray for their ego-centrism; the other who is "not-me" confirming the perceiving subject as "the One."[135] In "Stabat Mater," it is unclear whether Kristeva formulates herself as "the One" or the subordinate "other." She appears not to see any real autonomy or sovereignty for women.

Kristeva seems to confirm the intimation of Valerie Goldstein. Goldstein's 1960 article criticized the way several of her contemporary male theologians had pictured the human condition. They had ascribed man's "predicament as rising from his separateness and the anxiety occasioned by it."[136] Goldstein criticized their unconscious male bias, arguing instead that the female mode of experience was not separation but unremitting engagement with others, often at the expense of self. The distinctiveness of Kristeva's reported experience is her desire for psychic separation from her child. Unlike the usual coupling Goldstein had identified of separation and alienation, Kristeva's essay unexpectedly yokes *connection* with alienation. This unusual coupling potentially implies

134. Coakley, *God, Sexuality, Self*, 353.

135. Soskice, "Trinity and Feminism," 140.

136. Goldstein, "Human Situation," 100.

significant theological difficulties. Christian doctrine is based on an understanding of God as one who initiates, seeks, and desires an ongoing and
substantive relationship with each of his human creatures. God as infused
presence in creation, and present in multiple modes (in humans; in the
eucharistic presence; in holy scripture; in the church; and in those who
consciously know and abide in God) may imply, on Kristeva's reckon-
ing, a divine presence too ubiquitous; a relation too inescapably present.
Yet trinitarian doctrine, as explicated by Soskice, confirms John Paul II's
findings that subjectivity is configured by loving relations, not in solitude.

Kristeva's evocation of motherhood is limited by the parameters of
her psychoanalytic worldview, which offers no transcendence of either
personal, or social, past or present. For Kristeva, sexual difference functions culturally as negatively discriminatory for women (who, nevertheless, collude in their own discrimination). This worldview contrasts with
the Genesis stories where human sexual difference invites connection, and
through marriage and the family, is ordered towards founding a binding community of love. On the Kristevan account, sexual difference is a
polarity bridged only by the subsuming of women into the male symbolic,
rather than being something that tends towards binding the two in unity.
Kristeva's essay seeks to give a true account of her experiential knowledge
of early motherhood however her experience is self-interpreted in cultural
terms that do not offer a way out or forward.

Remaining

Symbiosis

The human placenta images symbiosis. It evades classification as either
maternal or *fetal* as it is formed from both maternal and fetal contribu-
tions. Upon implantation in the endometrium at about two weeks' post-
fertilization, the localized endometrial cells undergo cellular changes.
This reaction results in the part of the endometrium underlying the
implantation site forming a compact layer. This layer, the decidual plate,
forms the maternal part of the placenta. Microscopic villi extrude from
the extra-embryonic cellular membrane—the fetal contribution. The
placental villi allow for symbiotic exchange between mother and fetus:
maternal oxygen and nutrients diffuse through the walls of the villi to

enter the blood of the fetus; fetal carbon dioxide and waste products diffuse into maternal blood.[137]

In the placenta, *maternal* and *fetal* are each distinguishable, the two not admixed, yet forming a unity of substance and function which operates, and exists, only by virtue of its twoness-in-oneness. In this uni-duality, the placenta analogically images the hypostatic union: two *natures* present in the one hypostasis.[138] It is both fully of the mother and fully of the fetus. The placenta expands and elaborates the divine indicative of the two becoming one flesh (Gen 2:24). It is not only man and woman who shall mysteriously become one within their spousal relation; mother and child instantiate a related, though different, redrawing of the bounds of separateness and relationship. The fleshly unity of the placenta forecloses either party claiming *ownership* of it as it belongs to both simultaneously. Paul Ricoeur identified the hallmark of metaphor as being the simultaneous presence of *cataphasis* (it is) and *apophasis* (it is not). The metaphoric terms play off each other and with each other, dynamic interplay being the marker of "the truthful poetic image."[139] The metaphoric relationship opens the reader's capacity to see, and to see differently. The metaphoric terms the placenta invites us to see differently are those foundational to relationship: *I* and *you*. The placental organ seems especially to affirm the words of philosopher John Macmurray, as cited by Trevor Hart, that "the unit of the personal is not the 'I,' but the 'You and I.'"[140] More recently, Hart notes that David Ford has expressed a similar affirmation, that personal relations constitute personhood, with Ford asking rhetorically: "Is there any layer of self where there are no others?"[141]

The placental *selves* act in symbiotic harmony as to attempt otherwise, by for example, acting competitively or in isolation, would be to collapse the whole gestational relationship. The biblical creation narratives understand each human life as being a new instantiation of the creative act of God. Eve's cry upon the birth of Cain: "I have produced a man with the help of the Lord" (Gen 4:1 NRSV), acknowledges that human biology alone does not account for human generation. The divine-human relationship of creative cooperation is concretely and

137. Collins et al., *Oxford Handbook of Obstetrics and Gynaecology*, 18–25.

138. The similarity of metaphor to the hypostatic union is noted by Janet Soskice. See Soskice, *Metaphor and Religious Language*.

139. Hart, *Between Image and Word*, 25.

140. Macmurrray, *Persons in Relation*, 61.

141. Ford, *Shape of Living*, 1–3.

metaphorically represented in gestation, where one subject is enclosed within the nourishing, cleansing divine-maternal. Within the parameter of this metaphor, *human* is represented by the fetus. Disregard for the (divine) maternal context in which it lives would be analogous to disrupted placentation which, in a human fetus, may occasion intrauterine growth restriction, or miscarriage.[142]

Symbiosis is at the center of Glyn Maxwell's investigation into the nature and mechanics of poetry writing. Maxwell bathetically calls the poetic fundamentals "*something* and *nothing*."[143] Maxwell is keen to anchor poetry-making in the physical, so begins with a consideration of the blank whiteness of paper or screen ("nothing") in his chapter, "White." For Maxwell, the imagistic qualities of poetry do not in the first instance refer to literary device. Prior to any mental images a poem may evoke, it itself is an image on a page. Maxwell is suggesting that the boundaries between *text* and *image* are porous.[144] Concrete materiality of page or screen represents potentiality, and grounds the possibility of textual embodiment. Maxwell's thesis can be illustrated and supported by looking at a poem by R. S. Thomas, reproduced below,which makes deliberate and effective use of its whiteness.

R. S. Thomas, "The Annunciation by Veneziano"

The messenger is winged
            and the girl
haloed a distance
        between them
and between them and us
down the long path the door
through which he has not
          come
on his lips what all women
        desire to hear
in his hands the flowers that
        he has taken from her.

142. Fox, "Placentation."

143. Maxwell, *On Poetry*, 10.

144. In related vein, M. Wynn Thomas argues for not regarding the semiotic systems within which art and poetry function as being rigidly self-enclosed. In support of his proposition, he cites artistic images that fuse writing and painting. See Thomas, *Serial Obsessive*, 312–18.

Written as a poetic response to a medieval predella panel, the poem exploits the imagistic qualities of words on the page, printed form interacting symbiotically with poetic content. Thomas's poem mimetically positions the painted protagonists within his poem so they visually align with their position on the picture plane: "The messenger" on the left-hand side; "the girl" on the right. The poem's second line begins with a deep indent so that it appears to be a step down from the final word of the first line. This visual arrangement both retains a connection between the lines, and reorders their disconnection. The lines, like the painted protagonists, are each one's *other* yet their stepped relationship evokes their connectedness, as well as their metaphysical difference and distance. Thomas's eye is held by the empty space between the figures. It is *distance* which dominates his poem, the word itself suspended at the end of line three. Line four repeats the wide indent of line two, the arrangement of the words on the page registering spatial distance. There is a visual (and so, material) "gap" but one that can be "leant over"; the word placements register both space and a visual "bridge."[145] The spatial patterning and the syntax of the opening lines interact so that "haloed," appearing on the left-hand side of the text, is both the angel's, being on *his* side of the painting/poem, and Mary's, as the syntax makes clear. This shared holiness is the implied *bridge* between them.

It is Thomas's use of spatial form that redeems his poem from what would otherwise be, according to contemporary sensibilities, unacceptable patriarchy. Thomas's angel is gendered male and is imputed to know what it is that "all women desire to hear." This authorizes, by divine association, failure to invite, or listen to, a woman's words on the assumption that they will affirm those a male ascribes her. Such a reading would shut down the poem's possibility of communicating truth to contemporary readers. A way is available through this seeming impasse. In his exploitation of the gaps of lineation, Thomas has constructed a poem that offers a more benign reading that does not obliterate Mary's agency. The small clusters of words positioned at the ends of those *lines* which consist mostly of white spaces, can be read as their own vertical column of text, a literal subtext within the poem. These right-end words form a skeletal summary that enact the structure of erotic love, where it is precisely the *gap* of distance which is overcome: "and the girl," "between them," "come," "desire to hear," "he has taken from her." In this substructure,

---

145. These three images appear in another of Thomas's poems, "The Gap," from *Frequencies* (1978), which is discussed in Davis, *R. S. Thomas*, 87–90.

Mary's consent is intimated by her "desire to hear," the words now detached from the problematic line above. Mary is now the agent of desire where "hear" alludes to the traditional painterly motif of the conception taking place via Mary's ear; Word enters aural orifice. Thomas's technique of careful word placement on the page activates a two-fold symbiosis between the inspirational painting and his poetic response, rendered as image, and between the narrative content and its visual representation. Thomas's knowing manipulation of the white ground would seem to overthrow Maxwell's thesis, as blank space is here not passively present as "nothing." Maxwell himself, though, is aware that empty whiteness is not a *tabula rasa*, but for the poet "it's half of everything."[146] It signs both its own presence, and the potential of another presence. The whiteness, that is, operates in receptive mode; "white" and "black" are complementary and able to combine generatively.

Maxwell sees other symbioses between the human body and poetry. Having considered words as image, he then considers them as sounds and the feelings these induce in the body, in his chapters, "Pulse" and "Chime." In his discussion of rhythm and meter, he explores the symbiotic relationship between formal rhyme schemes and how these affect a sensitive delivery of the poem when read aloud. The metrical beats he likens analogously to the bar lines of musical notation, constituting a "silent skeletal frame."[147] While verse can be written as a strict, formal pattern of beats, it cannot be declaimed with the exact regularity of a metronome without damaging the effect of the poem. Read aloud sensitively, the beats are "as likely to fall through silence as upon sound."[148] This is not a novel insight of Maxwell's. He is describing the common practice of, for example, actors, who adjust their readings so as to accommodate the regular rhythms of poetry while allowing these rhythms to function in the background; they aim for a symbiosis between the regularized cadences of the synthetic scheme and those of daily speech, which can be thought of as the organic scheme.

146. Maxwell, *On Poetry*, 11.

147. Maxwell, *On Poetry*, 88.

148. Maxwell, *On Poetry*, 88.

Temporariness

The human placenta acts as the fetal "renal, respiratory, hepatic, gastrointestinal, endocrine, and immune systems."[149] The unit *mother-and-child* is, for the duration of gestation, a maternal-fetal-placental one. The placenta grows and differentiates extremely rapidly throughout its short lifespan, effectively *dying* upon delivery.[150] Uniquely among human organs, the placenta is designed to be temporary. For all its temporariness, its task completed upon delivery, it is increasingly seen to be an important indicator of long-term maternal and fetal health.[151] Its dysfunction is implicated in diverse chronic diseases and it is attracting considerable research attention.

The placenta can be read as metonymic of Christ.[152] As with the biological placenta, Christ offers himself as nourishment for the developing person, acting as the communicative interface between person and world, and person and the Father. The analogy can be developed further with the *in utero* person seen as metonymic of the whole human race. Once the child-person is sufficiently mature to survive *ex utero*, the placenta-Christ detaches. This reading harmonizes with the scriptural attestation of Christ's departure from the world in the Ascension where, placenta-like, he detaches-ascends, no longer visible to sight and no longer present in the world in the same way (Luke 24:51; Acts 1:9–11). The child-world is not left to starve. It continues to be fed by Christ but now in a veiled way via the eucharistic species of bread and wine.[153] Within this analogy, the loss of the placenta (Ascension of Christ) constitutes a first weaning. In this loss, though, is gain. The organs of the fetal body realize themselves upon delivery when they are in the world for which they were intended, developing through being exercised. Analogously,

149. Guttmacher et al., "Human Placenta Project."

150. James et al., "Can We Fix It?"

151. Nelson, "Does a Picture of the Human Placenta."

152. The placental Christ appears as a poetic motif in "Canto for a Summer Sunday in Ordinary Time": "Christ the placenta / self-addressed-stamped / envelops the world / embryo" (Bickimer, *Christ the Placenta*, 15).

153. This analogous talk of Christ's temporariness is not to gainsay the thrust of the Resurrection-Ascension testimonies, which affirm the permanence of Christ's earthly body, now relocated to the heavenly sphere. The mode of Christ's presence has changed from the straight-forwardly fleshly to the ritually-confected eucharistic signs. David Jones helpfully calls the Last Supper "abstract," rather than "representational" art. See Jones, "Art and Sacrament," 170.

the believer's faith (an *inner eye*) is developed when Christ's earthly flesh is no longer present.[154] The placenta is ordered towards growing the fetus so that extra-uterine life is possible, the placental-Christ so that post-mortem life is possible. The peeling-away of the *postpartum* placenta metonymically images all human persons who also, at death, detach from earthly life. Death as the peeling away of the fleshly body is anticipated in a progressive series of sloughings-off, visibly signed in the morphology of the aging body.[155]

Remainder

Flesh is remaindered at death, evacuated of life. The mystery of this state of affairs is that the body, which has lived as a unity of flesh and spirit, experiences a cleavage at death. This crisis presses against any certainty as to how human identity is constituted, let alone in what mode a person may be deemed to exist postmortem. There are biblical attestations of some persons exceptionally bypassing the norm of disincarnation: Elijah, who "ascended in a whirlwind into heaven" (2 Kgs 2:11 NRSV) and Jesus's post-resurrection Ascension (Acts 1:9–11). Additionally, Mary's assumption into heaven has been attested to in the early church, although not uniformly.[156]

The human body is treated with dignity and seriousness in the He-braic-Christian scriptures.[157] There is a dual sense of its being inherently

154. At his post-resurrection appearance to Thomas, which convinces the apostle of the truth of the Resurrection, Jesus says that those who believe the gospel without physically seeing the Christ are more blessed. See John 20:29.

155. R. S. Thomas uses a placental image in his poem, "Dialectic." His perspective on the placenta is darker than the reading above. The poem deals with the silence of God who implants his truth into persons, only to then be "sloughed off like some afterbirth of the spirit." See Davis, *R. S. Thomas*, 91.

156. O'Carroll notes that St. Epiphanius (c. AD 315–403) was non-committal in his writing on the subject, entertaining several possibilities about how Mary's life ended. He does suggest she may be the woman referred to in Revelation 12:14, who was "carried off." See the entries "Assumption of Our Lady" and "Death of Mary" in O'Carroll, *Theotokos*. The assumption of Mary was declared a dogma of the church by Pius XII on November 1, 1950, in the Apostolic Constitution, *Munificentissimus Deus*.

157. Respect for mortal remains persists within secular culture, even though its expression may be inconsistent. Follow-up reportage by the BBC of a Channel 4 *Dispatches* program registered the political fallout from an allegation that ten NHS trusts had been involved in the incineration of fetal remains, along with other clinical waste, at their hospitals. Some incinerated fetuses had been intentionally aborted. The

sacred and having the potential to become so. The Hebrew scriptures disallow heathen mourning practices that cut or tattoo the body (Lev 19:28). Leviticus 20 gives an extensive list of proscribed sexual practices which Paul draws upon in his letter to the Corinthians, exhorting them to practice sexual chastity (1 Cor 6:13–18). Paul's reasoning draws upon the strength of two metaphors: that the body of the believer is incorporated into Christ's body (1 Cor 12:27, *inter alia*), and that the believer is "a temple of the Holy Spirit" (1 Cor 6:19 NRSV). As sexual partners become "one flesh," having multiple or illicit sexual partners dishonors Christ. Paul's argument distinguishes sins "outside the body" from those "against the body itself," implying the latter's more damaging and more serious adverse effects. His maximal assessment of the body, and its especial status, sits in tension with the body's disintegration upon death when it becomes a problem to be disposed of.

John Paul II fleshes out the implications of the Pauline Corinthian epistle. The voluntary actions of the body are the actions of the person and, owing to a person's free will, indicate the internal character of that person. The consequence of the first sin was instability of the male-female union which John Paul sees as a cleavage in the personal subject. God indicates in Genesis 3:16 that the original, good desire for personal union will still operate but in compromised fashion. Such desires will henceforth be directed "toward the appeasement of the body, often at the cost of an authentic and full communion of persons" (*TOB* 31:3). The male-female relationship has changed from a "*communion of persons*" to "a relationship *of possession*" (*TOB* 31:3). Sin results in a distortion of the spousal meaning of the body, where "spousal meaning" is widely defined to include, but not be restricted to, sexual relations. It includes "the full consciousness of the human being" and "every effective experience of the body in its masculinity and femininity." Personal freedom to bestow oneself as gift has been thrown off balance and become deformed (*TOB* 31:6; 32:4–6). To speak realistically of humans post-Fall is to take account of this deformity. Jesus indicates as much when, in the Fourth Gospel, he

method of disposal elicited widespread criticism, and calls for the practice to end. While the reportage did not focus upon terminology, the different associations of *incinerate*, and *cremate*, registered differing moral attitudes. At stake is the dignity of the person, which extends to fitting disposal of carnal remains. The social ritual of cremation is deemed respectful of the deceased; incineration not. See "Warning Over Burning Aborted Foetuses."

expresses sensible mistrust of those who form a shallow commitment to him owing to the signs they see him perform (John 2:24–25; *TOB* 34:3).

The scriptural and papal explications above shed light upon why, in a few cases of exceptionally holy persons, their bodies are not left as a troublesome remainder upon earth. The assumption (or, in Jesus's case, Ascension) of these persons confirms their holiness. The saintly life is one of full integrity, meaning there is no cleavage between the inner life of thoughts and feelings, and the outer life of speech and actions. A few holy lives have been memorialized by the exceptional and supernatural preservation of their bodily remains, postmortem. A Pauline epistle gives the theological rationale for such a seeming impossibility: that in Christ, "the whole fullness of deity dwells bodily" (Col 2:9 NRSV). As Jesus is divine, those who dwell in him share in the fullness of his personal holiness. Such persons—saints—have so lived their lives that, even in death, their bodies continue to act as *signs*, pointing beyond themselves, to God.

Jesus's Ascension into heaven means his body is not remaindered on earth. It becomes available for those living on earth via his sent Spirit and eucharistic presence. The placental-Christic body, temporarily entombed, does not remain so, as Christ is more than a "temporary theophany," no longer needed.[158] Jesus's Ascension completes the process of birth, as does a placental delivery. The Ascension as completion of the Resurrection is implicit in the words of the Johannine Jesus: "No one has ascended into heaven except the one who descended from heaven, the Son of Man" (John 3:13 NRSV). Later in the gospel, in his first post-resurrection appearance, Jesus anticipates his Ascension: "Do not hold on to me, because I have not yet ascended to the Father" (John 20:17 NRSV).

Interface

The placenta is the organ of interface, instantiating *between-ness*. It is inside the mother's body, yet outside her own organ systems which sustain her life. The mother's pregnant body, protecting the fetal environment from pathogens, is a correlate of the "temple of the Holy Spirit" (1 Cor 6:19). Paul explains that sexual relations with prostitutes are analogous to profanation of the temple. The corporeal body, like the Jerusalem temple,

---

158. Resurrected and ascended, Christ's flesh is eternally with the Father: "The incarnation is not mere expediency" (Hart, *Between Image and Word*, 76).

acts as "in some sense, a barrier that separates the realm of purity inside from the evil cosmos outside."[159]

The maternal resonance in the remainder of 1 Corinthians 6:19, is strong: the Holy Spirit is "within you," is that "which you have from God," and means that "you are not your own." *Maternity* also associates with *temporariness*, as gestation is of fixed duration. This harmonizes with another Pauline metaphor for the body: "the earthly tent we live in" (2 Cor 5:1 NRSV). Paul contrasts the temporary body of flesh with our enduring, eschatological one: "a building from God, a house not made with hands." Nijay Gupta points out that neither is the physical body made by human hands, in contrast with that of idols. It is this contrast that makes Paul's temple analogy in 1 Corinthians, apposite.[160]

While the Corinthian epistles seem to imply that physical bodies are "dispensable visual aids,"[161] scriptural references to a general eschatological resurrection, which Jesus's Resurrection anticipates and makes possible, suggest otherwise. The body's status is more mysterious; *mystery* here understood not only as something closed off to knowledge, but, following David Jones's usage, that which discloses and shows forth something.[162] Such mystery is manifest in the physical remains of saints, which Roman Catholic, and Eastern Orthodox Christians, understand to be active interfaces between heaven and earth. Russian Orthodox priest and theologian, Sergius Bulgakov (1871–1944), is helpful in explaining how saints' relics are believed to function. He argues that the bodies of saints, having been sanctified by the Holy Spirit during their earthly lives, have undergone a substantive change. This is analogous to the substantive change effected in the eucharistic signs at the *epiclesis*. While continuing to be ordinarily visible to the eye, the bread and the wine are each now "an appearance, an opaque veil," the new reality present being "incorruptible holy flesh."[163]

While the call to sanctity is universal, saints are those whom the church confirms have actualized such holiness. Bulgakov uses a maternal image to illustrate personal saintliness: "man stops being man by making

159. Gupta, "Which Body Is a Temple?," 527.

160. Gupta, "Which Body Is a Temple?," 531.

161. Hart, *Between Image and Word*, 58.

162. Jones, "Preface to 'The Anathemata,'" 129.

163. Bulgakov, *Relics and Miracles*, 17.

of himself a place for God; but thereby he becomes truly man."[164] His words are prescient of John Paul's: that man finds himself in giving himself. A consequence of original man's first sin was the destabilization of the intimate relationship between flesh and spirit. As a result of original sin, the spirit of a person who dies is disincarnated; flesh reverts to matter. Even after the original sin was committed, each person still retained personal freedom; each remained a moral agent who could choose how to act, with each choice having consequences. It is therefore possible, by cultivating personal holiness—choosing to act aright—to reverse the ill effects of sin. One instantiation of this is the restoration of the original unity of flesh and spirit. Saints are those who have become holy; restored. Upon their deaths, even though their bodies may have suffered restrictions in function owing to illness or natural degeneration, they serve as confirmation of that to which Sarah Coakley draws attention in the writings of Gregory of Nyssa, that "change does not necessarily signal decay" but can be a mark of ongoing transformation, of the type Paul refers to in 2 Corinthians 3:18.[165]

Bulgakov argues that the real consequence of each human life is radical participation in the creation of his or her resurrection body. Although saints die, their life choices have so internalized God's transformative grace that they are, says Bulgakov, "in a special, transfigured state of spiritual body."[166] A saint acts as an interface between heaven and earth, abiding in both spheres. Saintly earthly remains are "living remains."[167] These may appear to be only the "dry bones" of Ezekiel (themselves placental in their status as remainder), or, less often, as incorrupt flesh. According to a metaphoric scheme of the obstetric body, saints' relics are placental, in being remainders, although their relics continue to act as interfaces between two environments, providing sustenance for those who come to them in faith.[168] To use the image of John Paul II, saintly remains

---

164. Bulgakov, *Relics and Miracles*, 19. Elizabeth A. Johnson summarizes the Kabbalistic doctrine of creation as being possible owing to God's free self-limitation. God contracts, so space is available for the world. The world is that which is brought forth from God while remaining in God. Johnson notes critically the use of this maternal figure, which invokes "quintessentially a female experience," by several theologians who nevertheless persist in using male imagery of God. See Johnson, *She Who Is*, 233–34.

165. Coakley, "Eschatological Body," 68.

166. Bulgakov, *Relics and Miracles*, 29.

167. Bulgakov, *Relics and Miracles*, 30.

168. The existence of saintly relics and of saintly incorrupt bodies steers a course

indicate the nuptial bonding between the saint and God, the consummate expression of which is the bond between Mary and her son.

Mary occupies a unique place in the panoply of saints. She is the mother of the Son, the first to be reborn of the Spirit at the Johannine crucifixion scene, and the fully realized disciple. No longer a pilgrim, she has reached the *telos* of her journey of faith, which is expressed in the church's confirmatory dogma of her assumption into heaven. Now fully present in heaven, no earthly remains of her exist, which could otherwise have been discovered and venerated as relics. Mary is the token and first-fruit of the transformation of the world, brought about through the life-death-resurrection of her son. The new and the old do not only coexist; they are now, in Mary, unified. Academic theologian and religious sister, Mary Timothy Prokes, expresses the relationship as, "a nuptial bonding between the already glorified and what remains in present dimensions of earth . . . there is an indissolubility between what is and what is to come."[169] Mary's body is no longer humanly limited. It now resembles, in some way, the body of her resurrected son. She, as he, is no longer subject to the restraints of time and space, so is able to be present both in heaven and on earth. She, as he, is now able to be sent on specific missions by the Father. Mary, sent from heaven, has manifested over the course of the centuries, to certain persons in specific locations, the greatest number of manifestations having occurred in the latter twentieth century. These visitations of the Virgin can prove to be highly contentious, mimetically acting out the dividing "sword" of her son's presence (cf. Matt 10:34). Marian apparitions or visitations tend to polarize opinion as to their veracity. The official Roman Catholic Church position is to treat purported

---

between two differing ways of understanding the body. One, indebted to Plato, sees the body as that existent behind which, or within which, veiled, is its meaning. This corresponds with the literary critical method of structuralism, which sees textual meaning hidden behind the text. The other, influenced by Aquinas, sees the body's material existence not as veil interposed between the body and its truth but rather that as which the subject lives. Critical attention is turned to the fabric of this veil rather than to something additional to it. This corresponds with the literary critical method of post-structuralism. See Barthes, "Theory of the Text," 39. The exceptionalism of the incorrupt saintly body draws attention to itself for the purpose of pointing, Marian-like, to Christ, whose ongoing life infused the saint's; immanence, and transcendence are co-present in the body-sign.

169. Prokes, "Nuptial Meaning of the Body," 168–69.

visions as private revelations, to be investigated, if warranted, thereby conveniently distancing the magisterium.[170]

The phenomenon of Marian apparitions lays open some attitudes of the church hierarchy towards both the laity, and the corporeal body. The phenomenon is nearly always laity-led and the visionaries are overwhelmingly women.[171] Michael O'Carroll notes the exegetical circle operative between clergy and laity regarding apparitions: the laity is instructed not to accept any apparition prior to its church approval; the church bases its decision on whether an alleged apparition warrants investigation upon the level of interest and belief displayed by the laity.[172] Furthermore, of the three types of visions listed by Richard Rutt: "corporeal," where a person is objectively seen; "imaginative," where the person appears in the mind of the witness; and "spiritual," where there is no image involved, the church esteems the latter most highly, "corporeal" least so.[173] As the phenomenon of Marian apparitions is largely female laity-led, and the catholic church hierarchy is exclusively male, the preference for a disincarnated mediation aligns with gender stereotypes (materiality associated with the female; rationality, esteemed more highly, with the male). This suggests a persistence in the marginalizing of the feminine, by imputing lesser importance to the dominant mode of Marian "interventions."[174] This preference sits in tension, seemingly overlooked, with the biblical instances of the vigorously faithful being blessed with what they physically see, notably Moses seeing the retreating glory of the Lord (Exod 33:18–23), and the Promised Land (Num 27:12); Simeon seeing Christ, the promise of Israel (Luke 2:25); the post-resurrection appearances of Christ, witnesses of which expressly attested to the corporeality of Christ's presence (Luke 24:42; John 20:27).

The locations of Marian apparitions qualify as *thin* places, a term used in Celtic spirituality. In these places, there is a palpable lessening of the usual sense of separation between this world and the spiritual realm. They are liminal places, where the interface of the temporal order and the supernatural order is perceived and for some, experienced. These *loci* function, although in expanded and amplified fashion, as do saintly

170. Rutt, "Why Should He Send His Mother?," 274.

171. Rutt, "Why Should He Send His Mother?," 274.

172. O'Carroll, "Apparitions of Our Lady," 288.

173. Rutt, "Why Should He Send His Mother?," 277.

174. Rutt, "Why Should He Send His Mother?," 277. This is Rutt's collective term for locutions, visions, and apparitions.

relics, prompting apprehension of spiritual presence through specific embodiments. They attest that even in the current period, the *metaxis* between Christ's Ascension and his Second Coming, it is possible to live a life that can, at least at times, penetrate the veil between the earthly and the spiritual. The world's *now* is *in-betweenness*, the figure of the placental Christ answered by the figure of the placental world.

Direct experience of Marian apparition sites is frequently reported as being transformative or *marking* in some way, another connection with the placental motif. The umbilical cord, attaching placenta and neonate, is clamped and cut after delivery. The umbilical stub finally detaches, but the site of its connection remains permanently visible upon the body. The umbilicus persistently and silently attests to the natal mother. It is a sign of radical connectedness and receptivity, of our bodies being our own, yet more than our own. Every human life begins within a mother, anchored in her. The umbilicus declares the m/other who m/othered me. Its presence also memorializes the placenta. Even that temporary organ is honored; corporeal utilitarianism is rejected. Concerning the body, *remainder* is not synonymous with *refuse*. Perhaps today, one of the most garrulous attestations of the umbilical and placental connection to the mystery of the body, and its divine Originator, is that of burgeoning placental and umbilicus stem cell research, carried out in the hope of renewal, regeneration and restitution of imperfect bodies.

6

Living Poem of the Father, for Christ

all men and women are entrusted
with the task of crafting their own life

. . . they are to make of it a work of art

—JOHN PAUL II, "LETTER TO ARTISTS"

THE JUDEO-CHRISTIAN UNDERSTANDING IS that the created order was gratuitously willed into being by God, from the excess of his love. All living things are alive by God's *fiat*. Being wanted and loved for oneself by God applies equally to all persons. This is the macro structure of creation. There is also a *micro* dimension to this structure: each person is called into being for a specific, God-ordained purpose; for a particular participation in, or contribution to, the ongoing outworking of salvation. To speak of a specific person's *purpose* or *reason* for existence is not to imply necessity on the part of God, nor compulsion on the part of the creature; neither is a divine utilitarianism at work. Having found God, and living in loving relationship with him, a primary task of the person is to discern and live out one's particular life's purpose. If received and responded to favorably, God endows each person with whatever is necessary to bring that life-task to fruition. Mary's divinely intended participation in salvation history is singular and exalted. Through her, salvation entered the world in the person of her son, Jesus, so Mary is the mother of salvation.

Christians believe Jesus to be equally divine as he is human, so Mary is also *Theotokos,* the mother of God.

The reciprocal nature of the divine-human relation (man dependent on God for life; God choosing to *depend* on man's agency) is seen most clearly and fully in the relation between Mary and God. Mary lives in the freedom of the covenant God made with her people. God had revealed to the Israelites how to live in a way pleasing to him, and Mary is faithful to this revelation. When, at the Annunciation, Mary hears of the extraordinary life task that God had prepared her for—to be the virginal mother of a son supernaturally conceived by the Holy Spirit—she accepts in the humility of trusting incomprehension.

Mary's maternal vocation means she is entrusted with authority over her developing child; an authority that derives from, and is confirmed by, her willingness to discern and serve her child's needs, upon which, she acts. In her maternal relation of support, Mary acts for the benefit of Christ's body, and in so acting, she grows in knowledge, love, and wisdom. Through exercising such knowledgeable and loving service, she aids and assists all persons. The shape of Mary's life is formed by her purposive orientation to God. She acted *for* the body of Christ when she elected to cooperate in realizing Christ's Incarnation; nurturing him to adulthood; supporting his project of realizing the "kingdom" of God on earth; and offering her supportive presence at his death.

Christ's body, towards which she is oriented, and whose interests she serves, is also her eschatological end, the destination she desires. Mary has already realized this destination, her *telos,* as the dogma of the assumption (1950) has formalized in church teaching. This dogma declares and affirms that Mary, at the end of her earthly life, was fit to enjoy the beatific vision, fully united with God, in every dimension of her personhood: mental, affective, spiritual, and physical. Even prior to Christ's conception, Mary had been saluted as "full of grace." This salutation signaled her readiness, and fitness, to receive God's Word as a living presence within her.[1] Her body (synecdochic of her person) is holy and set apart for God. The dogma of the assumption acts as attestation to Mary's lifetime faithfulness and intimacy with God. Although now assumed into the heavenly realm, Mary is understood to remain the definitive representative of her son, continuing to participate in his ongoing

---

1. Brant Pitre explicates and develops an early Christian theme of Mary as the ark of the covenant. Pitre charts five scriptural parallels between the two that were written into the Lucan gospel. See Pitre, *Jewish Roots of Mary.*

work of salvation. Wherever she manifests her presence, and whenever her name is invoked, she directs all persons to her son.

Her maternal body, occupied by Christ, was changed, as are all mothers' bodies. Following through the logic of the relational metaphors of *mother* and *spouse* indicates Mary's ontological alteration. Mary's body has been united with the Holy Spirit in an especial way. This real unity is realized and signed in the flesh of Christ whose materiality he received from Mary. The eucharistic body of the ascended Christ is a sign that also refers, in a secondary way, to the maternal body of his mother. The stronger the understanding of this symbolic signage, the more likely is there to be an accompanying acknowledgement of Mary's maternal presence during the celebration of the eucharistic sacrament. When the eucharistic body is maximally determined to not only indicate, but to actually make present, Christ's ascended, material body, then Mary's presence is always implicit; her maternal body continues to be given in the service of her son.

The Thinking Body

John Paul's central metaphor in his *Theology of the Body* was that of the body's *language*. While metaphors are linguistic usages, they also provide the frames within which thinking happens, so structuring, in Janet Soskice's words, not only "what sort of answers we get, but what kinds of questions we ask."[2] Metaphor is not just a way of describing the world but a way by which we make sense of it. This type of sense-making is not only an interior, intellectual process, involving perception and language, but one that results from a fuller relationship between language and body.

Cognitive scientist, Benjamin K. Bergen, has demonstrated how language in any mode, literal or metaphorical, engages perceptual simulations in the body.[3] This "embodied simulation" is a form of knowing wherein "language about actions engages the parts of the brain responsible for performing those same actions."[4] Even grammatical structure, Bergen explains, contributes its own meaning to such mental simulations. This being so, it significantly bolsters talk of a connection between *language* and *body*, expanding our thought about the range and type of

2. Soskice, *Metaphor and Religious Language*, 63.

3. Bergen, *Louder Than Words*, 263.

4. Bergen, *Louder Than Words*, 78.

bodily participation in speech. It strengthens a sense of the unity of the body if the linguistic domain and the physical domain are seen to be so closely related that *mental* acts or speech acts are more truly thought of as *embodiments*.

If thinking within a metaphoric frame guides perception, then how to account for any metaphor's arising in the first place? Writer and journalist, James Geary, argues that so-called primary metaphors, for example, size indicating importance; heat indicating anger; height indicating happiness, indicate their experiential origin, taking us back to the body.[5] These are metaphors with their roots in physiologic experience—the heightened blood flow of anger; the sense of walking tall when happy. These metaphors suggest that the experience of living in the world leads persons to think metaphorically. The origin of metaphor may be less about how we perceive the world; more about how we perceive ourselves within the world.

This position informs the thinking of Elizabeth Sewell in her book, *The Human Metaphor*.[6] Sewell makes an elevated claim for metaphor: that it does not just admit the phenomenal world as a way of thinking, but constitutes the structure of thought; that because we think metaphorically, language is that way. Sewell thus refers to metaphor as the human "method" of relating to the world. It shapes the person who, in turn, is always part of the cosmic whole that is constantly being renewed and reshaped. This is not to suggest, for Sewell, the imposition of mind upon matter but instead to follow such thinkers as Teilhard de Chardin, who postulated an *inwardness* to matter, as human consciousness arose from it.

Sewell was influenced by Michael Polanyi's hypothesis concerning the relation between thinking and the body. Polanyi's observations and analyses of the performance of skills by highly competent practitioners led him to conclude that such was their mastery, the skills they were exercising in the performance of the task had receded into the cognitive background where they behaved as tacit knowledge. This subconscious engagement of assimilated skills, he hypothesized, may also apply to the intellectual life, hence *body* may legitimately be said to be an integral part of thinking. Sewell found that postulate compelling, citing in support the sense some writers have expressed of not being fully conscious of what

5. Geary, *I Is an Other*.

6. Sewell, *Human Metaphor*. Sewell's book title is a borrowing from Novalis, by way of Dylan Thomas.

they are doing in the process of composition; of being guided, and of finding the final result "amazing" for its "congruence and foresight."[7]

Physiology's relation to thought processes and language—words triggering simulations in the mind; mind having so integrated physical skills as not to have to consciously attend to their exercise—says much about how we negotiate the world, and provides insights into our experience of living. It does not, though, disclose how it is that one person's life becomes biographically shaped in a particular way. It has been the premise of this book that all of nature functions as a sign of its creator; humans are a supreme and privileged type of sign (*image*).[8] The nature and purpose of an image is to be recognizably similar to, although not identical with, its original. The similarity between *sign* and *signified* should present no impediment to others recognizing it; it should be "transparent."[9] The person is a sign in his total personhood, but that sign can be parsed so that each constituent of the person is seen as a *signum*; so too, the linguistic sign-system within which he or she lives. The summation of a person's life, their biography, is the representative sign by which their sign-status is adjudicated for its level of transparency to its Original. The definitive personal biography has already been lived, so Christians believe, by Jesus; Jesus, that is, is fully *sign*. Nothing in his life fails to signify the Father. His life, offered to, accepted, and confirmed by the Father, is the measure for every human life; living in conformity with Christ's life is the realization of authentic personhood.

Within this comprehensive natural sign-system, where the person is the privileged sign, there are also linguistic signs with privileged status. Two with which this book has been concerned are poems and metaphors. If *metaphor* is the term we give to indicate a linguistic expression which is not only the outcome of *a priori* perception and thought, but the *a priori* structure of thinking (Sewell's "method" by which we relate to the world), then metaphor is privileged in two senses: it is the somatically generated ground of personal relations with the world, and the foundational way of expressing those relations. A human life has the multivalences and profusion of meaning that is achieved linguistically with metaphor, one of those linguistic forms that Rowan Williams attributes to the "pressure" of some phenomena; his metaphoric frame implies its eruptive potential,

7. Sewell, *Human Metaphor*, 124.

8. Augustine's *De Doctrina* claimed that not all things were signs. It does imply that all things are potential signs. See Ticciati, *New Apophaticism*, 141.

9. Carpenter, *Theo-Poetics*, 112.

with all the danger, disruption, and transfixion that his choice of (meta-phoric) noun evokes.

The Body as a Poetic Sign

Although he does not explicitly use the terms *poem* or *poetry* in his *Theology of the Body*, John Paul bases his anthropology upon the premise that the human body is not only meaningful, but poetic. Persons inhabit a symbolic cosmos, saturated with signs. The body is part of this semi-otic context, intended to be comprehended; it is a sign, intended to be disclosive and interpretable. While knowledge of the body is accessible to the natural sciences, the type of knowledge the body mediates (gift-edness, relationality, mutuality, openness) is outside the scope of those disciplines. The body's form and content, structure and meaning, are a seamless whole; the body is a *poem*, with its own inviolable, irreducible integrity. Not only can the body be known via the metaphor, *poem*, the body originates and mediates literary poems which are forms of linguis-tic embodiment. The embodied person is a poetic sign and the summit of the created order. These persons, living in community, develop their own human sign-systems which generate, receive, interpret, and de-liver meaning.[10] The structure of human-world encounters inscribes a feedback loop: the more fully the body is known, the more the body's ultimate Source is known; the more that Source is known, the more the body knows itself.

A poem, though, can be distinguished from poetry. It is the hope of a poet, I have suggested, to construct poems that manifest poetry, un-derstood to be an abstract quality mediated by the poem, through which it may be accessed. *Poetry* is a term notoriously elusive of definition. It refers to some arresting quality which is recognized, or known, when it is perceived or experienced. A general definition would be: poetry is that transformed and potentially transforming quality of a poem that persists in its reader's mind and senses, not letting go. It may be instantly identifi-able (the *yes!* moment) or may seep slowly into a life, gradually saturating it. It is absorbing and absorbed. It can be recognized, perhaps inchoately, as manifesting truth by recipients who, in Ricouer's term, "stand before" the poem, in an attitude of receptive openness. The relation between

---

10. Talk of the natural world, or human language, signifying God, is analogical. See Ticciati, *New Apophaticism*, 135.

poem and poetry can be well represented by either the spousal metaphor (each a "gift" for the other, in an exclusive and particular way) or, better, the maternal (poetry dwelling within the poem, the relationship between them irrevocable). The distinction in terminology allows a distinction to be made between body-viewed-as-poem, and the greater or lesser degree to which that somatic poem may be infused with poetry.

The Poetics of the Maternal Body

John Paul's theological anthropology devotes much of its analytic attention to what may be called the *other-centeredness* (giftedness) of the person which he finds to be a foundational characteristic of personhood. This structural openness and outward orientation proceeds from the other-centeredness of God. Being constituted relationally is one of the indelible markers of being human which is signed in each person's entering the world through the body of another. The spousal relation expresses in a unique way the desire to give and receive love without reserve; its particular state signals the universal human inclination towards others. The spousal relationship is established by intention which is then acted upon in word and deed. The covenantal words of marriage effect the bond which is then sealed with the act of spousal coitus. That consummation effects substantive change, the real unity of the two, expressed in Genesis as the two becoming "one flesh." This is extremity of language communicating extremity of personal relation. In sexual relations, each participant remains a personal center of subjectivity, yet the male and female behave together as a single biological organism. As the sexual gametes of each sex contain only one set of chromosomes, their potential fertility awaits timely and unimpeded sexual union when male and female gametes may meet and fuse, each giving to each a complementary set of chromosomes. When this happens, two haploid cells become one diploid cell. Spousal coitus, through which conception may occur, draws the couple together in a cooperative act which, of its nature, confirms and strengthens their mutual love.

Rowan Williams, writing in *The Edge of Words*, includes within his category of "extreme" language such constructions as metaphor, paradox, and irony, whose purpose is to enlarge our understanding not only of their referent, but of how language can speak truthfully of a thing.[11]

---

11. Williams, *Edge of Words*, 128.

They function, he says, "by pushing habitual or conventional speech out of shape,"[12] an image strongly connotative of the gestational body. Using Williams's image in conjunction with John Paul's terms, we could say that the extreme language of the two-in-one spousal body becomes physically signed in any resultant pregnancy in two ways: the maternal body becomes a morphing extreme of body-text that rewrites the conventional speech of the non-pregnant body, and secondly, the developing child is a concrete manifestation, an outward and visible sign and confirmation, of the spouses' invisible but real unity.[13] The meaningful biology of gestation and birth deepens and reconstitutes relational possibility, superseding the oppositional *you versus me*, and transcending the amicable *you and me*, transforming it into the relational apex, *you in me*. This relation of spousal equality and mutuality is encoded in the genomic patterning of any conceptus, half of whose DNA is donated by its mother, half by its father. Each *me* proceeds from the bonding of two *yous*. The escalating triad of one-within-another progresses from the transience of each act of spousal coitus, to the more indelible (although also temporary) gestational presence, to the permanent fusion of twoness in a related but different third. Belonging together, expressed gestationally in the strongest possible spatial terms, applies not only to the child but to the mother. The child becomes the encompassing form of the mother's life, the context in which she lives. Mother and child figure and refigure each other's identities.

In its changing shapes, the obstetric body constitutes a communicative sign-system, or language. It is an analogical signifier of the dynamism of spoken language, changing as it adapts itself to new needs. Meanings disclose themselves in the somatic adaptations as the maternal processes body forth. The creative refiguration of the obstetric body is a type of carnal *poiesis*; the unfolding processes are a type of performance art.

Gestational language, or the *poem* of the obstetric body, seems to have inspired Paul Ricoeur's reflective analysis of the revelatory function of poetic discourse (which he does not limit to the literary poetic genre) in his essay, "Metaphor and the Central Problem of Hermeneutics." Ricoeur sees a correlation between the "suspension" of the descriptive function of discourse and the revelatory function. His reasoning is that descriptive veracity is measurable according to its degree of adequation; that is, how

12. Williams, *Edge of Words*, 150.

13. "They give rise to another being similar to themselves, about which they can say together, 'It is flesh of my flesh and bone from my bones'" (*TOB* 22:3).

close the description is to the real object which is its referent. Any description is liable to empirical verification. Ricoeur, though, sees the value in poetic discourse in its not opposing text and object, following the structure of "objects opposed to a subject," in the manner of description.[14] Rather, he sees poetic language as preceding that capacity, restoring the reader to a state of participation-in or belonging-to an order of things. Ricoeur's scheme has a deeply maternal structure which draws upon the earliest life experiences of each personal subject, initially enclosed within another, followed by a protracted *postpartum* dependent attachment to another. Consciousness of oneself as a center of autonomous will, which can be opposed to other autonomous centers, develops later. The poetic function for Ricoeur is analogous to the maternal function as, in both instances, truth is revealed not via oppositional self-consciousness, nor logical thought patterns, but as a place of manifestation. Benignly confronting that text, or *locus*, can make possible self-understanding.[15] The response invited is not "obedience" to the text's vision, but an appeal to the imagination which recognizes the text "as a Poem."[16]

The maternal gestating body is intended to affirm and expand the reciprocally-expressed language of the couple: *gift of self in love for the other*. Pregnancy, once initiated, progresses according to a series of mechanical somatic responses to changing chemical signals which sequentially refashion the mother's body, independent of her will. The acts of the gestating body reiterate the spousal language of love: orientation towards the good of another in total acceptance of that intimately, yet imperfectly known, other. This is signed in expansive uterine accommodation, increased cervical tensile strength, and the exceptional generation of a single-use organ.

A literary poem is also that which exists *for* others. How it is related to by its auditors or readers varies according to whether its mediation is oral or written. Literary poems which exist in written form have, as Paul Ricoeur has noted, a universalized potential audience. The cost of this

<hr/>

14. Ricoeur, "Metaphor and Hermeneutics," 137.

15. Ricoeur, "Metaphor and Hermeneutics," 152.

16. Ricoeur, "Metaphor and Hermeneutics," 152. C. S. Lewis makes a similar point in his essay "Bluspels and Flanansferes" (1939). Metaphors, he says, are intended to help us make meaning to arrive at knowledge. One of the conditions of seeing a correct meaning is to keep in mind the metaphorical nature of metaphor—that it is not "fact"—while also noting that some things we can know in no other way than through what he calls "magistral" metaphors.

expanded readership is the loss of public communal recitations, which had shared the function of religion in binding a community together. The act of reading, on the other hand, is private, individualized, and interiorized. Ricoeur has noted that, paradoxically, written text which is most closely linked to materiality in being legibly recorded, becomes spiritualized upon being "liberated from the narrowness of the face-to-face situation" of oral performance.[17] Writing becomes a means by which a Cartesian split is effected between bodies and minds. As Edwin Muir has attested, once a poem is bound as a book, it tends to unbind the community from whom, and for whom, it sprang.[18]

If it is granted that poems have an internal pressure towards oral expression, with the fluidity, flexibility, and communal participation which that allows, this may intimate poetry's particular affinity with the body, and its social dimension. A poem publicly recited participates in the real historicity of embodied life which is spoken and spent. The poem's transient participation in the elusive present is poignant with associations of life's inexorable progression towards death. It paradoxically evokes the preverbal state as words become breath, the very mark of our being. A communal recitation assembles a body of auditors around an orator who not only mediates the poem but who becomes the "site of encounter."[19] The relationship is stronger than mediation, as the orator's body becomes, in Les Murray's words, "the material in which a work is realized."[20] A poetic declamation is an ontological statement making concrete and experiential what a poem is: a body-of-words that proceeds from matter-which-speaks.

The two dominant biblical motifs associated with the Word of God: the Man-God, and the scriptural gospel, integrate the two modes of formal linguistic mediation: speaking and writing. God's expressive word, as encountered in the world, is the meeting point where durable permanence (law) meets labile motility (body of Christ). If it is allowed that

17. Ricoeur, "Speaking and Writing," 31.

18. Muir, "Natural Estate," 11. Most of the ballads from the Orkney Islands, where Muir was born and raised, ceased to live in the community once they were written down. The organic, imaginative inheritance slid into decline. Prior to their formal recording, they had been orally redacted over centuries, the fruit of generations of recipients who were also participants in their composition. Once written, one version became the standard and its communal currency deflated with fixity. See Muir, "Natural Estate," 15.

19. Rosen, Art & Religion in the Twenty-First Century, 32.

20. Murray, "Embodiment and Incarnation," 32.

formal language, connected with rules, law, and boundary enforcement, is the domain of the father, and that poems are the linguistic places where this law communes with the pre-verbal maternal of pulses, rhythms and musicality, then Mary is the person where the two domains meet. Mary's presentation within scripture does not comply with the usual way women are referred to, as she is both personally named, and given her own direct speech. Her declamation of the Magnificat on the occasion of the Visitation to Elizabeth (Luke 1: 39–45) is not only useful for narrative purposes, confirming her as "Daughter Zion." It functions as a composite presentation of the language of the father (multiple quotations from, or allusions to, several books from the formal record of the Hebrew scriptures), and of the poetic language domain associated with the mother (quotations and allusions are to Wisdom literature, hymnody from the psalms, and prophecy). Mary is figured as the symbiosis of culture and nature.

The Poetics of Mary's Maternal Body

The two types of self-donative love with which this book is primarily concerned: that of the maternal, gestational body, and that of a literary poem, offer two interpretive introits to the Annunciation.

Annunciation: Speaking Life

The merits of Mary's *fiat* are attributable to her having acted according to her personal freedom. Her *yes* is both the summit of her lived human experience, and the product of it. Mary is able to consent as she has already heard, internalized, and lived the words of God. This internalization is externalized in the way she lived, and is a moral virtue, as it resulted from her free cooperation with grace. So, although her motherhood in the temporal order preceded her discipleship of her son, her discipleship of God had gone before, creating the ground of her assent; she is already formed as a *yes* to God before she is asked to formally and specifically articulate that *yes* at the Annunciation. John Paul's early philosophical work offers another depth of understanding to the significance of the Marian *fiat*.

In *The Acting Person*, Wojtyła wrote that an authentically human act is one where the person not only acts but reflexively recognizes him- or herself as the cause of that act. The personal subject is an actor who enacts and is simultaneously aware of being that acting subject. There is a distinction, therefore, which Wojtyła makes, between such self-aware acts, and events that merely *happen* to a person. A personal act has two objects: the intended object of the will, and the subject's own ego (*ego* here as both subject and object of a person's action). As Deborah Savage explicates, this means that every human action is not reducible to a matter of volition or intentionality because "it will always include an element of self-determination, an act of the person."[21] Actions are not only, that is, the externalization of will. They are also that which shape the person who has chosen so to act. The acting person is aware of this constitutive connection between acts and personhood. Mary's *fiat,* seen in this light, is something deeper than agreement informed by faith in the One who asks, as meritorious as that is. Her *yes* was the historic moment of real coalescence between the divine and human wills. Mary, acting in her own capacity, but also as representative of humankind, is acting without self-interest. She is not seeking to gain, or increase, mastery over a situation or person, but acts wholly in voluntary submission to God (contra Eve who sought to grasp the power of ultimate discrimination, hence of judgement, for herself). Mary is thereby conforming herself to God, fashioning herself as the true, restored image.

Wojtyła schematizes constitutive action (which includes thought and speech) in the following way. First, truth is cognized, prior to its becoming an object of the will. This ordering makes rational sense, as only that which is known can be recognized, and once recognized, become an object of desire.[22] The will is ordered towards recognition of the good. Notwithstanding the strong attraction that the good exerts, a person may choose to resist it. Free will persists. Rather, the good has a strong attractive power, an allure. A person's acceptance or rejection of this allure determines "the maturity and the perfection of the person."[23] Each decisive moment when a person decides "I will," determines who that person is becoming. Wojtyła therefore speaks of decision-making as being "an instance of threshold." Acting upon an inclination to the good by moving towards it, involves, according to Wojtyła, personal self-transcendence in two different directions: horizontally, towards an external object in the world; and vertically, outside the world, so as to transcend one's "own

---

21. Savage, "Wojtyła's Account of the Person," 41.
22. Wojtyła and Tymieniecka, *Acting Person*, 114.
23. Wojtyła and Tymieniecka, *Acting Person*, 127.

previously constituted boundaries." Mary as presented in the Lukan Annunciation is at the threshold of self-transcendence when she questions
the angel. In accepting his answer, she accepts the real possibility of transcending, through faith in God, her own borders and limits.

This deliberate release of the self is an ever-present possibility
for persons. Just as *Eve* and *Adam*, in making the choices they did, are
morally and ethically responsible for what subsequently befell them, so,
inversely, does Mary's choice redound to her credit. The Annunciation
pericope re-personalizes free will. It is not an abstraction in the gospel,
attributable to human nature, but a property of the personal subject.
Wojtyła's personalistic insights—that personal actions continually form
and re-form the actor—allow for the sign of Mary's perpetual virginity
to be read more expansively than only pointing narrowly to her sexual
chastity. Her personal response to God was total. She withheld nothing from the full integrity of her person, body, mind, and spirit. Just as
her motherhood anchors unseen reality in concrete, visible flesh, so is a
carnal sign of her corporeal integrity, fitting. This idea of propriety, or
conveniens, was a term used theologically in the high medieval period
by such theologians as Anselm, Aquinas, and Bonaventure, to express a
satisfying symbiotic relation between a thing and something with which
it fits. The notion avoided the polarities of *necessity* and of *contingency*.
The term therefore had the quality of a bridging term that expressed a
yes-and-no; the copresence of seeming contradictories acts as a defense
against contrastive opposition.[24] Mary's intact hymen signifies fittingly
the totality of her gift of self to God; it is a sign that binds together the
virginal and the spousal, so transcending the either/or which those states
would usually indicate.

The poetics of Mary's virginal *intactus* can be read according to
boundary crossing and boundary enforcement. Affirming, with her act
of consent, that the person may be taken up into the boundless possibilities of God, Mary transcends the bounds of human possibility, redrawing
their contours by becoming *virgin mother*. The conception of her son transcends the boundary of the human *soma*, the transcendence signed in the
preservation of Mary's virginity. This sign is structured as a layered treble
paradox. The legible sign of Christ's presence inscribes itself invisibly, literally veiling the mystery in flesh, in a metaphoric microcosm of the Incarnation. As a metaphoric reworking of the signage of consummation, it

24. Turner, *Julian of Norwich*, 38–40.

reverses the signage of male dedication to God in circumcision; retention of genital flesh, not its removal, signifies Mary's consecration. Thirdly, the sign of Christ's transcendence of the norms of human conception happens at the point of his immanent manifestation within the womb of Mary.

Read according to John Paul's spousal characteristics of mutuality and reciprocity, the exchange between the angelic messenger and Mary respects, yet is unrestricted by, the bounds of Mary's embodiment: her temporality and spatial fixity. Those bounds are invited into the boundlessness of God. Spatial constraints and norms are transformed but temporality is not erased. Temporality is invited to donate itself to eternity, which is effected by eternity's entering into time. This is the structural conceit that shapes Edwin Muir's "Annunciation," and is present in Noel Rowe's "*Magnificat:* 1. Annunciation" where the divine eternal waits upon Mary's response, outside her room. The possibility of mutuality within this divine-creaturely exchange is skeptically quizzed in Elizabeth Jennings's poem of the event.

If Mary's virginity deals in the poetics of self-giving, then her spousal relation deals in the poetics of knowledge. Les Murray coined his neologism, "wholespeak," to express language that fuses analytic, orderly, and conscious cognition, with the subconscious locutions of dreams and imagination. Mary's brief dialogue with the angel demonstrates such fullness and balance in her thinking and speaking. She tries to understand rationally, with cognitive consonance, which is insufficient for the situation. She enters into God's alternative vision which she cannot clearly see, nor understand, but trusts. The event continues to live in her mind as she contemplates all that had happened to her. Contemplation is both a form of cognitive processing and the work of a reflective imagination. The fullness of language that she exhibits is layered and complex, Murray's wholespeak now appearing to be a form of Marian-speak.

Mary speaks in the manner of an artist, saint or seer. She acts trustingly with that which she sees, knows, or intuits, breaking new ground in the process. Her *knowing* included the apophatic darkness of incomprehension as well as the radiance of illumination. Rowan Williams has spoken of prayer running ahead of systematic thinking.[25] Mary's *fiat* seems to function in that way: a response from the heart that does not

25. Williams, *Tokens of Trust*, 63.

wait for the understanding of the mind.[26] This is not to imply that such committed action as Mary's is precipitate or irrational. What it does indicate is an alignment of her vision with the revealed vision of God. Under such circumstances, her *fiat* constitutes an imaginative leap of creative faith which is supremely rational. In Mary's *fiat*, as in poetic composition, there is, in Williams's words, an "appropriate rigour" to the task, whereby poetic utterances are measured against the truths of lived life and the revelation of God.[27]

Pietà: Eucharistic Sign

The *Pietà* motif recognizes and honors the particular nature of maternity where the bond formed *in utero* is a unique type of bodily communion, grounded in, but somatically exceeding, the intimacy of sexual congress. The poetic challenge is to work it into words that do not overwhelm its speaking silence. One way to achieve this restraint is to restrict the length of a poem, as is notably the case with the three *Pietà* poems considered in this book. Their brevity (ten lines; fourteen lines; twelve lines) is apposite, organically related to the content of the image: the death of the definitive Word. The brevity of the poems speaks to the peak emotional content of the image, and to the seeming implosion of words' power to communicate.

The silence associated with the *Pietà* completes a metaphoric circle, taking the viewer back to the beginning of Jesus's life, at the Annunciation. Mary then had heard, and listened to, the word of the Father, mediated via the angel. Silence is the ground of hearing. Silence after the deposition of Christ's body from the cross is the silence of trauma, where human words fail. It points to the provisional character of human language. The limitations of our human languages indicate a *more,* an *other,* where words cannot fail. Silence of this type is the excess beyond even extreme language, and refers human words to God's one complete and final Word, the only word of sufficient plenitude to never be exhausted, depleted, or evacuated by circumstance.

26. Williams said of the New Testament writers that they were working out something that had "long since happened to the heart and imagination" (Williams, *Tokens of Trust*, 63).

27. Williams, *On Christian Theology*, xiv.

As an imaginative augmentation of scripture and dogma, the *Pietà* motif has proven itself resilient and enduring, securely integrated within the Catholic symbolic. As an image, it offers rich poetic valences. It is a dual lament for the irretrievable poems: the silenced Word, and the mother unmade by the death of her only issue. The drama of the image lies in its spatial integration of mother and child at the point of devastating disintegration of that particular mother-child bond but also the collapse of the proto-community, or more fundamentally, the implosion of the possibility of human community. Emotionally intense situations, where words struggle, or surrender, are those where, in Les Murray's terms, the "forebrain" is demoted, the "limbic" promoted. The poetic translation of this emotional pattern, and its effect on the body, is realized convincingly in James McAuley's "Pietà" poem where words cede to gesture. McAuley's poem is structured around an affecting pun where maternal taction touches the reader with elegiac affectivity. To touch is to confront the fleeting present within the boundaries of the spatiotemporal world.

The *Pietà* image represents the hiatus and tension of Holy Saturday. The risk of the whole salvific project waits upon whether Christ's Passion will be received and interpreted as sign, or whether his poetic endeavor will be misconstrued, misunderstood, ignored, or passed over with a literalist reading. Here is object like any other (a corpse) and not like any other (depending upon whose, one believes, is the corpse). If the living Jesus were a sign, as he himself claimed to be ("If you knew me, you would know my Father also," John 8:19b NRSV), then how does his death affect the truth of his claim? Is the claim invalidated? How could this dead man be a sign of God? If it is the case that a sign is, in Elizabeth Sewell's words, "the beginning of a progression, a clue to directed motion," then is this sign forward leading or backward looking?[28] If the body had correctly been supposed to be the body of one enthroned, as is God (cf. Mark 16:60–64; Dan 7:13–14), then how is that body now the sign of God? The deposed Christ-corpse in the arms of his mother is a figure with the highest "level of indeterminacy."[29] The *Pietà* is a threshold image, pointing to the course of Jesus's life having seemingly gone disastrously awry. How can such apparent *wrongness* be read aright? How can the

---

28. Sewell, "Reading of Signs," 155.

29. Sewell, "Reading of Signs," 162. The phrase is used by Michael Polanyi in speaking of the relation between scientific discovery and prophecy: scientific theory anticipates something which is far beyond what either the theory is then able to express, or what the founder of the discovery is then able to know.

valid credulity of faith be kept alive without opposing faith to reason? Is it possible that *corpse* is in some sense, still *corpus*?

Some Purposes of Poems

Although a poet may feel driven to write, a poem is neither a necessity, nor a contingency. A poem is written, and read, for its own sake. It is an act of discretionary freedom which manifests some of those characteristics that John Paul II identified as being foundational to the person: mutuality (poem and reader each hoping for the other), reciprocity (each giving and receiving from the other), and generativity (new insights; different ways of seeing; fresh interpretations resulting from their union). A reader's act of reading can enact the spousal vow ("I take you to be mine"), the reading experience as intense as wanting to inhabit the poem.[30]

A writer of a poem labors to compose a piece that poetically reveals or expresses some reality. The labor involves finding, then arranging, a right and satisfying pattern of words. Poems which resonate in a community, perhaps entering a cultural canon, are valued because of their relationship with truth, reminding their auditors and readers that the primary task—and possibility—of man is to abide in truth. At their best, they confer the gift of sight. This may be the sight afforded when something overlooked, marginalized, misunderstood, or undervalued, has been illuminated; things once not seen, now made visible. The writer is acknowledged to have, in some measure, penetrated the surface of some reality. Albeit partially, or imperfectly, a poet aims, whether consciously or not, to retrieve that original purity of vision about which John Paul II has spoken, whereby persons and things were seen in their ontological truth. This purity of vision was, as earlier indicated, directly related to the state of the beholder's heart, as authentic vision proceeds from love. Even in a fractured world, it remains possible to experience the gift of authentic inner vision. This type of vision is received and imparted by the seer. Speaking not of artists but of viewers, Cardinal Joseph Ratzinger (Benedict XVI) echoed John Paul II when, in 2002, he spoke of the edifying experience of contemplating Christian icons, and masterpieces of Christian art. Seeing them, he said, was a way to purify both one's sight

---

30. See Murray, "Poems and Poesies." Murray's description of the experience of art is expressed in strongly erotic terms.

and one's heart. Through their beautiful presence, "we are brought into contact with the power of the truth."[31]

Poetic truthfulness honors its subject. It also honors the openness and power of words; the possibility that words can express reality. Edwin Muir has written that one of the chief concerns of a poet is to render truthful images: "If the image is true, poetry fulfils its end."[32] Poetry, that is, says Muir, has a *telos*. Muir's statement begins from the assumption that there is such a thing as *truth*, and, proceeding from this, that truth can be humanly perceived, and truthfully expressed. The Judeo-Christian belief is that the God who revealed himself is the one in whom all truth subsists; that God *is* truth. Any quest for truth, including literary truth, is therefore, at some level, a quest for God. Christian theology holds that those who seek truth will be aided and directed by God's Spirit, present and active in the world. The Holy Spirit enlightens, allowing us to *see* what something means. Divine illumination increases the more it is sought and honorably received, the more the seeker surrenders to the vision of God.

Seeking a true poetic image is transferring into literary endeavor the foundational calling of every life: to be a living image of God. For a poet, this end is achievable when s/he loses self-consciousness and self-concern. This is one aspect of the transcendent element in authentic composition. It entails a preparedness to surrender in humility to the words, foregoing an absoluteness of authorial will. The *self* who composes steps aside for the sake of the composition, in an act of self-effacement. George Orwell famously ended his 1946 essay, in which he addressed his motivations for writing, by declaring: "one can write nothing readable unless one constantly struggles to efface one's own personality. Good prose is like a window pane."[33] Orwell's parting simile extolls humility as a necessary virtue for writers who would be "good"—for those who want the real and the true to be seen through their work. This insight aligns with the gospel injunction to act in such a way that onlookers see God (the Real and the True) through those actions (see Matt 5:16). The artistic and the Christian vocation is to be glasslike, so the Light can shine through.

The desire, and attempt, to call things by their proper names, is a desire to participate in truth, an expression of grace. Acknowledging, and

---

31. Ratzinger, "Feeling of Things" 13.
32. Muir, "Public and the Poet," 108.
33. Orwell, "Why I Write," 10.

opening to, a transcendent element in composition, can clarify one's inner vision. Under these conditions, a writer may have a sense that words find him. This is the literary correlate of the paradox of personal giving, elucidated by John Paul: that in giving to another, the donor finds herself. Such giving involves detachment from the ego. It is this very detachment that, in literary composition, enables the exercise of an unsentimental critical faculty—what Les Murray calls the "calmly ruthless judgement."[34] The authorial aim of self-surrender, stripped of egotistical desires, is a metaphoric nakedness.[35]

If, as George Steiner suggests, one of the purposes of poems (or any artform) is to suggest change by intimating new possibilities for living;[36] that is, to suggest conversion, then Mary is the one whose life indicates the possibilities of a life converted to her son. Such a relationship is one lived in close and loving relationship. The closest relationship, expressed in terms of physical proximity, is one of inherence and adherence, typology that is strongly maternal. To inhere is only possible having first gained access. In the eucharistic words of institution, Jesus opens the way to himself by breaking open his body; his words evoke the foundational human trope of the mother whose body, in birth, is a metaphor of fracture. Fracture is what makes life possible. The creation narrative of Genesis 2 lends itself to such an interpretive linkage. The male is symbolically *broken* so as to form the female—action that ends, or breaks, mankind's solitude. Generativity—ensuring the permanent end of solitude—is henceforth possible. God's creative breakage reciprocally enriches both male and female whose bodies are now able to be sexually given to each other. The gospel passion narratives also indicate generative fracture. The Johannine trope of Christic fracture at the Crucifixion is, reading inter-textually, registered in Mary who felt the force in her own person. The symbol they share is expressive of their spousal unity. Both suffer together for the sake of others, their spiritual children. Mother and son, in their shared, generative suffering, are figured as "a subject in unity" (*TOB* 32:4), who act as a single organism of "one flesh"[37]; that is, as a spousal couple. The Christ corpus, pierced at the cross, is a metonym of fecund breakage. The broken Word penetrates Mary, where it germinates, in

34. Murray, "Embodiment and Incarnation," 324.

35. Spender, *Making of a Poem*, 59–60.

36. Steiner, *Real Presences*, 142.

37. This expression from Genesis 2:4 indicates sexual union. It also includes multiple other dimensions, including the ethical, the theological, and the sacramental. See *TOB* 9:5.

a metaphoric reprise of the Annunciation event. The birth of the new covenant at the cross does not avoid the costliness of love. Rather, costly love delivers as does a laboring woman: at the juncture where living in surrender to another becomes an act of loving sacrifice.

The Poetry of the Mary-Poem

Historically, artistic representations of the Virgin Mary have been shaped by concerns to honor her by protecting her physical modesty. She can, though, in the sense used above, be fruitfully thought of in terms of "original nakedness." The Genesis creation texts give an account of the true and uncorrupted *text* of the created order, as it was in the beginning. God, the complete utterance, does not revise his own Word. Neither does God, who is love, compel speech. The apex of the created order—the human—is a creature of radical freedom. The divine intention is that each one made in the divine image (that is, all human beings) would be free to respond to that divine Word of creative love by becoming a creaturely word of responsive love. This original relationship was mortally wounded by primordial man's act of radical mistrust of God's Word. The structural potential for the intended relationship remained, although vastly more costly, and difficult, to realize. Being a truthful image (*imago Dei*) remained the human calling. Mary is the creature in whom the image was fully restored. She, in her earthly life, received and returned God's love unreservedly. No aspect of her life contradicted the originating Word, so she sought no cover. Her person reiterates the original psychic nakedness of man which the naked body had originally signified. Mary is the longed-for dialogue partner of the Father by virtue of her having realized the truth content of personhood: being an image of God in a way which wholly corresponds with the original intention of the Creator.

It has already been noted that poet, Bruce Dawe, has suggested that the task of a poem is not to judge, but to formulate questions. These questions are ordered towards arriving at truth and, hopefully, a measure of understanding. Mary offers an image of someone who has arrived at both truth and understanding. We may say, therefore, that she fulfils in her person the task of a poem. For what is a poem but an attempt to enter more deeply into the world, to penetrate the truth of things, and then to share that vision with others? ("Vision" here may amount to seeing the questions that need to be asked.) Poems, at their best, attempt to see a thing with the heart, as only such *seeing* can restore true sight. Christian doctrine teaches that a receptive heart is one converted to God. Mary imitates God's act of superabundant donation: God entered the world so that the living Word could be seen, heard, and recognized; Mary gave herself as the way for the corporeal Word to make that entry. All persons have the potential and the vocation to respond as did Mary, imparting God to others; all are called to make Truth recognizable in human embodiment. Thinking of Mary as the *poem* of the Father is not to spiritualize her, as her whole person, in her concrete materiality, is a living poem. Her body became a corporeal temple, infused with the Holy Spirit, who we may think of as the *poetry* of God.

As figure of the church, Mary is the one who dwells entirely in Christ, who reciprocally dwells in her. This is the maternal structure of indwelling and the spousal structure of mutuality that is offered as a lived possibility for all persons. Mary, though, occupies a unique and elevated place within the ecclesial body. In the temporal order, she was the one mother of the one Son. Given to the church by Christ from the cross, she is the mother in the spiritual order of that same son's mystical body. Christ's incarnational indwelling of Mary is uniquely recorded within her maternal body. In human pregnancies, fetal cells enter the maternal blood circulation. Their presence persists in maternal blood and tissues for decades *postpartum*, even from pregnancies not carried to term. Some of these transferred cells appear to have multilineage capability, which may offer the mother assistance in the case of injury to her body. This being so, the intimacy of Christ's presence within Mary is of a different order from the rest of the faithful. Jesus's presence is encoded in her blood. In words forcefully resonant of the Johannine Christ's, it may be said that those who have seen her, have seen the Son (cf. John 14:9).

Mary is graced and chosen to be the mother of the Word. She who was saluted as "full of grace" lived a life as God originally created all human lives to be lived: in the unashamed nakedness of her personal solitude before God. Mary is able to endure the holy presence because of her steadfast and obedient faith. Oriented to God, she fixes her eyes on him with whom she desires communion. This desire was met in her in extraordinary fashion. Her maternal body constitutes an act of faith in the words of God received, interpreted, and preserved, by her faith community. Her body is affirmation and act of faith—that words matter, mean, and can be truth-bearing. Mary exemplifies such faith in the emissive Word of the Father, making it her own. She receives his dense utterance and allows it to infuse her whole person, making her its carrier and its realization. Mary's motherhood sits at the juncture of transcendence (Mother of God) and immanence (Mother of the Church). Her maternal body offers nurturance and sustenance, protective hospitality and strength. Mary becomes, by virtue of how she chooses to live her life, the incarnation of the poetry of the Father. Her body, portal of the Word's entry as matter into the material universe, remains the site of the Word's gestation, always and only delivering Jesus. This is her creative task. This is her life lived as poem of the Father.

Bibliography

Abrams, M. H. "Kant and the Theology of Art." In *The Fourth Dimension of a Poem and Other Essays*, by M. H. Abrams, 151–94. New York: Norton, 2012.

———. "The Language and Methods of Humanism." In *The Fourth Dimension of a Poem and Other Essays*, by M. H. Abrams, 93–105. New York: Norton, 2012.

Atkinson, Joseph. "The Experience of the Body and the Divine: A Scriptural Perspective." *Communio: International Catholic Review* 37.2 (2010) 309–28.

Austin, J. L. *How to Do Things with Words.* 2nd ed. The William James Lectures Delivered at Harvard University in 1955. Oxford: Oxford University Press, 1976.

Barker, Margaret. "Atonement: the Rite of Healing." *Scottish Journal of Theology* 49.1 (1996) 1–20.

———. *The Gate of Heaven: The History and Symbolism of the Temple in Jerusalem.* London: SPCK, 1991.

———. *The Mother of the Lord.* Vol. 1. London: Bloomsbury, 2012.

———. "The Veil." In *The Gate of Heaven: The History and Symbolism of the Temple in Jerusalem*, by Margaret Barker, 104–32. London: SPCK, 1991.

Barnard, Alan. *Genesis of Symbolic Thought.* Cambridge: Cambridge University Press, 2012.

Barthes, Roland. "Theory of the Text." In *Untying the Text: A Post-Structuralist Reader*, edited by Robert Young, 31–47. London: Routledge & Kegan Paul, 1981.

Beattie, Tina. *God's Mother, Eve's Advocate: A Marian Narrative of Women's Salvation.* London: Continuum, 2002.

———. *Woman.* London: Continuum, 2003.

Benedict XVI. *Jesus of Nazareth: The Infancy Narratives.* Translated by Philip J. Whitmore. London: Bloomsbury, 2012.

Bergen, Benjamin K. *Louder Than Words: The New Science of How the Mind Makes Meaning.* New York: Basic, 2012.

Berry, Wendell. "Standing by Words." In *Standing by Words: Essays*, by Wendell Berry, 24–63. Berkeley, CA: Counterpoint, 1983.

Bickimer, David Arthur. *Christ the Placenta: Letters to My Mentor on Religious Education.* Birmingham, AL: Religous Education, 1983.

Boss, Sarah Jane. "The Development of the Virgin's Cult in the High Middle Ages." In *Mary: The Complete Resource*, edited by Sarah Jane Boss, 149–72. Oxford: Oxford University Press, 2007.

———. *Mary.* New Century Theology. London: Continuum, 2003.

———. "The Naked Madonna." *The Tablet*, February 17, 2001. 235.

Boyarin, Daniel. "Jewish Masochism: Couvade, Castration and Rabbis in Pain." *American Imago* 51.1 (1994) 3–36.

Brady, Veronica. "Female Imagery and Imaging and the Experience of Theology." In *Gospel and Gender: A Trinitarian Engagement with Being Male and Female in Christ*, edited by Douglas A. Campbell, 124–33. Studies in Theology and Sexuality. London: SCM, 2003.

Branham, Joan R. "Bloody Women and Bloody Spaces: Menses and the Eucharist in Late Antiquity and the Early Middle Ages." *Harvard Divinity School* 30.4 (2001) 15–22.

Bruzelius, Margaret. "Mother's Pain, Mother's Voice: Gabriela Mistral, Julia Kristeva, and the Mater Dolorosa." *Tulsa Studies in Women's Literature* 18.2 (1999) 215–33.

Bulgakov, Sergius. *Relics and Miracles*. Translated by B. Jakin. Cambridge, UK: Eerdmans, 2011.

Bulzacchelli, Richard H. "Mary and the Acting Person: An Anthropology of Participatory Redemption in the Personalism of Karol Wojtyła/Pope John Paul II." PhD diss., University of Dayton, 2012.

Bynum, Caroline Walker. *Jesus as Mother: Studies in the Spirituality of the High Middle Ages*. Berkeley: University of California Press, 1984.

Carpenter, Anne M. *Theo-Poetics: Hans Urs von Balthasar and the Risk of Art and Being*. Notre Dame, IN: University of Notre Dame, 2015.

Casad, Andrew. "Blood, Sex, and the Eucharist: A Discourse Analysis on the Reception of the Precious Blood." *New Blackfriars* 88.1015 (2007) 313–21.

Coakley, Sarah. "Creaturehood before God: Male and Female." *Theology* 93.755 (1990) 343–54.

———. "The Eschatological Body: Gender, Transformation, and God." *Modern Theology* 16.1 (2000) 61–73.

———. *God, Sexuality, and the Self: An Essay "On the Trinity"*. Cambridge: Cambridge University Press, 2013.

———. "Is There a Future for Gender and Theology? On Gender, Contemplation, and the Systematic Task." *Svensk Teologisk Kvartalskrift* 85.2 (2013) 52–61.

———. *Powers and Submissions: Spirituality, Philosophy, and Gender*. Challenges in Contemporary Theology. Oxford: Blackwell, 2002.

Collins, Sally, et al. *Oxford Handbook of Obstetrics and Gynaecology*. 2nd ed. Oxford: Oxford University Press, 2011.

Davis, William V. *R. S. Thomas: Poetry and Theology*. Waco, TX: Baylor University Press, 2007.

Dawe, Bruce. "Australian Poets in Profile: 1 Bruce Dawe." *Southerly* 39.3 (1979) 235–44.

DeLamater, John D., and Janet Shibley Hyde. "Essentialism vs. Social Constructivism in the Study of Human Sexuality." *The Journal of Sex Research* 35.1 (1998) 10–18.

Dickenson, Donna. *Property in the Body: Feminist Perspectives*. Cambridge Law, Medicine, and Ethics. Cambridge: Cambridge University Press, 2007.

Drury, John. *Painting the Word: Christian Pictures and their Meanings*. New Haven, CT: Yale University Press; London: National Gallery, 1999.

Dunn, Rose Ellen. "Let It Be: Finding Grace with God through the *Gelassenheit* of the Annunciation." In *Apophatic Bodies: Negative Theology, Incarnation, and Relationality*, edited by Chris Boesel and Catherine Keller, 329–48. New York: Fordham University Press, 2010.

Evdokimov, Paul. "*From* The Sacrament of Love: The Nuptial Mystery in the Light of the Orthodox Tradition." In *Theology and Sexualtiy: Classic and Contemporary Readings*, edited by Eugene F. Rogers Jr., 179–93. Blackwell Readings in Modern Theology. Oxford: Blackwell, 2002.

Finch, Martha. "Rehabilitating Materiality: Bodies, Gods, and Religion." *Religion* 42.4 (2012) 625–31.

Fingesten, Peter. "Topographical and Anatomical Aspects of the Gothic Cathedral." *The Journal of Aesthetics and Art Criticism* 20.1 (1961) 3–23.

Ford, David F. *Christian Wisdom: Desiring God and Learning in Love*. Cambridge Studies in Christian Doctrine. Edited by Daniel W. Hardy. Cambridge: Cambridge University Press, 2007.

———. *The Shape of Living*. 1997. Reprint, Norwich: Canterbury, 2012.

Fox, H. "Placentation in Intrauterine Growth Retardation." *Fetal and Maternal Medicine Review* 9.2 (1997) 61–71.

Fox, James. "The Riddle of Kate Moss." *Vanity Fair*, December 2012. 36–49, 97–99.

Freitag, Barbara. *Sheela-Na-Gigs: Unravelling an Enigma*. London: Routledge, 2004.

Gambero, Luigi. *Mary and the Fathers of the Church: the Blessed Virgin Mary in Patristic Thought*. San Francisco, CA: Ignatius, 1999.

Gaventa, Beverly Roberts. *Mary: Glimpses of the Mother of Jesus*. Personalities of the New Testament. 1995. Reprint, Edinburgh: T&T Clark, 1999.

Geary, James. *I Is an Other: The Secret Life of Metaphor and How It Shapes the Way We See the World*. 2011. Reprint, New York: Harper Perennial, 2012.

Gentner, Dedre, and Brian Bowdle. "Metaphor as Structure-Mapping." In *The Cambridge Handbook of Metaphor and Thought*, edited by Raymond W. Gibbs Jr., 109–28. Cambridge Handbooks in Psychology. Cambridge: Cambridge University Press, 2008.

George, Marie I. "What Does 'Made in the Image of God' Mean?" Lecture delivered at the Third Annual Conference of the Society of Catholic Scientists, University of Notre Dame, South Bend, IN, June 7–9, 2019. Online. https://www.catholicscientists. org/idea/what-does-made-in-image-of-god-mean.

Gershoni, Moran, and Shmuel Pietrokovski. "The Landscape of Sex-Differential Transcriptome and its Consequent Selection in Human Adults." *BioMed Central Biology* 15.7 (2017). Online. doi: 10.1186/s12915-017-0352-z.

Glick, Leonard B. *Marked in Your Flesh: Circumcision from Ancient Judea to Modern America*. Oxford: Oxford University Press, 2005.

Goldstein, Valerie Saiving. "The Human Situation: A Feminine View." *The Journal of Religion* 40.2 (1960) 100–112.

Gousmett, Christopher John. "Shall the Body Strive and Not Be Crowned? Unitary and Instrumentalist Anthropological Models as Keys to Interpreting the Structure of Patristic Eschatology." PhD diss., University of Otago, 1993.

Granados, Jose. "The Body, the Family, and the Order of Love: The Interpretative Key to Vatican II." *Communio: International Catholic Review* 39.1–2 (2012) 201–26.

———. "Embodied Light, Incarnate Image: The Mystery of Jesus' Transfiguration." *Communio: International Catholic Review* 35.2 (2008) 6–45.

Green, Arthur. "Shekhinah, the Virgin Mary, and the Song of Songs: Reflections on a Kabbalistic Symbol in Its Historical Context." *Association for Jewish Studies Review* 26.1 (2002) 1–52.

Guite, Malcolm. *Faith, Hope, and Poetry: Theology and the Poetic Imagination.* Ashgate Studies in Theology, Imagination, and the Arts. Farnham: Ashgate, 2010.

Gupta, Nijay K. "Which Body Is a Temple (1 Cor 6:19)? Paul Beyond the Individual/ Communal Divide." *The Catholic Biblical Quarterly* 72.3 (2010) 520–36.

Gurtler, Gary M. "Plotinus on the Limitation of Act of Potency." *The Saint Anselm Journal* 7.1 (2009) 29–43.

Gurtner, Daniel M. *The Torn Veil: Matthew's Exposition of the Death of Jesus.* Society for New Testament Studies Monograph Series. Cambridge: Cambridge University Press, 2007.

Guttmacher, A. E., et al. "The Human Placenta Project: Placental Structure, Development, and Function in Real Time." *Placenta* 35.5 (2014) 303–4.

Hanvey, James. "Tradition as Subversion." *International Journal of Systematic Theology* 6.1 (2004) 50–68.

Hart, Kevin. *The Trespass of the Sign: Deconstruction, Theology, and Philosophy.* Cambridge: Cambridge University Press, 1989.

Hart, Trevor A. *Between the Image and the Word: Theological Engagements with Imagination, Language, and Literature.* Ashgate Studies in Theology, Imagination and the Arts. Edited by Jeremy Begbie and Trevor Hart. Farnham: Ashgate, 2013.

Harvey, A. E. *Renewal through Suffering: A Study of 2 Corinthians.* Studies of the New Testament and its World. Edinburgh: T&T Clark, 1996.

Hill, John Lawrence. *After the Natural Law: How the Classical Worldview Supports our Modern Moral and Political Values.* San Fransisco, CA: Ignatius, 2016.

Horan, Daniel P. "Beyond Essentialism and Complementarity: Toward a Theological Anthropology Rooted in Haecceitas." *Theological Studies* 75.1 (2014) 94–117.

Horne, Donald. *The Lucky Country: Australia in the Sixties.* Melbourne: Penguin, 1964.

Howell, Kenneth. "Mary's Bodily Participation in the Redemption of Christ." In *The Virgin Mary and the Theology of the Body*, edited by Donald H. Calloway, 199–226. West Chester, PA: Ascension, 2007.

Humphreys, Colin J., and W. G. Waddington. "Astronomy and the Date of the Crucifixion." In *Chronos, Kairos, Christos: Nativity and Chronological Studies Presented to Jack Finegan*, edited by Jerry Vardaman and Edwin M. Yamauchi, 165–82. Winona Lake, IN: Eisenbrauns, 1989.

International Theological Commission. "Communion and Stewardship: Human Persons Created in the Image of God." 2004. Online. http://www.vatican.va/roman_curia/congregations/cfaith/cti_documents/rc_con_cfaith_doc_20040723_communion-stewardship_en.html.

Irigaray, Luce. *This Sex Which Is Not One.* Translated by Catherine Porter. New York: Cornell University Press, 1977.

Jakobson, Roman. "Closing Statement: Linguistics and Poetics." In *Style in Language*, edited by Thomas A. Sebeok, 350–77. 1960. Reprint, Cambridge, MA: MIT Press, 1964.

James, Clive. *Poetry Notebook 2006–2014.* London: Picador, 2014.

James, J. L., et al. "Can We Fix It? Evaluating the Potential of Placental Stem Cells for the Treatment of Pregnancy Disorders." *Placenta* 35.2 (2014) 77–84.

Jay, Nancy B. *Throughout Your Generations Forever: Sacrifice, Religion, and Paternity.* Chicago: University of Chicago Press, 1992.

Jennings, Elizabeth. *Every Changing Shape: Mystical Experience and the Making of Poems.* Manchester: Carcanet, 1996.

———. "The Uses of Allegory: A Study of the Poetry of Edwin Muir." In *Every Changing Shape: Mystical Experience and the Making of Poems*, 148–62. Manchester: Carcanet, 1996.

Joel, Daphna. "Genetic-Gonadal-Genitals Sex (3g-Sex) and the Misconception of Brain and Gender, or, Why 3g-Males and 3g-Females Have Intersex Brain and Intersex Gender." *Biology of Sex Differences* 3.1 (2012). Online. doi: 10.1186/2042-6410-3-27.

John Paul II. "*Familiaris Consortio:* On the Role of the Christian Family." Apostolic Exhortation given November 22, 1981. Online. http://w2.vatican.va/content/john-paul-ii/en/apost_exhortations/documents/hf_jp-ii_exh_19811122_familiaris-consortio.html.

———. "*Fidei Depositum:* On the Publication of the Catechism of the Catholic Church Prepared Following the Second Vatican Ecumenical Council." Apostolic Constitution given October 11, 1992. Online. http://www.vatican.va/content/john-paul-ii/en/apost_constitutions/documents/hf_jp-ii_apc_19921011_fidei-depositum.html.

———. "*Fides et Ratio:* On the Relation Between Faith and Reason." Encyclical given September 14, 1998. Online. http://w2.vatican.va/content/john-paul-ii/en/encyclicals/documents/hf_jp-ii_enc_14091998_fides-et-ratio.html.

———. "*Gratissimam Sane:* Letter to Families." Letter given February 2, 1994. Online. https://w2.vatican.va/content/john-paul-ii/en/letters/1994/documents/hf_jp-ii_let_02021994_families.html.

———. "Holy Mass In Phoenix Park, Dublin, Ireland." Homily given September 29, 1979. Online. http://www.vatican.va/content/john-paul-ii/en/homilies/1979/documents/hf_jp-ii_hom_19790929_irlanda-dublino.html.

———. "Letter to Women." Letter given June 29, 1995. Online. http://www.vatican.va/content/john-paul-ii/en/letters/1995/documents/hf_jp-ii_let_29061995_women.html.

———. *Man and Woman, He Created Them: A Theology of the Body.* Translated by Michael Waldstein. Boston, MA: Pauline, 2006.

———. "*Mulieris Dignitatem:* On the Dignity and Vocation of Women." Apostolic Letter given August 15, 1988. Online. http://www.vatican.va/content/john-paul-ii/en/apost_letters/1988/documents/hf_jp-ii_apl_15081988_mulieris-dignitatem.html.

Johnson, Elizabeth A. *She Who Is: The Mystery of God in Feminist Theological Discourse.* New York: Crossroad, 1996.

———. *Truly Our Sister: A Theology of Mary in the Communion of Saints.* New York: Continuum, 2006.

Jones, David. "Art and Sacrament." In *Epoch and Artist: Selected Writings*, edited by Harman Grisewood, 143–79. 1955. Reprint, London: Faber and Faber, 1959.

———. "The Preface to 'The Anathemata.'" In *Epoch and Artist: Selected Writings*, edited by Harman Grisewood, 107–37. 1955. Reprint, London: Faber and Faber, 1959.

Kelly, A. J. "Mary and the Creed: Icon of Trinitarian Love." *Irish Theological Quarterly* 69.1 (2004) 17–30.

Kerr, Fergus. "The Need for Philosophy in Theology Today." *New Blackfriars* 65.768 (1984) 248–60.

Kitzberger, Ingrid R. "Stabat Mater? Re-Birth at the Foot of the Cross." *Biblical Interpretation* 11.3–4 (2003) 468–87.

Kraus, Helen. *Gender Issues in Ancient and Reformation Translations of Genesis 1–4.* Oxford: Oxford University Press, 2011.

Kristeva, Julia. *Revolution in Poetic Language.* New York: Columbia University Press, 1984.

——. "Stabat Mater." In *The Kristeva Reader*, edited by Toril Moi, 160–86. 1986. Reprint, Oxford: Blackwell, 1996.

Kwok, Piu-Lan. "Engendering Christ." In *The Strength of Her Witness: Jesus Christ in the Global Voices of Women*, edited by Elizabeth A. Johnson, 255–69. Maryknoll, NY: Orbis, 2016.

Lagrand, James. "How Was the Virgin Mary 'Like a Man'? A Note on Matt 1:18b and Related Syriac Christian Texts." *Novum Testamentum* 22.2 (1980) 97–107.

Lakoff, George, and Mark Johnson. *Metaphors We Live By.* Chicago: University of Chicago Press, 2003.

Lavin, Marilyn Aronberg. "The 'Stella Altarpiece.' Magnum Opus of the Cesi Master." *Artibus et Historiae* 22.44 (2001) 9–22.

Leach, Edmund. *Genesis as Myth and Other Essays.* London: Jonathan Cape, 1969.

Lee, Patrick, and Robert P. George. *Body-Self Dualism in Contemporary Ethics and Politics.* Cambridge: Cambridge University Press, 2008.

Leo XIII. "*Divinum Illud Munus*: On the Holy Spirit." Encyclical given May 9, 1897. Online. http://www.vatican.va/content/leo-xiii/en/encyclicals/documents/hf_l-xiii_enc_09051897_divinum-illud-munus.html.

Levin, David Michael. *The Body's Recollection of Being: Phenomenological Psychology and the Deconstruction of Nihilism.* London: Routledge & Kegan Paul, 1985.

Lewis, C. S. "Bluspels and Flanansferes: A Semantic Nightmare." In *Selected Literary Essays*, edited by Walter Hooper. 1961. Reprint, New York: HarperCollins, 2013. Kindle ed.

——. "On Three Ways of Writing for Children." In *On Stories and Other Essays on Literature*, by C. S. Lewis, 31–44. 1966. Reprint, Orlando, FL: Harcourt, 1982.

——. "Transposition." In *The Weight of Glory and Other Essays*, edited by Walter Hooper, 91–115. 1962. Reprint, New York: HarperCollins, 2001.

Leyerle, Blake. "Blood is Seed." *The Journal of Religion* 81.1 (2001) 26–48.

Loughlin, Gerard. "Myths, Signs and Significations." *Theology* 89.730 (1986) 268–75.

——. "Nuptial Mysteries." In *Faithful Reading: New Essays in Theology in Honor of Fergus Kerr, OP*, edited by S. Oliver et al., 173–92. London: T&T Clark, 2012.

Lubac, Henri de. *The Motherhood of the Church.* Translated by Sergia Englund. San Francisco: Ignatius, 1982.

Lundell, Torborg. "Couvade in Sweden." *Scandinavian Studies* 71.1 (1999) 93–104.

Margalit, Natan. "Priestly Men and Invisible Women: Male Appropriation of the Feminine and the Exemption of Women From Positive Time-Bound Commandments." *Association for Jewish Studies* 28.2 (2004) 297–316.

Markus, R. A. "St. Augustine on Signs." *Phronesis* 2.1 (1957) 60–83.

Marshall, Graeme. "The Problem of Religious Language 'Look at It This Way' (Wittgenstein)." *Sophia* 51.4 (2012) 479–93.

Martin, Francis. "Male and Female He Created Them: A Summary of the Teaching of Genesis Chapter One." *Communio: International Catholic Review* 20 (1993) 240–65.

Mathetes. "The Epistle to Diognetus." In *Ante-Nicene Fathers: The Apostolic Fathers with Justin Martyr and Irenaeus,* edited by Alexander Roberts et al. Christian Classics Ethereal Library. Online. https://ccel.org/ccel/mathetes/epistle_of_mathetes_to_diognetus/anf01.iii.ii.html.

Maxwell, Glyn. *On Poetry.* London: Oberon, 2012.

McAuley, James. *Poetry, Essays, and Personal Commentary.* St. Lucia: University of Queensland Press, 1988.

McDonnell, Kilian. "Feminist Mariologies: Heteronomy/Subordination and the Scandal of Christology." *Theological Studies* 66.3 (2005) 527–67.

McFague, Sallie. *Metaphorical Theology: Models of God in Religious Language.* Philadelphia: Fortress, 1982.

McLauchlan, Richard. "R. S. Thomas: Poet of Holy Saturday." *The Heythrop Journal* 52.6 (2011) 976–85.

Macmurray, John. *Persons in Relation.* London: Faber and Faber, 1961.

Miles, Margaret R. *Augustine on the Body.* Dissertation Series: American Academy of Religion. Missoula, MT: Scholars, 1979.

———. *Carnal Knowing: Female Nakedness and Religious Meaning in the Christian West.* New York: Vintage, 1991.

———. *A Complex Delight: The Secularization of the Breast, 1350–1750.* Berkeley: University of California Press, 2008.

———. "God's Love, Mother's Milk: An Image of Salvation." *Christian Century* 125.2 (2008) 22–25.

Miller, Sarah Alison. *Medieval Monstrosity and the Female Body.* Routledge Studies in Medieval Religion and Culture. Edited by George Ferzoco and Carolyn Muessig. New York: Routledge, 2010.

Ming, John. "Concupiscence." In vol. 4 of *The Catholic Encyclopedia,* edited by Charles George Herbermann et al. New York: Robert Appleton, 1908. Online. http://www.newadvent.org/cathen/04208a.htm.

Monti, Anthony. *A Natural Theology of the Arts: Imprint of the Spirit.* Aldershot: Ashgate, 2003.

Morgan, Barry. "Kyffin Williams and R. S. Thomas—Attitudes to Wales and to Faith." Lecture delivered at The Kyffin Williams Trust Annual Memorial, Oriel Ynys Môn, Llangefni, Anglesey, Wales, May 10, 2013.

———. *Strangely Orthodox: R. S. Thomas and His Poetry of Faith.* Llandysul, Ceredigion: Gomer, 2006.

Moynihan, Robert, ed. *Let God's Light Shine Forth: The Spiritual Vision of Pope Benedict XVI.* London: Hutchinson, 2005.

Muir, Edwin. *An Autobiography.* 1954. Reprint, Edinburgh: Canongate, 1993.

———. "The Natural Estate." In *The Estate of Poetry: Essays,* by Edwin Muir, 1–22. 1962. Reprint, Saint Paul, MN: Graywolf, 1993.

———. "Poetry and the Poet." In *The Estate of Poetry: Essays,* by Edwin Muir, 78–93. 1962. Reprint, Saint Paul, MN: Graywolf, 1993.

———. "The Public and the Poet." In *The Estate of Poetry: Essays,* by Edwin Muir, 94–110. 1962. Reprint, Saint Paul, MN: Graywolf, 1993.

———. *Selected Poems.* London: Faber and Faber, 2008.

Murray, Les. "Embodiment and Incarnation." In *A Working Forest: Selected Prose,* by Les Murray, 309–25. Potts Point, NSW: Duffy & Snellgrove, 1997.

————. "On Being Subject Matter." In *A Working Forest: Selected Prose*, by Les Murray, 30–44. Potts Point, NSW: Duffy & Snellgrove, 1997.

————. "Poems and Poesies." In *A Working Forest: Selected Prose*, by Les Murray, 372–85. Potts Point, NSW: Duffy & Snellgrove, 1997.

————. *Subhuman Redneck Poems*. Manchester: Carcanet, 1996.

————. "The Trade in Images." In *A Working Forest: Selected Prose*, by Les Murray, 344–50. Potts Point, NSW: Duffy & Snellgrove, 1997.

Naumann, M. Isabell. "The Anthropology of Father Josseph Kenterich and the Image of Mary." In *The Virgin Mary and the Theology of the Body*, edited by Donald H. Calloway. Stockbridge, MA: Marians of the Immaculate Conception, 2005.

Nelson, D. M. "Does a Picture of the Human Placenta Predict the Future?" *Placenta* 31.11 (2010) 943.

Newton, William. "John Paul II and *Gaudium et Spes* 22: His Use of the Text and His Involvement in Its Authorship." *Josephinum Journal of Theology* 17.1 (2010) 168–93.

Norris, Thomas. "Mariology a Key to the Faith." *Irish Theological Quarterly* 55.3 (1989) 193–205.

O'Carroll, Michael. "Apparitions of Our Lady." In *Mary is for Everyone: Essays on Mary and Ecumenism*, edited by William McLoughlin and Jill Pinnock, 285–91. Leominster: Gracewing, 1997.

————. *Theotokos: A Theological Encyclopedia of the Blessed Virgin Mary*. Wilmington, DE: Michael Glazier; Dublin: Dominican, 1982.

O'Connell, Helen E., et al. "The Anatomy of the Distal Vagina." *Journal of Sexual Medicine* 5.8 (2008) 1883–91.

Orwell, George. "Politics and the English Language." In *Why I Write*, by George Orwell, 102–20. 1946. Reprint, London: Penguin, 2004.

————. "Why I Write." In *Why I Write*, by George Orwell, 1–10. 1946. Reprint, London: Penguin, 2004.

Ory, Steven J., and Marcelo J. Barrionuevo. "The Differential Diagnosis of Female Infertility." In *Principles and Practice of Endocrinology and Metabolism*, edited by Kenneth L. Becker. Philadelphia; London: Lippincott Williams & Wilkins, 2001.

Pattison, Stephen. *Seeing Things: Deepening Relations with Visual Artefacts*. London: SCM, 2007.

Paul, Ian. "Metaphor and Exegesis." In *After Pentecost: Language and Biblical Interpretation*, edited by Craig Bartholomew et al., 387–402. Carlisle, CA: Paternoster, 2001.

Paulsell, Stephanie. *Honoring the Body: Meditations on a Christian Practice*. The Practices of Faith Series. San Francisco: Jossey-Bass, 2002.

Pechey, Graham. "'Frost at Midnight' and the Poetry of Periphrasis." *Cambridge Quarterly* 41.2 (2012) 229–44.

Pfeffer, Naomi. "Older Mothers and Global/National Responsibilities." *Bio-News*, February 8, 2010. Online. https://www.bionews.org.uk/page_92145.

Pitre, Brant. *Jesus and the Jewish Roots of Mary: Unveiling the Mother of the Messiah*. New York: Image, 2018.

Pius XII. "*Humani Generis:* Concerning Some False Opinions Threatening to Undermine the Foundations of Catholic Doctrine." Encyclical given August 12, 1950. Online. http://www.vatican.va/content/pius-xii/en/encyclicals/documents/hf_p-xii_enc_12081950_humani-generis.html.

Premack, David. "Human and Animal Cognition: Continuity and Discontinuity." *Proceedings of the National Academy of Sciences* 104.35 (2007) 13861–67.

Prokes, Mary Timothy. "The Nuptial Meaning of the Body in Light of Mary's Assumption." *Communio: International Catholic Review* 11.2 (1984) 157–76.

Pybus, Cassandra. *The Devil and James McAuley*. 2nd ed. St. Lucia: University of Queensland Press, 2001.

Rahner, Karl. *Faith and Ministry*. Translated by Edward Quinn. Vol. 29 of *Theological Investigations*. London: Darton Longman Todd, 1984.

———. *Further Theology of the Spiritual Life*. Translated by David John Bourke. Vol. 8 of *Theological Investigations*. London: Darton Longman Todd, 1971.

———. *More Recent Writings*. Translated by Kevin Smyth. Vol. 4 of *Theological Investigations*. London: Darton Longman Todd, 1966.

———. *Science and Christian Faith*. Translated by Hugh M. Riley. Vol. 21 of *Theological Investigations*. London: Darton Longman Todd, 1988.

———. *Theology of the Spiritual Life*. Translated by Karl H. Kruger and Boniface Kruger. Vol. 3 of *Theological Investigations*. London: Darton Longman Todd, 1974.

Ratzinger, Joseph. *Called to Communion: Understanding the Church Today*. Translated by Adrian Walker. 2nd ed. San Francisco: Ignatius, 1991.

———. *Daughter Zion: Meditations on the Church's Marian Belief*. Translated by John M. McDermott. 1977. Reprint, San Francisco: Ignatius, 1983.

———. "The Feeling of Things, The Contemplation of Beauty." Message delivered to the Communion and Liberation Meeting at Rimini, Italy, August 24–30, 2002. Online. http://www.vatican.va/roman_curia/congregations/cfaith/documents/rc_con_cfaith_doc_20020824_ratzinger-cl-rimini_en.html.

———. "Letter to the Bishops of the Catholic Church on the Collaboration of Men and Women in the Church and the World." Delivered May 31, 2004. Online. http://www.vatican.va/roman_curia/congregations/cfaith/documents/rc_con_cfaith_doc_20040731_collaboration_en.html.

Reece, E. Albert, and J. C. Hobbins, eds. *Clinical Obstetrics: The Fetus and the Mother*. 3rd ed. Malden, MA: Wiley-Blackwell, 2008.

Retief, F. P., and L. Cilliers. "Christ's Crucifixion as Medico-Historical Event." *Acta Theologica* 26.2 [s7] (2006) 294–309.

Riches, Aaron. "Deconstructing the Linearity of Grace: The Risk and Reflexive Paradox of Mary's Immaculate Fiat." *International Journal of Systematic Theology* 10.2 (2008) 179–94.

Ricoeur, Paul. "Metaphor and the Central Problem of Hermeneutics." Translated by David Pellauer. In *Hermeneutics: Writings and Lectures*, edited by Daniel Frey and Nicola Strickler, 45–64. Cambridge: Polity, 2013.

———. "The Problem of Hermeneutics." Translated by David Pellauer. In *Hermeneutics: Writings and Lectures*, edited by Daniel Frey and Nicola Strickler, 1–44. Cambridge: Polity, 2013.

———. "Speaking and Writing." In *Interpretation Theory: Discourse and the Surplus of Meaning*, by Paul Ricoeur, 25–44. Fort Worth, TX: Texas Christian University Press, 1976.

Rogers, Eugene F., Jr. *Sexuality and the Christian Body: Their Way into the Triune God*. Oxford: Blackwell, 1999.

Rosen, Aaron. *Art & Religion in the Twenty-First Century*. London: Thames & Hudson, 2015.

Rowe, Noel. "James McAuley: The Possibility of Despair." *Southerly* 60.2 (2000) 26–38.

———. *Next to Nothing*. Sydney: Vagabond, 2004.

———. "'Will This Be Your Poem, or Mine?' The Give and Take of Story." In *Ethical Investigations: Essays on Australian Literature and Poetics*, edited by Bernadette Brennan, 13–29. Sydney: Vagabond, 2008.

———. *Wings and Fire*. Hunters Hill, NSW: Marist Promotions Team, 1984.

Rubin, Miri. *Mother of God: A History of the Virgin Mary*. London: Penguin, 2009.

Ruether, Rosemary Radford. *Sexism and God-Talk: Towards a Feminist Theology*. London: SCM, 1983.

Rutt, Richard. "Why Should He Send His Mother? Some Theological Reflections on Marian Apparitions." In *Mary is for Everyone: Essays on Mary and Ecumensim*, edited by William McLoughlin and Jill Pinnock, 274–84. Leominster: Gracewing, 1997.

Savage, Deborah. "The Centrality of Lived Experience in Wojtyła's Account of the Person." *Annuls of Philosophy* 61.4 (2013) 19–51.

Sacred Congregation for the Doctrine of the Faith. "*Inter Insigniores*: On the Question of Admission of Women to the Ministerial Priesthood." Declaration given October 15, 1976. Online. http://www.vatican.va/roman_curia/congregations/cfaith/documents/rc_con_cfaith_doc_19761015_inter-insigniores_en.html.

Second Vatican Council. "*Dei Verbum*: Dogmatic Constitution on Divine Revelation." November 18, 1965. Online. https://www.vatican.va/archive/hist_councils/ii_vatican_council/documents/vat-ii_const_19651118_dei-verbum_en.html.

———. "*Gaudium et Spes*: Pastoral Constitution on the Church in the Modern World." December 7, 1965. Online. http://www.vatican.va/archive/hist_councils/ii_vatican_council/documents/vat-ii_cons_19651207_gaudium-et-spes_en.html.

———. "*Lumen Gentium*: Dogmatic Constitution on the Church." November 21, 1964. Online. http://www.vatican.va/archive/hist_councils/ii_vatican_council/documents/vat-ii_const_19641121_lumen-gentium_en.html.

———. "*Nostra Aetate*: On the Relation of the Church to Non-Christian Religions." October 28, 1965. Online. http://www.vatican.va/archive/hist_councils/ii_vatican_council/documents/vat-ii_decl_19651028_nostra-aetate_en.html.

———. "*Sacrosanctum Concilium*: Constitution on the Sacred Liturgy." December 4, 1963. Online. http://www.vatican.va/archive/hist_councils/ii_vatican_council/documents/vat-ii_const_19631204_sacrosanctum-concilium_en.html.

Scarry, Elaine. *The Body in Pain: The Making and Unmaking of the World*. New York: Oxford University Press, 1985.

Schiller, Britt-Marie. "Representing Female Desire within a Labial Framework of Sexuality." *Journal of the American Psychoanalytic Association* 60 (2012) 1161–97.

Schindler, David L. "Being, Gift, Self-Gift: A Reply to Waldstein on Relationality and John Paul II's Theology of the Body (Part One)." *Communio: International Catholic Review* 42 (2015) 221–51.

Scola, Angelo. "The Nuptial Mystery at the Heart of the Church." *Communio: International Catholic Review* 25.4 (1998) 630–62.

Sell, Nancy A. "The Magnificat as a Model for Ministry: Proclaiming Justice, Shifting Paradigms, Transforming Lives." *Liturgical Ministry* 10.1 (2001) 31–40.

Sered, Susan Starr. *Women as Ritual Experts: The Religious Lives of Elderly Jewish Women in Jerusalem*. Oxford: Oxford University Press, 1992.

Sewell, Elizabeth. *The Human Metaphor*. University of Notre Dame Press, 1964.

———. "The Reading of Signs, in Thinking and Poetry." In *To Be a True Poem: Essays by Elizabeth Sewell*, edited by William E. Ray, 153–67. Winston-Salem, NC: Hunter, 1979.

Shivanandan, Mary. "Body Narratives: Language of Truth?" *Logos: A Journal of Catholic Thought and Culture* 3.3 (2000) 166–93.

Soskice, Janet Martin. "Blood and Defilement." In *Feminism and Theology*, edited by Janet Martin Soskice and Diana Lipton. Oxford: Oxford University Press, 2003.

———. *Metaphor and Religious Language*. Oxford: Clarendon, 1985.

———. "Monica's Tears: Augustine on Words and Speech." *New Blackfriars* 83.980 (2002) 448–58.

———. "Trinity and Feminism." In *The Cambridge Companion to Feminist Theology*, edited by Susan Frank Parsons, 135–50. Cambridge: Cambridge University Press, 2002.

Spender, Stephen. *The Making of a Poem*. Edited by S. O. Agrell and Georgina Mase. London: Hamilton, 1955.

Stadlen, Naomi. *What Mothers Do: Especially When it Looks like Nothing*. London: Piatkus, 2004.

Steinberg, Leo. *The Sexuality of Christ in Renaissance Art and in Modern Oblivion*. 2nd ed., revised and expanded. Chicago: University of Chicago Press, 1996.

Steiner, George. *Real Presences: Is There Anything in What We Say?* London: Faber and Faber, 1989.

Storkey, Elaine. "Who Is the Christ? Issues in Christology and Feminist Theology." In *The Gospel and Gender: A Trinitarian Engagement with Being Male and Female in Christ*, edited by Douglas A. Campbell, 105–23. Studies in Theology and Sexuality. London: T&T Clark.

Strhan, Anna. "Religious Language as Poetry: Heidegger's Challenge." *The Heythrop Journal* 52 (2011) 926–38.

Sutton, Agneta. "The Complementarity and Symbolism of the Two Sexes: Karl Barth, Hans Urs von Balthasar and John Paul II." *New Blackfriars* 87.1010 (2006) 418–33.

Sylva, Dennis D. "The Temple Curtain and Jesus' Death in the Gospel of Luke." *Journal of Biblical Literature* 105.2 (1986) 239–50.

Taylor, Charles. *A Secular Age*. Cambridge, MA: Belknap, 2007.

Thomas, M. Wynn. *R. S. Thomas: Serial Obsessive*. Cardiff: University of Wales Press, 2013.

Ticciati, Susannah. *Job and the Disruption of Identity: Reading Beyond Barth*. London: T&T Clark, 2005.

———. *A New Apophaticism: Augustine and the Redemption of Signs*. Studies in Systematic Theology. Leiden: Brill, 2013.

Tillard, Jean-Marie R. "The Marian Issues." In *Studying Mary: Reflections on the Virgin Mary in Anglican and Roman Catholic Theology and Devotion*, edited by Adelbert Denaux and Nicholas Sagovsky, 4–11. London: T&T Clark, 2007.

Tonstad, Linn Marie. "Sexual Difference and Trinitarian Death: Cross, Kenosis, and Hierarchy in the *Theo-Drama*." *Modern Theology* 26.4 (2010) 603–31.

Turner, Denys. *Julian of Norwich, Theologian*. New Haven: Yale University Press, 2011.

———. *Thomas Aquinas: A Portrait*. New Haven: Yale University Press, 2013.

Valenza, Gaetano, et al. "Revealing Real-Time Emotional Responses: A Personalized Assessment Based on Heartbeat Dynamics." *Scientific Reports* 4 (2014) 1–13.

Vanhoozer, Kevin J. "Discourse on Matter: Hermeneutics and the 'Miracle' of Understanding." *International Journal of Systematic Theology* 7.1 (2005) 5–37.

Waldstein, Michael. "Index." In *Man and Woman, He Created Them: A Theology of the Body*, by John Paul II, 677–730. Translated by Michael Waldstein. Boston, MA: Pauline, 2006.

―――. "Introduction." In *Man and Woman, He Created Them: A Theology of the Body*, by John Paul II, 1–128. Translated by Michael Waldstein. Boston, MA: Pauline, 2006.

Wallace, David Foster. "The Empty Plenum: David Markson's *Wittgenstein's Mistress*." In *Both Flesh and Not: Essays*, by David Foster Wallace, 73–116. London: Penguin, 2013.

Ward, Graham. "The Displaced Body of Jesus Christ." In *Men and Masculinities in Christianity and Judaism: A Critical Reader*, edited by Bjorn Krondorfer, 98–112. London: SCM, 2009.

Warner, Marina. *Alone of All Her Sex: The Myth and the Cult of the Virgin Mary.* 1976. Reprint, New York: Vintage, 1983.

Warner, Martin. *Say Yes to God: Mary and the Revealing of the Word Made Flesh.* London: Tufton, 1999.

"Warning Over Burning Aborted Foetuses." *BBC News*, March 24, 2014. http://www.bbc.co.uk/news/health-26716924.

Willemien, Otten. "Christ's Birth of a Virgin Who Became a Wife: Flesh and Speech in Tertullian's 'De Carne Christi.'" *Vigiliae Christianae* 51.3 (1997) 247–60.

Williams, Rowan. *The Edge of Words: God and the Habits of Language.* London: Bloomsbury, 2014.

―――. *Grace and Necessity: Reflections on Art and Love.* London: Continuum, 2005.

―――. "Language, Reality and Desire in Augustine's 'De Doctrina.'" *Literature and Theology* 3.2 (1989) 138–50.

―――. "On Being a Human Body." *Sewanee Theological Review* 42.4 (1999) 403–13.

―――. *On Christian Theology.* Oxford: Blackwell, 2000.

―――. *A Ray of Darkness.* Lanham, MD; Plymouth, UK: Cowley, 1995.

―――. "The Seal of Orthodoxy: Mary and the Heart of Christian Doctrine." In *Say Yes to God: Mary and the Revealing of the Word Made Flesh*, edited by Martin Warner, 15–29. London: Tufton, 1999.

―――. *Tokens of Trust: An Introduction to Christian Belief.* Norwich: Canterbury, 2007.

Wojtyła, Karol. *Love and Responsibility.* Translated by H. T. Willetts. Rev. English ed. San Francisco, CA: Ignatius, 1981.

Wojtyła, Karol, and Anna-Teresa Tymieniecka. *The Acting Person.* Translated by Andrzej Potocki. Rev. ed. Analecta Husserliana. Dordrecht, Holland: D. Reidel, 1979.

Subject Index

Scripture Index

Revelation